Stress and Challenge at the Top:
The Paradox of the Successful Executive

Stress and Challenge at the Top:
The Paradox of the Successful Executive

James Campbell Quick, PhD

The University of Texas at Arlington, USA

Debra L. Nelson, PhD

Oklahoma State University, USA

Jonathan D. Quick, MD

*Management Sciences for Health, USA
and Peshawar, Pakistan*

JOHN WILEY & SONS

Chichester · New York · Brisbane · Toronto · Singapore

18 SEP 1990

Other Wiley Editorial Offices

John Wiley & Sons Inc., 605 Third Avenue
New York NY 10158-0012, USA

Jacaranda Wiley Ltd, G.P.O. Box 859, Brisbane,
Queensland 4001, Australia

John Wiley & Sons (Canada) Ltd, 22 Worcester Road,
Rexdale, Ontario M9W 1L1, Canada

John Wiley & Sons (SEA) Pte Ltd, 37 Jalan Pemimpin #05-04,
Block B, Union Industrial Building, Singapore 2057

Library of Congress Cataloging-in-Publication Data:

Quick, James C.
    Stress and challenge at the top: the paradox of the successful
executive/James Campbell Quick, Debra L. Nelson, Jonathan D.
Quick.
        p.   cm.—(Wiley series on studies in occupational stress)
    Includes bibliographical references (p.   ).
    ISBN 0 471 91983 7
    1. Job stress—Prevention.   2. Stress management.   3. Executives.
I. Nelson, Debra L., 1956 –   .   II. Quick, Jonathan D.   III. Title
IV. Series.
    HF5548.85.Q54   1990   89-28138
658 4'09'019—dc2   CIP

British Library Cataloguing in Publication Data:

Quick, James C.
    Stress and challenge at the top.
    1. Managers. Stress
    I. Title   II. Nelson, Debra L.   III. Quick, Jonathan D.
    658.4'095

ISBN 0 471 91983 7

Typeset by Inforum Typesetting, Portsmouth
Printed in Great Britain by Biddles Ltd, Guildford, Surrey

Dr James Campbell Quick
and
Dr Jonathan D. Quick
wish to dedicate this book to the memory of
their maternal grandfather
Professor Dr Otto Alois Faust
1887–1989
and
to our families

Dr Debra L. Nelson
wishes to dedicate this book to
her parents
Ronald J. and Dianne Nelson

Contents

Acknowledgments ix

Series Preface xi

Preface xiii

1. Successful Executives: A Profile of Drive and Ambition 1

2. Executive Stress: The Risks of Success 21

3. Preventive Stress Management: What Works and
   What Doesn't! 45

4. Profiles of Male Executives: Able Men in Trying Times 69

5. Profiles of Female Executives: The Ladies at the Top 105

6. Meeting the Challenge: Messages from the Top 133

7. Loneliness: A Lethal Problem 147

8. Forming Healthy Attachments: Key to the Paradox 163

Appendix: Creating a Personal Stress Management Plan 185

Bibliography 193

Index 203

Acknowledgments

In addition to our Wiley Series Editor, Professor Cary L. Cooper, we would like to thank a number of individuals who have helped us in the development of this work, either conceptually or administratively. These include Wayne Bodensteiner, James E. Dalton Jr, Michael Hitt, Lisa Kennedy, Dianna Nelson, Adele E. Neupert, James F. Quick, Tina B. Quick, Sheri Schember Quick, and Margaret White. We would like to thank W. Warner Burke and Jerry B. Harvey for their developmental assistance to us concerning attachment behavior and its theoretical underpinnings. We would like to thank Cynthia Ryder for her assistance in drafting many of the figures, and Ann Anderson, Libby Dotson, Sue Hundley, Brenda Lott, Linda Norris, and Connie Rozelle for their assistance in the development of the executive profiles.

We are indebted to Bob Perkins, Dean of the Graduate School, The University of Texas at Arlington for the funding support provided in the early stages of the research through the Organized Research Fund. Support from the Dean's Excellence Fund, College of Business Administration, Oklahoma State University was important in the later stages of the reseach.

To improve euphony and to avoid clumsy locutions, such as 'his/her' or 's/he', we have used the traditional masculine form to apply to both sexes until otherwise specified.

Series Preface

The Wiley Series on Studies in Occupational Stress has made a major contribution to the literature in the field of occupational and organizational stress over the last decade. The main objective of this series was to help review existing work in the field and to map out the future of research in this burgeoning and increasingly important area of organizational behavior and occupational health. The early books set the stage in trying to develop an understanding of various occupational groups, such as blue collar workers, white collar and professional workers, health care professionals, etc. Gradually the emphasis shifted to important conceptual issues such as control and autonomy in the workplace, coping with stress, and the link between stress and health. These early books tended to be edited volumes of discrete, integrated topics, which were appropriate at the time given the 'state of the art' of occupational stress research. As more and more research is being pursued and published in the journals, it is important that we now begin to consolidate this literature and to provide more comprehensive and in-depth accounts of particular topical concerns in the field. The books which will follow, therefore, will be author-written books which focus on an issue or topic of interest, in a more pragmatic sense, for people in the workplace: managers, trade unionists, occupational psychologists, occupational medics, and the myriad of others involved in the health and well-being of people at work. This book represents this new dimension to our series.

CARY L. COOPER
University of Manchester, UK

Preface

The pursuit of top level positions in a corporation is challenging, requiring both drive and ambition, and sustaining one's success at the top is challenging and stressful, due in part to the 'loneliness of command' and in part the vagaries of corporate warfare. Corporate warfare places not only top level executives at risk, but also an organization's other human resources, as we have learned in one study of mergers, acquisitions, downsizing, and plant closings conducted through our Center for Research on Organizational and Managerial Excellence (CROME).

Prevention is an extraordinarily powerful notion in dealing with the risks and stresses of corporate life. Once an executive has a health catastrophe, it is frequently impossible to return to the health condition he or she enjoyed prior to the catastrophe. Why not prevent the problem in the first place? The public health notions of prevention and preventive medicine have been instrumental in the 50% increase in life expectancy which Americans have enjoyed in this century.

This book is for behavioral scientists, executives, and others interested in the study of executive life. Chapter 1 looks at the distinguishing features of executives' lives, from their drive and ambition to their leadership and need for achievement. The lives of most executives are challenging, exciting, demanding, stressful, and a feature of industrialized nations.

Chapter 2 identifies what stress is and what the costs of mismanaged stress are. We adopt the original thrust of Walter B. Cannon's work which suggests that stress is a naturally occurring human response consisting of a complex of neurological and endocrinological activities. As an emergency response, it prepares us to effectively manage the legitimate demands and emergencies of life, achieve peak performances and overcome environmental threats to our well-being. Hence, stress is inevitable and, when properly used, very beneficial.

However, there are a host of psychological, behavioral, and medical disorders which constitute distress. These frequently result from the mismanagement of our stress response. Early detection is the best preventive action in these matters.

While distress is the bad news in the field of stress, there are a range of responsible prevention strategies which executives may employ to manage the inevitable stresses of work and personal life. These strategies are reviewed in Chapter 3, which is based upon our ideographic research with executives as well as an understanding of the stress literature.

In Chapters 4 and 5 we present six idiographic profiles of men and women executives who have successfully managed the stresses and demands of their professional and personal lives. Each of these men and women has a unique story to tell. They are Purvis Thrash, Otis Engineering Corporation; Gordon Forword, Chaparral Steel; Jody Grant, Texas American Bancshares; Ebby Halliday, Ebby Halliday REALTORS; Catherine Crier, 162nd Judicial District Court; and Kim Dawson, The Kim Dawson Agency and Dallas Apparel Mart.

Chapter 6 draws the parallel between the challenges of corporate warfare, in which executives are all too often cast in the role of battle commanders, and military warfare. In addition, the chapter contains a set of five Messages from the Top, drawn from the executives we have studied, including those profiled in Chapters 4 and 5.

Chapter 7 is focused on the 'loneliness of command' feature of executive life, looking at the forces which contribute to casting an executive into a lonely, isolated position. In addition, the psychological and health risks associated with loneliness are addressed. Loneliness may truly become a lethal problem when it is chronic.

Chapter 8 is the key to the book and the concluding chapter. It is here that we address the paradox of the successful executive. We have found that the self-reliant executive is one embedded in a rich network of professional and personal relationships which sustain and nurture the executive without smothering him or her. Each executive has an autonomous life apart from a specific relationship, yet invests in the relationship in a healthy way. Hence, the executive is neither over-dependent nor counter-dependent.

Harold Geneen once said, 'If I had enough arms and legs and time, I would do it all myself.' Self-reliant executives recognize the fatal flaw in this fanciful wish. They are able to meet the stress and challenge at the top by depending upon other people who have their best interests at heart.

Chapter 1

Successful Executives: A Profile of Drive and Ambition

Are professional success and personal well-being incompatible goals for executives in the world of the 1990s? Does the stereotypic hard-driving executive with limited time for family and less time for personal reflection represent the only viable pattern for achieving a high level of individual success in an increasingly competitive environment? Numerous examples of executives who have become leaders in their fields while living balanced and healthy lives suggest that professional success and personal well-being are not mutually exclusive. But why do some executives thrive on the challenges, stress, and pressures of executive life, while others suffer a variety of personal or physical problems under similar demands? What are the distinguishing characteristics which separate executives who are invigorated by the process of achieving from those who are drained by the process?

In attempting to deal with these questions, we began in 1983 a series of in-depth interviews with male and female chief executives using a standard interview protocol. Recently much attention has been focused on the factors which lead to individual and organizational excellence. At the same time, other investigators have focused on factors which create stress at work and which lead to negative health consequences. In choosing male and female executives, we looked for individuals who have both achieved sustained success in their careers and maintained their health and well-being in the face of myriad trials and challenges. We were concerned not simply with success or with well-being, but with the characteristics of executives who had achieved *sustained* professional success *and* personal well-being.

In Chapters 4 and 5, we will present in-depth profiles of three male and three female chief executives. In addition to these primary source data, we will draw on numerous examples from historical figures and other contemporary executives. The executives who are profiled have allowed us to get to know them through close and personal examination of their professional and personal experiences. In interviewing them, observing their behavior, and gathering insights from those who work closely with them, we have come to appreciate the many different paths to success, yet the many similarities which successful individuals share.

In his 35 year follow-up of the Harvard Class of 1942, Vaillant (1977) concluded that he found no life story in which there had not been some trauma or adversity. But it was not the trauma or adversity which was the distinguishing feature of individual lives; rather, it was how well the individual did in spite of the challenge. His conclusion was that it is the effective management of the stresses of life that enables us to live and to live well. Similarly, the six detailed profiles presented in Chapters 4 and 5 and the other examples cited throughout clearly demonstrate that, while stress is an unavoidable, even necessary part of working life, its unhealthy consequences can be avoided.

Before turning to the executive profiles, we will look first in this chapter at the dimensions of an executive's personality which are associated with drive and ambition. In the next chapter, we will consider some of the health consequences of executive stress and, in particular, some of the factors associated with staying healthy under stress. Finally, in Chapter 3 we will review methods which successful executives have used to manage the stress generated by lives of striving and achievement.

EXECUTIVE PERSONALITY AND BEHAVIOR

Executives are personalities with a natural drive and ambition to succeed in the world. There are four relevant dimensions of an executive's personality and behavior which we will discuss in this chapter. These are leadership, power and control, stress, and risk-oriented behavior (see Figure 1). While there will be natural variance on these four dimensions for a given group of successful executives, none will be passive followers with a low need for power who have low stress and avoid risk. It is primarily at the high ends of the scale that we will focus our attention.

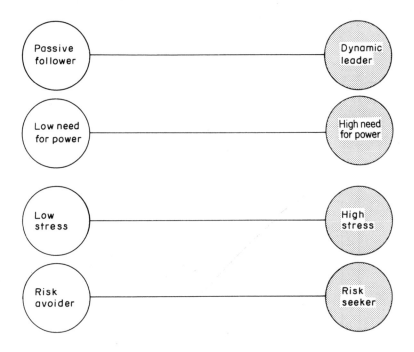

Figure 1   Dimensions of executive personality and behavior

Active Leadership

Executives are active personalities as opposed to passive personalities. Their activity may be manifested in physical action or in high levels of psychological activity. This does not preclude their being peaceful or calm, for they can be that while achieving a great deal. While their activity is usually externally directed, its source lies within their own personalities—it is their strong sense of self which is the root of their energy.

Their strong sense of self is embodied in what Freud (1933) called the ego-ideal. This element of the personality is the map that is used, often unconsciously, in directing behavior and shaping the environment. The image of the ideal is crucial as a basis for action. For example, in building Hospital Corporation of America, Dr Tom Frist, Jr, President and Chairman, started with the image of technical excellence in health care, originating from his medical training. To this he added the Holiday Inn model, creating an image of a hospital chain paralleling the

Holiday Inn chain of motels throughout the country. The blended images created an ideal which was the basis for extraordinary corporate growth over a sixteen year period from the late 1960s through the mid-1980s.

The ego-ideal is not a fixed element in the healthy executive personality. It is an elastic and dynamic standard which becomes modified over time with changing reality. The senior vice president of an oil field service organization had looked forward to spending several peaceful years as president before his retirement. This was his image during the late 1970s. Near the end of the first quarter following his assumption of the president's duties, the bottom fell out of the oil industry. His whole concept of what he needed to do was revised dramatically. He entered a two year struggle to downsize his company in terms of personnel (40% reduction) and capital expenditures (over 50% reduction). His ego-ideal changed through the experience so that growth was no longer necessarily desirable, nor was expansion to be sought after.

Executives also play a key, active function in shaping the organizational ideal. Schwartz (1987) calls the organizational ideal the 'perfect person' for the organization. In some companies, this ideal is strongly defined and well expressed, while in others it is much fuzzier and more diffuse. Executives embody elements of their organization's ideal through their attitudes and behaviors. Executives strive for the ideal. This sort of symbolic activity is embodied in the roles we have seen Lee Iacocca (of Chrysler) play. His strong, active image on television ads captures the essence of this symbolic ideal.

In addition to being contributors to the creation of the organizational ideal, executives play an important role by participating in the extension of an ideal. The engineering vice president of a manufacturing firm talked about the general excitement in his job as the most rewarding aspect of his work. On closer examination, it became clear that he was actually the originator of most of the challenge and excitement himself. He did this by embracing the basic participative philosophy of the firm's president. He accepted the overall ideal forged by the president and translated that through the engineering function of the company. Prior to his arrival in the early 1980s, the engineering function had been largely a passive element of the company. His arrival energized and activated the engineers, encouraging them to go into the different work areas of the company, to visit with their counterparts, and to look for problems they might help solve.

While the ego-ideal and the images in an executive's mind are primary energizing forces in the personality, that energy is directed outward. Executives vary in their reality orientation; that is, how much they are in touch with and aware of the realities within their companies and within the environment in which the company operates. The failure to maintain a strong reality orientation leads to miscalculations that are often problematic and occasionally disastrous. A young insurance company executive was very occupied with increasing his position and power at work. He realistically viewed himself as articulate, professionally competent, and very much the master of his job. He judged himself to be ready for a new challenge. While his immediate boss was on a two week Hawaiian anniversary vacation, the executive approached the relatively new division executive about his interest in advancement. He did not approach him with a clear or well-formulated plan, apparently believing that the energetic new division executive would create one for him. The net result was that his immediate boss dismissed him shortly after his return, believing he could no longer fully trust him. The executive's failure was in misunderstanding the complexities of the political realities of the insurance company.

While some executives, like the insurance executive, do a poor job of reality testing prior to acting, others use various methods to reality test on an ongoing basis. An example comes from the behavior of a senior military general. He is a man who is particularly concerned with how his staff will react to change, uncertainty, and stress. He develops realistic information about key people in his work environment by testing and challenging them, in part to observe the response or reaction. Through this process he learns how these men and women are likely to react. In essence, he elicits a response to get better information for the future prediction of behavior. His method gives him a solid reality base for understanding his key personnel. Some who do not understand his approach become defensive, for which the general does not give one high marks.

Another form of reality testing is less interpersonal and more technological. Chaparral Steel is an American mini-mill company that has been interested in leading its sector of the steel industry. The executive team has a strong organizational ideal that is consistent across individuals. In translating their images, goals, and ideals into action, these executives spend time with steel companies and corporations in Japan, West Germany, Scandinavia, as well as universities throughout Canada and the US. This behavior is targeted at reality testing and learning. They want to answer questions like: How do these people perform a specific operation better than we do? How do they do it less expensively? How do they do it differently than we do?

The executive's activity is goal directed, the goal being to achieve the ideal image in the mind. As reality requires, this ideal is modified and shaped so that the result is achievable. The interaction between the ideal and reality is not a one way street, however. Opportunities and niches are created by executives who work to alter external reality to correspond to the ideal as well as altering the ideal to reflect reality. An example of this has been achieved in the nutrition and health care industries with low-sodium products. Product executives are attempting to educate and reshape some of the eating behavior of consumers. Other examples abound in the consumer products area.

As active leaders within their organizations, executives are critical to a whole variety of organizational outcomes. They influence both the shape and the direction which an organization takes over time. This may be seen in the words of the chairman of a bank in describing his role.

> Well, as chairman of the bank, I am the leader so to speak, and supposed to establish the tone and the work ethic. And I think if I serve the role from a leadership point of view that is an integral part of it. Aside from that, the job itself is what the job of a chairman should be in most organizations. That is to be involved in policy and selection of leaders, to delegate to those leaders and to control their activities, but not too closely. Not to the extent that we stifle creativity. And yet we control them so that they are never out of control.

Power and Control

The second theme of executive life is power and control. Executive work involves the control of resources, including people, money, material, and time. For some, the drive is to dominate. A division executive in a service industry had approximately 34 managers under his supervision and a total of 300 employees. One of his strategies was to periodically move his managers around to see how they responded to different challenges and functions. He did not do this wholesale, but on a selective basis so that only two or three managers moved at a time. He saw the business as a chess game and the managers as chess pieces to be moved. This view of power and control is that of dominion over others.

The commander of a military airlift wing had a different perspective. While he was the final decision maker, his staff officers all were active participants in the decision process. Rather than dominating them, he used them as important sources of information. His staff meetings often appeared chaotic because of the nature of the dialogue; expressions of opinion were diverse and unrestrained. The commander's studied attention to each officer's opinion was in contast to the animated expression of thoughts and ideas. In essence, the commander exercised control through channeling the energy and drive of his staff.

The exercise of control does not necessarily mean authoritarian or dictatorial action, though that is sometimes the case. The chairman of the large commercial bank illustrates this kind of behavior pattern and the complications that can go along with it.

> He has a very authoritarian and highly directive management style in all of his working relationships, often instructing subordinates with a shaking, pointed index finger and an angry voice. He goes to unusual lengths to avoid depending on others, maintaining a withdrawn and aloof posture with managers and staff in the bank. In addition to typing all of his own memos and failing to confide in either staff or colleagues, he periodically causes conflict by involving himself in details rather than leaving them to others. For example, the chairman frequently interferes with his loan department by directing that certain pet loans be made while others be turned down. His decisions in these cases are not based on the bank's guidelines, but on individual whims and personal preferences that are never clear to his loan officers. His behavior communicates a lack of trust in his loan officers and creates an uncertain and unpredictable atmosphere for them. (Quick, Nelson and Quick, 1987, p. 143).

Control should not be equated with dictatorialness or self-centeredness. Control exercised by an executive may also be developmental and positive. McClelland (1925) has discussed this positive, other-centered aspect of power and control. Executives who possess this characteristic identify their interests with those of the group they are managing, forming a collaborative relationship with others in the group. They identify with and understand the needs of the members of the group. And they direct or channel the energy and actions of the members of the group. This is done through positive as opposed to punitive dynamics.

Power and control in a social system is estimated by the number of successful influence attempts which occur. There are three basic ways in which a single influence attempt may be concluded. The first is for the executive's influence attempt to be carried out exactly as intended. When Oscar Wyatt, Chairman of Coastal States Gas, relocated the company's headquarters from Corpus Christi, Texas, to Houston, he simply did it. Staff moved or made alternative arrangements. This sort of straightforward successful conclusion of an influence attempt is not common because of the complexities of an executive's environment.

The second way to conclude an influence attempt is through a series of reciprocal influence attempts and responses that conclude in a measure of success. In this sort of exchange, an executive's intentions and attempts are modified through interaction with individuals and events in the environment. This second way of concluding an influence attempt is usually protracted and involves much exchange and negotiation. A prime example of this sort of exchange occurs in labor–management negotiations. Here the goals of the two groups are incompatible, to some degree, and require negotiations to avert direct opposition on the part of one group to the other. To avoid rendering himself powerless, the executive must be able to modify and change positions based on new, different, or more complete information. The underlying dynamic is aimed at achieving a result as near to the original intention as possible. This is the most common way for influence attempts to be played out in the workplace.

The third way an influence attempt may conclude is through failure. The net result of this is a loss of power for the executive and the system as a whole. Organizations in which there are numerous failed influence attempts are powerless ones, full of frustration. While an executive cannot control the response of another to his influence attempts, he does have control over his response to the other's influence attempt with him. Thus, the complete block of another person's effort has far different consequences than the attempt to reshape that effort into a more acceptable direction. An example of failure is the case of Howard Putnam at Braniff Airways. Having left a highly successful position as chairman of Southwest Airlines, Putnam made an attempt to rescue Braniff in the early 1980s. His attempts failed, ended in bankruptcy, and led to his departure from the airline industry.

The exercise of power involves understanding different personalities and how to interact with them. A division executive in the defense industry described the notable differences in the personalities of the three managers who worked for him. The first manager was an unusually enthusiastic, energetic man with strong initiative. The executive found that to effectively manage this man involved occasional support and little else. The second manager had a clear understanding of the executive's intentions and objectives, always asking if uncertain. This manager needed minimum attention and direction. The third manager, at the other extreme, was one who needed forceful direction. Once he had it, he was successful and productive. The executive simply had to tell him frequently and forcefully what needed to be done.

One of the failures of some executives is the inability to understand that they cannot control another person, only the circumstances and consequences of behavior. The belief that one can control another's behavior is a fantasy of omnipotence which may be an occupational hazard for anyone who *does* have control over a wealth of resources. The confusion concerns what is being controlled. The resources, such as money, benefits, and opportunities, are controlled for the purpose of influence; however, the underlying dynamic is calculated and contractual. The manager, peer, or subordinate who does not accept this calculated arrangement cannot be controlled by the consequences of the behavior.

An excellent example of a strongly autonomous personality that would fit this category is General George Patton. He was at times an unusually difficult subordinate for Generals Eisenhower and Bradley to supervise. Neither of these generals had fantasies of omnipotence; they were therefore able to manage the complications of Patton's personality.

At the other extreme of the executive with fantasies of omnipotence is the one who believes himself powerless. If the underlying feeling is one of powerlessness, then the only way to counter this feeling is through aggressive and/or defensive behavior that demonstrates clear, observable consequences. An executive with this problem will not nurture and develop subordinates because the development of their power and competence is interpreted as a threat to his own. This type of manager exercises power through domination over others, not cooperation with them.

Executives with either set of fantasies create various conflicts and problems in the workplace related to the lack of reality contact. These conflicts all center around the defensive behaviors the executives exhibit. The central purpose of the defensiveness is the protection of the fantasy. The alternative to either of these extremes is the executive who understands the realities and limitations of his power. This executive establishes a very nondefensive work environment in which power and influence operate in reciprocal ways, not just unilaterally. This pattern of behavior leads to an increasingly powerful, influential work environment.

Stress

The third theme in executive life is stress, an inevitable characteristic of

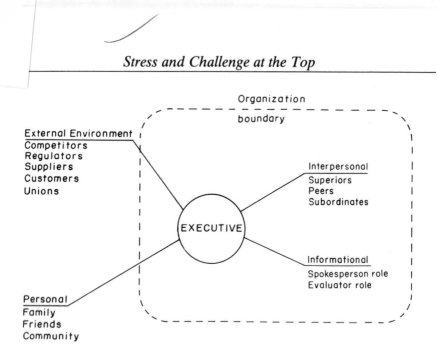

Figure 2   Environmental sources of executive stress

professional and personal life. This is not necessarily bad because stress is a very useful asset in responding to legitimate emergencies and challenges at work. Not all stress is caused by emergencies, however. The two major sources of stress for an executive are internal and external demands. The internal demands which executives face are found in the ego-ideal element of the personality. This personality element places pressure on the other elements of the personality to respond and adjust. Examples of internal demands would be expectations to achieve certain promotions or to achieve specific social status positions. All elements of the personality would be required to cooperate in this effort. The external demands which create stress for an executive are complex and varied. The major categories of demands are represented in Figure 2. They are (1) elements in the external environment; (2) interpersonal demands in the workplace; (3) informational demands; and (4) personal demands.

An executive is a key point of contact for his organization with its external environment. Competitors, regulators, suppliers, customers, and unions are all key elements in the external environment. While some of the relationships with these environmental elements are basically competitive in nature, others are more cooperative. All of the relationships place pressure on the executive to behave in ways advantageous to other members of the relationship. The president of a rug manufacturing company found his relationship with the local union president among the most stressful of his working relationships. The confrontations were often acrimonious, heated, and frustrating for both men. There were constant arguments over salary issues, benefits, and working conditions. The company president was able to change the relationship markedly by an effort one day to listen patiently to the union president. While there was not always agreement on issues thereafter, the tense confrontation was eliminated from the relationship. Chrysler President Lee Iacocca attempted a variation on this by placing Douglas Fraser, President of the United Auto Workers (UAW), on Chrysler's Board of Directors in the early 1980s. By doing so, he achieved a more cooperative labor–management relationship for a time.

Customers represent a different sort of stress for an executive. While there is not the same sort of conflict as with unions or regulators, the relationship often becomes strained out of customer frustration. Our work with customer service executives demonstrates their recognition of the importance of customer satisfaction and their stereotypic perception of the customer as an angry, frustrated person. One service executive in the real estate industry found that his service representatives had a pattern of tension headaches generated by angry customer calls. While not having a direct impact on the executive, the customer complaints had a secondary impact due to the time he needed to devote to the problems created for his service representatives. The external environmental problems thus create some interpersonal demands within the workplace.

The interpersonal demands of different constituencies create several competing demands on an executive. The different categories of relationships shown in Figure 2 may serve as sources of demands and/or sources of support. The absence of a positive interpersonal bond between an executive and his superior(s) will create distress due to lack of predictability and trust. The executive's primary emotional and psychological attachment in the workplace is with the superior. The emotional charge makes this a very significant dependency relationship in terms of the executive's well-being, with a strong potential for high levels of stress. The inability to trust and predict one's superior's behavior leads to the distress seen in the case of one senior executive:

> I spent five years in an organization working for a fellow who was a brilliant man, one of the few people I have ever known who had real

charisma about him. But he had problems of his own. He had a manic depressive type personality and he was either so high or so low that I couldn't relate to him and we never connected. So I had no one to talk to, to counsel with me, to think with me. It was just a very difficult situation. My wife would tell me every Sunday afternoon you're tightening up and withdrawing. It was just like you had to get ready to go do battle for the week. He always kept me off balance.

Executive relationships with peers create a different sort of interpersonal demand. The underlying dynamic in the relationship is not dependency; rather it, is competition. The competition is over resources of all kinds, including financial, material, time with superiors, and personnel. The dilemma of the peer relationship is that undue competition creates divisiveness in the relationship; hence, the internal conflict in creating a cooperative relationship. This entails sublimating the drive to pursue self-interest at the expense of the peer's self-interest. The importance of communicating in peer relationships is noted by an operating company president in the health care industry:

So I guess I emphasize communication as much as anything else. I worry about it sideways as I spend a lot of my time wandering around in our organization. We have five operating companies of which I am the president of one. I spend a lot of time with the other four, not very productive from the point of view of anything that relates to my bottom line or my organization, but making sure our relationship is a sound one so that if something is important to me, they're going to go along with me. And I know what's important to them so I know I can support them when it's appropriate.

The demands which subordinates place on an executive are different again. The underlying dynamic is neither dependency nor competition if it is a healthy relationship. The need for restraint is greater than in the peer relationship because of the natural power advantage built into the relationship. Excessive use of the power advantage tends to crush the initiative in the subordinate but excessive restraint on the part of the executive results in an unrestrained subordinate. The executive as leader draws out the subordinate for greater development. In addition to the demands for self-management in the relationship with subordinates, there are the demands which subordinates place directly on the executive. These are time and resource demands of various kinds. Some subordinates will be more demanding than others by nature, especially those who are achievement-oriented, aggressive, and/or abrasive.

The relationship with a subordinate whom an executive chooses to mentor will become more stressful, and potentially much more rewarding, than the relationship with other subordinates. This is due to the additional time, energy, and responsibility demands which go along with that sort of involvement. The other aspect of the mentor–understudy relationship which makes it stressful centers around the inherent conflict of the later stages in the understudy's development. The junior executive will arrive at a developmental point when breaking the bond with the mentor is in the junior executive's long-term best interest.

In addition to the interpersonal demands of the work environment are the informational demands. An executive must engage in the representational role of spokesperson for his organization, shaping the attitudes and behaviors of other toward the organization. The executive engages this role in a variety of settings, from television advertising to direct customer interactions to regulator interfaces. This is exemplified in the case of Tom Wageman, Chief Executive of Sunbelt Savings and Loan Association of Texas in the mid-1980s. During one difficult year in the industry, Wageman aggressively represented his organization, resulting in an increase in deposits of nearly $500 million in one twelve month period.

A second aspect of informational demands concerns the acquisition and evaluation of information from all sorts of channels. Trends, environmental changes, threats, and opportunities which affect the organization must be evaluated by an executive to determine their impact and to determine the correct response to these events. For example, American automobile executives during the 1970s and 1980s were confronted with an increasing amount of foreign competition from West German and Japanese auto makers while also being challenged by consumers who were interested in small, more fuel efficient automobiles. Evaluating this information required determining whether the trends were long-term or temporary, what nature of technological response was required, and the whole range of response options that was needed to adjust to the change.

The final set of demands that creates stress for an executive falls in the personal arena. Some of these personal demands intersect with work demands. Community service activities, for example, may be expected of an executive. While some companies, like Eastman Kodak, provide some work time allocations for community activities, other organizations expect executives to engage in these activities in their personal time. The military services label these sorts of activities 'additional duties.'

With many executive work weeks well in excess of 40 hours, there is an inevitable clash between personal and professional demands. The time limit of 168 hours per week is universally applicable, regardless of occupation or personal preference. While conflict and competition may develop between the home and work environments, such conflict is not inevitable, as we see in the case of an oil field industry executive:

> About fifteen years ago—I was not upper management, I was in middle management at the time—the company decided that they would have the middle and upper management be interviewed and evaluated by an industrial psychologist's firm. This is the type of thing that you go in and have a pre-interview and then you take the test and you can go back in for a post-interview. So, I went through all of this, and went back in for the post-interview and the industrial psychologist said to me, 'You know it's evident here that you probably do pretty good at the job you have now, but you're just going to have to make up your mind to it that you're not ever going much higher in this company, and you're certainly never going to be the president and chief executive officer.' Well this kind of startled me. I said, why do you say that, and he said, 'You're too good a family man.' he said, 'You are not willing to make the sacrifices of your family time, interest, all this for your job and that's going to limit your career.'

This executive's subsequent progress to the roles of president and chief executive officer (CEO) shows the fallacy of the psychologist's conclusion.

While the executive's external demands are complex and varied, so too are the ego-ideal elements which provide the internal drive and motivation for action. Figure 3 depicts the three fundamental aspects of personality identified by Freud (1949): the 'it' (originally translated as 'id'), the 'I' (originally translated as 'ego'), and the 'above-I' (originally the 'super-ego'). The above-I consists of the internalized values, restraints, and model behavior patterns towards which an individual strives. An important element of the above-I is the ego-ideal. The deeper psychic elements of the ego-ideal are the fundamental basis for the executive's drive and ambition. These elements come from at least three separate sources in the individual's development and are identified in Figure 3.

First, the child internalizes elements of the parental model. This does not always have to be a parent of the same sex. In the case of a young female engineer, the dominant model she had chosen and internalized for her professional development was her father. Second, images in the

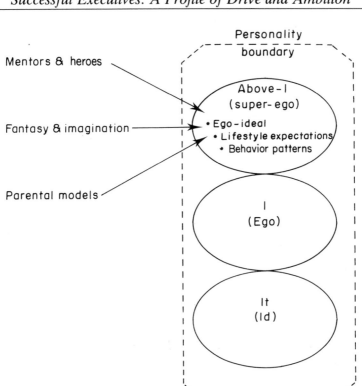

Mentors & heroes

Fantasy & imagination

Parental models

Figure 3   Development of the ego-ideal

ego-ideal emerge from elements of fantasy and magical thinking. In the US culture, these elements of fantasy and magical thinking are reflected in our superheroes, such as Superman and Captain Marvel. There has been a whole range of these superheroes that have emerged in cartoon strips and television series over the past 40 years. The same underlying psychic process that gives rise to these magical heroes contributes elements or characteristics to the ego-ideal. One example might be the characteristic of being so powerful that pain makes no impact at the emotional level. This may be an ideal, but it is certainly not an achievable ideal.

The third element which contributes to the modification of the ego-ideal is mentors and role models, especially early in the career. These play important roles because the ego-ideal, at least within the healthy personality, is always in the process of modification and change based on new experience. A leading steel executive's philosophy of management was

significantly influenced by the chairman of his corporation who counseled him to always 'work himself out of a job.' By this the chairman
meant he should work to develop his subordinates, cultivate their
talent, and delegate authority to them. This counsel became incorpor-
ated into the executive's ego-ideal and served as a standard toward
which he still strives.

These internal driving forces bring the executive's ambition into
contact with the opportunities and constraints of the real world. For an
executive to establish his ambition in the world involves risk.

Risk Taking

Risk taking is a key feature of executive life. Executives who do not take
risks are the managers of the status quo. While these individuals provide
some stability and continuity to every organization, they are not the
architects who build and create. The architects who build, create, and
take risks are the leaders of any industry. Effective risk takers are not
executives who respond totally intuitively or from the hip. Rather, they
are individuals who exercise good conscious and unconscious judgment
based upon accumulated experience. They make risky decisions that
pay off more often than not.

Decision making patterns may be classified into one of three categories. These categories are (1) intuition, (2) judgment, and (3) problem-
solving. Intuitive decision making is creative and spontaneous. It may
be highly appropriate to artistic endeavors and also valuable as input to
judgmental decision making. As a basis for significant decisions,
however, it has limited value for executives.

Problem-solving decision making lies at the other end of the continuum from intuitive decision making. It is methodical, data based,
mathematical, and systematic. This type of decision making requires a
theoretical or conceptual equational model into which information can
be put. The equation is worked and the problem solved. New plant
location decisions are good examples where such a decision formula
may prove quite useful. Factors such as natural or essential resource
availability, labor availability, transportation channel presence, and
other relevant criteria for a good plant location site would be placed into
the model to compare various alternative sites. The bottom-line comparisons thus lead to the final decision.

Again, this approach has limitations as well as value. It also may be used as a tool and input to judgmental executive decision making. This is the most likely form of decision making for risk taking executives because within this category, the executive accepts full responsibility for the final decision. General George Patton argued for judgmental decision making with two key guidelines (Williamson, 1979). First, each strategic decision has a window of opportunity. If the decision maker waits too long, the opportunity is lost and the lack of decision becomes a negative decision. On the other hand, if the decision maker decides precipitously, he may miss key information essential to the exercise of good judgment. Hence, there is the risk of not taking advantage of a good opportunity because insufficient information is developed prior to action. And, there is the risk of a lost opportunity due to total inaction.

The second guideline is that each business decision creates stress, uncertainty, and fear. Fear has both a functional and dysfunctional role in decision processes. The value of fear is that it draws the decision maker's attention to the risks and uncertainties involved in the decision. The decision maker may benefit from the explicit enumeration of the risks and losses that may result from the various decision alternatives. Thus, the fear motivates the executive to develop information as a defense against the uncertain outcomes. The dysfunctional aspect of fear is that it may cause the decision maker to freeze. There may be sufficient uncertainty in the decision situation that a conscious decision not to act is the best decision. Such conscious choice is distinct from the emotional paralysis that results from intense fear and anxiety.

As Drucker (1974) has pointed out, executives should not be avoiding risky decisions. Rather, they should be taking the right risks. What are the 'right' risks? Estimating risks is a judgmental process based on experience. This would support an argument for executives to become specialists in a particular line of business or industry. They must learn the business. The notion of the interchangeability of executive talent across industries or lines of business, while popular for a time, is argued against by Iacocca (1984). This does not mean that the education of the executive should be highly specialized. On the contrary, there is support for a broad, diversified educational experience coupled with a con-centration within one industry.

The reasoning for this perspective concerns the understanding and estimation of risk taking. The more experience an executive develops in one industry, the better the understanding of how the industry works, of the forces that operate within the industry, and of the implications of various decision alternatives. This understanding leads to a greater ability to predict and to control events within the organization and the industry. Understanding, predictability, and control all play a functional role as antidotes to distress (Sutton and Kahn, 1987). They also are central to the estimation of risk and the choice of decision risks. The net result of concentrating in one industry and line of business should be a greater ability to make good quality decisions and assume risks with greater payoff potentials.

Paradoxically, this concentrated focus also demands diversity. The reason for diversity emerges from the possibility of developing tunnel vision with regard to problems and decisions in the industry, pointing to the value of an unspecialized education. A broad education and continuing broad educational experiences give an executive new perspectives on old issues. AT&T (American Telephone & Telegraph) recognized the need for this educational breadth among their more technically trained specialists, such as in accounting, finance, and engineering, over 25 years ago. Through a collaborative relationship with Williams College, an Executive Program was designed which exposed mid-level executives to five intensive weeks of education in the humanities and social sciences. This Williams College Executive Program has evolved to the point where approximately 30 select executives are exposed to music, literature, art, psychology, and other liberal arts disciplines. The educational experience is designed to broaden their perspective, provide them with new and different frameworks for thinking about their work, and prepare them to be better decision makers.

In addition to the need for flexibility and/or diversity of perspectives on the part of an executive, there is also a need for some diversity within the line of business. A good example of that need is reflected in the Texas banking system of the 1980s as well as some of the international banks. Excessive loan investments in the oil industry or foreign investments in the Latin American countries created a highly concentrated risk exposure for those banks. The principle is applicable to other industries as well.

A key aspect of executive risk taking concerns personal exposure. Some executives do not assume any personal risks and they avoid them through contractual arrangements or golden parachutes which protect them. They develop a financially secure position and then defend it, assuming no risk. John Deere (manufacturers of large farm equipment) exemplified an alternative which resulted in strong growth for his company in the early years. He reinvested much of the profit from the business back into the business, either in the form of improved production methods or in research and development.

SUMMARY

Executive life is risky, personally and professionally. However, successful executives are not risk avoiders; they are risk seekers. They attempt to control the risks by placing their best bet and then changing the odds even more in their favor. The risks create stress, which is also caused by a range of environmental and internal factors. This stress carries with it a set of health risks which will be discussed in detail in the next chapter. One of the key internal sources of stress for executives is the ego-ideal which activates their personality and drives them to positions of leadership where they can exercise their need for power, influence, and control. Their active, stressful, risky lifestyle need not necessarily lead to the problems all too common in corporations around the world.

FURTHER READING

Cooper, C. and Hingley, P. (1985). *The Change Makers*, Harper & Brothers, New York.

Drucker, P. F. (1974). *Management: Tasks, Responsibilities, Practices*, Harper and Row, New York.

Levinson, H. (1963). What killed Bob Lyons? *Harvard Business Review*, **36**, 127–43.

Levinson, H. (1975). *Executive Stress*, New American Library, New York.

Levinson, H. (1981). *Executive*, Harvard University Press, Cambridge, Mass.

Quick, J. C., Nelson, D. L. and Quick, J. D. (1987). Successful executives: How independent? *Academy of Management Executive*, **1**(2), 139–45.

Schwartz, H. W. (1987). On the psychodynamics of totalitarianism, *Journal of Management*, **13**(1), 41–54.

Sutton, R. I. and Kahn, R. L. (1987). Prediction, understanding and control as antidotes to organizational stress. In J. W. Lorsch (ed.) *Handbook of Organizational Behavior*, Prentice Hall, Englewood Cliffs, New Jersey.

Chapter 2

Executive Stress: The Risks of Success

—In 1981, Alvin L. Feldman, Chairman of Continental Airlines, died in his office of an apparently self-inflicted gunshot wound.
—W. Howard Beasley III was transforming Lone Star Technologies, Inc. as Chairman, President, and CEO. In 1989, he was advised to take a medical leave because of Hodgekins lymphoma.
—Bill McGowan founded and built MCI Communication Corporation over a 20 year period. In 1986, at age 59, he had a heart attack. He survived and in 1987 received a heart transplant.

The consequences of executive stress? Perhaps—at least in part. Death from a heart attack can be the extreme individual consequence of ineffectively managed stress. Peptic ulcers and tension headaches are other individual consequences. Poor performance, decline in morale, and loss of organizational vitality are potential organizational costs of mismanaged stress. But stress is not necessarily destructive or bad: it can provide the eleventh-hour burst of creativity needed to finalize a major ad campaign or close a pivotal real estate deal. Channeled properly, stress can be energizing, stimulating and growth producing.

Though our wisdom about stress provides some useful insights, it also contains some concepts which may not stand up to careful scrutiny. For example, it appears that it is not the people who openly express their anger who develop heart disease, but those who repress it and turn it in on themselves (Gentry *et al.*, 1982). And the 'executive heart attack' may be more common among mid-managers who have not made it to the top than among the executives who have (Moss, 1981).

The executives profiled in Chapters 4 and 5 have all experienced significant levels of stress during their professional lives, but all have lived—even thrived—to tell about it. Why do some people experience the negative consequences of stress, while others do not? This chapter will review the dynamics of stress, the stress response, and the potential health consequences of stress. It will consider why some executives show signs of distress, while others appear resistant to harmful effects from lifestyles which, to the outside observer, appear highly stressful. Finally, it will provide some guidance on assessing one's own stress levels.

The underlying theme of this chapter is that, while stress is an inevitable and perhaps even necessary component of executive success, its negative consequences are neither inevitable nor necessary. By studying executives who have been successful in their careers while maintaining their personal well-being, we hope to better understand what makes a 'healthy success.'

THE DYNAMICS OF STRESS

For many of us, 'stress' has only negative connotations; it is an experience to be avoided, a source of anxiety, tension, and discomfort. Yet the occurrence of stressful events is a universal part of daily life, particularly in the working world. Stress is a naturally occurring experience essential to our growth, development, and performance both at work and at home. The ultimate outcome depends not simply on the occurrence of stress, but more importantly on individual and organizational responses to stress.

'Stress' has become a purposefully ambiguous term used variously to refer to (1) stressful events ('stressors'), (2) the psychological and physiological stress response, or (3) the eventual individual and organizational consequences of stress. Figure 1 summarizes the relationships between these three distinct aspects of stress.

Stress has its origins in the demands of organizational and personal life. *Stressors* are the physical or psychological demands encountered in the course of individual, community, and organizational life. As noted in Chapter 1 and summarized in Figure 1, managers and executives face a variety of organizational and personal demands. Stressors are often negative or unpleasant such as an unhappy spouse who decided to leave with the children. But situations which create great excitement, joy, and positive arousal are also demanding. Thus, a successful merger, a long-awaited promotion, or the birth of a child are all stressors. What matters in determining the degree of stress that an individual experiences is the intensity of the perceived demand for readjustment or adaptation. The

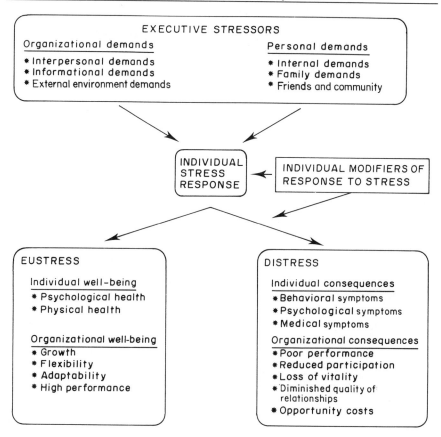

Figure 1   Stressors and their consequences (adapted from Quick and Quick, 1984, p. 44)

stress response occurs as a result of the individual's reaction to the stressor or perceived demand.

The *stress response* is the generalized, patterned, unconscious mobilization of the body's natural energy resources when confronted with a stressor. This mobilization occurs through the combined action of the nervous and hormonal systems. The four cardinal characteristics of the stress response are: (1) heightened sense of alertness; (2) elevated heart rate and blood pressure; (3) release of glucose and fatty acids from their storage sites into the blood stream; and (4) reduction of less emergent activities such as digestion and immune function.

Stressful events are inevitable, but the destructive or distressful effects of these events are not inevitable. In general, stressful events or stressors can lead to one of two outcomes: individual strain and distress, or individual well-being and eustress (Figure 1). *Eustress* is the healthy, positive, constructive outcome of the stress response. It includes the individual and organizational well-being associated with growth, flexibility, adaptability, and high performance levels. Conversely, *distress* is the unhealthy, negative, destructive outcome of the stress response. Distress refers to both adverse organizational consequences and adverse individual consequences (Quick and Quick, 1984; Selye, 1976).

THE STRESS RESPONSE

When confronted with news reports and journal articles describing the spectrum of conditions which have been associated with stress and stressful events, it is reasonable to ask, 'How can this be?' 'How can accidents, heart attacks, and diabetes *all* be associated with something such as stress?' The answer lies in the psychological and biological linkages which govern inner human workings and which have now begun to be understood. Through the work of medical scientists, psychologists, and other researchers, many of these linkages are now known.

The nature of the stress response was first studied at the beginning of the century by the Harvard physician-researcher Walter Cannon and in the mid-1920s by Hans Selye, known to many as the 'Father of Stress.' As a young medical student, Selye became curious about the general phenomena of 'being sick.' He noted that patients suffering from a variety of ills showed many similar physiologic responses.

Through human and animal research Selye (1973) discerned a rather predictable pattern of responses which he termed the 'general adaptation syndrome (GAS).' He identified three stages to the GAS: the alarm reaction, the stage of resistance, and the stage of exhaustion. The 'alarm reaction' is the immediate, predictable response to any type of stress, often called the 'emergency reaction,' or simply the 'flight-or-fight' response.

The pattern of the alarm reaction—the immediate stress response—is familiar. Imagine, for example, that you have been leading the team to develop the strategy for a major new initiative. You will be presenting to the board of directors the team's recommendations, in which you have a considerable personal and professional investment. You expect resistance from some members simply because it's a new concept. From others you expect strategic or technical questions—possibly some your team has not considered. Others you hope to look to for support. You've rehearsed the presentation, but the uncertainty is still there.

As the chairman begins to introduce the topic, you scan your notes. In about 30 seconds you'll be the focus of the meeting with only your notes and a few charts to present. Pause and observe your own body: despite the air conditioning, your brow and palms are moist, dampening your carefully prepared notes. You notice a pounding in your chest—your heart is beating 100 times a minute, rather than its usual 60 times, and each beat is more powerful as it raises your blood pressure. You feel a little queasiness—a gnawing in the pit of your stomach. Your breathing is deeper, yet tighter.

As you clear your throat and begin to speak you realize your mouth is dry, cottony. You take a sip of water, raising the glass with a slightly tremulous hand. Your muscles are tense as you rock forward in your chair. All your attention is focused on the board members and the comments you are about to make.

You are experiencing Selye's alarm reaction, the fight-or-flight response. At this point the flight option may seem very attractive. Through biological mechanisms developed in our primitive past, your body is preparing for a physical response to a challenging situation.

The stress response consists of an immediate, unconscious, well-orchestrated pattern of sympathetic nervous system and endocrine (hormone) system reactions, the combined effects of which are the four basic psychophysiological changes noted above:

1. Increased alertness.
2. Release of glucose and fatty acids for energy from their storage sites into the blood stream.
3. Redirection of blood flow to the brain and large muscle groups.
4. Reduction of less emergent activities such as digestion and immune system functions.

The stress response is controlled primarily through the sympathetic nervous system. The human nervous system has two major divisions: the somatic nervous system, which controls skeletal muscles, and the autonomic nervous system, which controls basic life functions such as breathing, heartbeat, blood pressure, and digestion. The autonomic nervous system is further divided into the sympathetic and parasympathetic nervous systems. The parasympathetic nervous system stimulates vegetative or reparative activities.

The *sympathetic nervous system* stimulates activating functions generally identified with the stress response. Much of our basic understanding of the role of the sympathetic nervous system and, in particular, the role of epinephrine (adrenaline) comes from the work of Walter B. Cannon and his colleagues at Harvard. Sympathetic responses result from the direct action of sympathetic nerves on target organs such as the heart, blood vessels, and muscles and from the release of catecholamines, primary epinephrine, and norepinephrine, into the blood stream. Circulating catecholamines have a direct activating effect on the central nervous system, leading to the awake, alert state which usually occurs in stressful situations.

The other system involved in the stress response is the hormone or *endocrine system*. Much of the information regarding the role of the endocrine system in stress derives from Selye's research. Hormones are chemical messengers released by endocrine glands to travel in the blood stream to stimulate specific responses in a variety of organs. Adrenocorticotropic hormone (ACTH), cortisol, glucagon, epinephrine and norepinephrine are the most important stress hormones.

Within seconds after the onset of a stressful stimulus, ACTH is released from the pituitary gland, deep in the brain, and travels through the blood stream to the adrenal glands, which sit atop each kidney. Here ACTH stimulates the conversion of cholesterol to cortisol and related hormones. Cortisol, in turn, mobilizes stored energy reserves by stimulating the liver to release and replenish glucose and stimulating fat cells to release fatty acids. Cortisol has several other effects with potentially negative outcomes. It causes a breakdown of protein for use as energy, inhibits immune and inflammatory responses, shrinks lymphoid tissue involved in fighting infection, and weakens bones. Moderate levels of cortisol strengthen muscle contraction, but prolonged or excessively high doses weaken muscles. Other hormones also act to stimulate increased blood glucose, release of fatty acids, increase in heart rate, and increase in blood pressure.

Thus, the sympathetic nervous system and the endocrine system work together to mobilize the body's various resources. The stress response is rooted in man's evolution. It was essential for survival in an environment of primarily physical challenges such as warring tribes and the pursuit of wild game. The response is still functional. If channeled wisely, it can improve performance in work and recreation environments, both physical and intellectual. But if the alarm reaction is elicited too intensely and too frequently over an extended period without an effective outlet, a stage of exhaustion is reached. As Selye (1973) notes, 'One would think that once adaptation has occurred and ample energy is available, resistance should go on indefinitely. But just as any inanimate machine gradually wears out, so does the human machine sooner or later become the victim of constant wear and tear.'

It is at the stage of exhaustion that many of the undesirable consequences of stress occur. These may include behavioral changes such as increased alcohol consumption, psychological effects such as depression, or medical consequences such as the onset or worsening of heart disease. These are the individual manifestations of *distress*—stress mismanaged.

WHEN STRESS BECOMES DISTRESS: THE HEALTH CONSEQUENCES OF STRESS

Properly monitored and managed, the stress response contributes to a state of optimum health and well-being by stimulating productivity and supporting performance. But when the stress response is elicited too intensely or too often and the individual is unable to rapidly dissipate the effects of the stress response, the result can be individual *distress*. The distress resulting from mismanaged stress may be manifested by any of several behavioral, psychological, or medical problems listed in Table 1. These problems will be considered before turning to the potential health benefits of stress.

Behavioral Consequences

Behavioral changes are among the earliest and most overt signs of rising levels of stress. Increased cigarette smoking, greater alcohol and drug

Table 1   Individual consequences of distress

Behavioral consequences	Psychological consequences	Medical consequences
Smoking	Burnout syndrome	Heart disease
Alcohol abuse	Family problems	Cancer
Drug abuse	Sleep disturbance	Respiratory illness
Accident proneness	Sexual dysfunction	Backache and arthritis
Violence	Depression	Ulcer disease
	Psychogenic disability	Headache

abuse, accident proneness, and violence are among the changes which research has associated with increased stress.

Cigarette consumption may serve as pleasure smoking, social smoking, or stress smoking. Russek (1965) surveyed 12 000 professional men in fourteen occupational categories and used 32 expert judges to categorize the occupations as high-stress or low-stress. He found 46% of men in high-stress occupations to be smokers compared with 32% in low-stress occupations. Both stress and cigarette consumption were related to the incidence of heart disease. Similarly, Conway and colleagues (1981), in a study of US Navy petty officers, found a significant correlation between occupational stress and cigarette smoking. In an attempt to address the cause–effect relationship, studies by Lindenthal and associates (1972) and Hillier (1981) demonstrate that increases in smoking under stress are proportional to the number of stressors within a given period of time. Increased levels of stress also appear to lead to increased alcohol consumption and drug abuse. Although moderate and occasional alcohol consumption appear to have some important beneficial health effects (Neff, 1985), the negative consequences are substantial. About 10 million Americans, up to 10% of the work force, are alcoholics. Alcohol consumption is a major factor in one-half of the country's homicides and motor vehicle fatalities, one-third of reported suicides, the majority of the nation's 30 000 annual deaths from liver cirrhosis, and a substantial number of serious birth defects (Trice and Roman, 1981). The economic cost of alcoholism is equally staggering: an estimated national cost of $43 billion in 1975, including about $20 billion in lost production.

In addition to these most visible effects of alcohol are its insidious effects on work performance, on judgment, and on professional and personal relationships. These subtler effects may contribute to a downward spiral of stress, alcohol consumption, declining performance, increasing stress, increasing alcohol consumption, and so on. Without the firm intervention of a colleague or family member (who demonstrates true concern by acting, rather than tolerating the situation), this downward spiral may continue until professional or personal self-destruction occurs.

While alcohol abuse continues to be the most visible form of drug abuse, over the last two decades 'recreational drugs'—principally cocaine—have gained a disturbing popularity and prestige among young professionals. As with smoking, drug abuse can be thought of as fulfilling pleasure-seeking, social, or stress-reduction needs. Whatever the stimulus, when drug abuse begins to affect work performance and individual relationships it becomes part of the same downward spiral that characterizes alcohol abuse.

Individuals may respond to stress with markedly increased appetite or markedly decreased appetite, either of which can lead to unhealthy consequences. Stress resulting from work overload—real or perceived—also leads some people to unhealthy diets such as high-fat fast foods.

Finally, a subtler, but still potentially lethal effect of stress is to predispose the individual to industrial, automobile, and other forms of accidents. Violence on the part of the stressed individual is one of the more extreme, but less common manifestations of individual distress. Incidents of family violence, including spouse and child abuse, are increasing. As a result of public concern about becoming victims of violence, the US Public Health Service recently expanded its health promotion and disease prevention objectives of the nation to include the control of stress and violent behaviors (Silver, Goldston and Silver, 1985).

Psychological Consequences

Closely related to the behavioral consequences of distress are the psychological consequences. Among the problems to consider are the burnout syndrome, family problems, sleep disturbances, sexual dysfunction, depression, and psychogenic disability.

'Burnout' is a relatively recent term which has rapidly gained acceptance and popularity in both the lay and professional stress literature (Maslach and Jackson, 1981). It is perhaps a milder form of the popular concept of 'nervous breakdown'—psychiatrically speaking, in most instances, a reactive depression. Burnout refers to a pattern of physical and emotional exhaustion, performance changes, and behavioral symptoms. Burnout tends to occur in professions characterized by a high degree of personal investment in work and high performance expectations.

Executives with a strong emotional commitment to work, with much of their self-image derived from success in their work, and a decreased emphasis on family and community relationships, may be particularly prone to burnout (Levinson, 1981). Investment in work can limit the amount of time spent in family and recreational activities. When difficulties arise at work or when there are insufficient signs of success, burnout-prone individuals begin to invest even more time at work and further neglect outside supports. Later stages of burnout are characterized by increasing use of alcohol or tranquilizers, increased rigidity, waning self-confidence and confidence in others, and an increase in time spent working combined with a dramatic decline in real productivity.

Marital discord and family conflict result from a variety of sources; the combination of home and work stress appears to have been a particularly significant factor in the last several decades. Burke, Weir, and DuWors (1979) examined the view of women married to men who exhibited unbalanced professional striving and competitive overdrive. The wives of men with such characteristics reported greater levels of depression, less satisfaction, fewer friends and less contact with those friends, and more feeling of tension, anxiety, isolation, worthlessness, and guilt. Handy (1978), studying the marriages of 23 successful mid-career executives, found four principal marital patterns, as defined by the attitudes and values of each spouse. Certain patterns were associated with resentment and discontent, while other patterns were associated with low stress and supportive relationships. The data suggest that the impact of organizational stress on a marriage is in part determined by the underlying structure of the relationship.

Insomnia each year affects up to 30% of the general population. Worries over promotion, conflict at work, and project deadlines frequently cause difficulty in falling asleep. Evidence on alcohol metabolism indicates that this common home remedy for insomnia may actually contribute to the problem. The initial depressant effect of the alcohol helps a person to fall asleep, but also disrupts sleep cycles because of a rebound increase in epinephrine later in the night. This can lead to a self-replicating cycle of stress–alcohol–awakening–fatigue–stress etc. Because sleep deprivation has a negative impact on mood and performance, it can exacerbate the work situations which caused the sleep disturbance in the first instance. Thus sleep disturbance should be recognized as a symptom of stress, as a possible source of stress, or both. The problem should be dealt with directly through efforts to reduce stress levels, to plan activity and exercise patterns to promote sound sleep, or, for temporary help, to obtain safe and effective sleeping medications.

Other potential psychological consequences of stress include sexual dysfunction, depression, and psychogenic disability. Stress has been shown to reduce interest in lovemaking not only because stress-related problems are distracting, but also because stress alters both men's and women's hormone physiology. Since satisfying sexual relations can be an important part of one's mental health and well-being, preventing or resolving sexual dysfunction is a necessary element of stress management. Clinical depression can result from work-related stressors, from stressors outside the workplace, or from biological factors seemingly unrelated to any circumstances in a person's life. Identification of the cause and prompt treatment is important to minimize the impact of a depressive episode on an individual's personal life and career development. Finally, psychological trauma or conflict can sometimes be expressed as a frank physical disability—acute laryngitis, acute blindness, weakness of one hand, and so forth. Frequently such a psychogenic disability or 'conversion reaction' is of brief duration and resolves without intervention. At times, however, conversion symptoms can be quite disabling and require skilled psychiatric care.

Medical Consequences

While the behavioral and psychological effects of stress can be substantial in themselves, they may in turn contribute to even more devastating and irreversible medical problems. When these are at the asymptomatic stage, they often go undetected. This can be particularly frightening in the case of heart disease because the first symptom may be sudden death.

Numerous studies reviewed elsewhere have associated work overload, job dissatisfaction, job insecurity, role conflict, interpersonal demands, and a variety of other work stressors with classic 'stress symptoms' such as headache, heartburn, backache, musculoskeletal conditions, and generalized fatigue (Quick and Quick, 1984). Table 2 lists the ten leading causes of mortality in the US during 1985 and summarizes examples of research linking work stress to morbidity or mortality from each of these ten leading killers. Although genetics, biological development, and many other factors influence the appearance and course of these conditions, there is a growing body of empirical evidence suggesting that stress plays a role in hastening the appearance of disease or in worsening the impact of the disease.

Each year over 900000 men and women in the US die from heart disease and strokes (Table 2). Since heart disease is the leading cause of death among men over age 25, large numbers of cardiac events among executives and middle management should be expected. But a variety of

Table 2   Work stress and illness

Rank	Cause of death	Number of deaths (1985)	Examples of research linking work stress to morbidity and mortality
1	Heart disease	975 660	For a controlled study of 453 male post-heart attack patients, a stress reduction program reduced later deaths (Frasure-Smith and Prince, 1985)
2	Cancer	457 200	A prospective study of 208 female breast cancer patients showed higher stress levels associated with decreased survival (Funch and Marshall, 1983)
3	Stroke	153 300	Positive correlation between stressful events and hypertension, which is the leading risk factor for stroke (Julius, 1984)
4	Accidents, injuries, etc.	91 690	According to insurance industry data, 75–85% of accidents at work are stress-related (Jones, 1984)
5	Chronic lung disease	73 430	Review of 90 references finds positive correlations between cigarette smoking, work stress, and chronic lung disease and lung cancer (Schilling, Gilchrest and Schinke, 1985)
6	Pneumonia and influenza	65 230	Study of 114 healthy people with high life change stress who had low natural killer cell activity, suggesting stress may negatively affect immunity (Locke *et al.*, 1984)
7	Diabetes	37 640	In a study of 66 insulin dependent diabetics, 75% had clinical symptoms or abnormally high blood sugars following stressful events (Kisch, 1985)
8	Suicide	27 350	In an analysis of US mortality data, there was a pattern of stress-induced self-destructive behaviors in seven stress-related causes of death, including suicide and homicide (Karcher and Linden, 1982)
9	Liver cirrhosis	26 740	In a screening program of 7948 males involved in a preventive medical program, mortality data were compared to the nonparticipant population, and the death rate due to alcohol-related diseases was five times higher in the nonparticipant group (Trell, Kristenson and Peterson, 1985)

Table 2 Continued

Rank	Cause of death	Number of deaths (1985)	Examples of research linking work stress to morbidity and mortality
10	Homicide	19310	Among 148 former mental patients and 245 respondents from the general population, self-reports of frequency of life stress events were positively correlated with increased frequency of four types of aggressive behavior ranging from arguments to assaults with weapons (Steadman and Ribner, 1982)

Source for Mortality Statistics: *Monthly Vital Statistics Report*, Vol. 34, No. 9 (December 16, 1985) National Center for Health Statistics. Figures are for the annual period September 1984 through August 1985.

studies and anecdotal evidence suggest that fatal and nonfatal heart attacks occur more frequently among individuals experiencing high levels of distress. The oil engineering executive profiled in Chapter 4 notes, for example, that during the 1982 to 1987 oil industry upheaval senior management remained healthy, while several individuals in middle management experienced nonfatal heart attacks.

The most important factors contributing to these deaths are family history of cardiovascular disease, smoking, hypertension, blood lipids (cholesterol and triglycerides), diabetes, and possibly Type A personality. Lack of exercise and poor diet are also contributing factors. With the exception of family history, there is evidence relating each of these factors to stress, in general, and in several cases to work stress, in particular.

The relationship between work stress and smoking was noted above. The onset or worsening of high blood pressure or hypertension has also been associated with psychological stress (Henry, 1976). Recent studies have reemphasized the role of cholesterol levels in the development of heart disease and these levels appear to be related to stress. Friedman and associates (1958) in one of the earliest studies of this relationship, found that among tax accountants cholesterol levels increased as the deadline for filing federal income tax returns approached.

Within the last decade evidence has developed which suggests that a significant portion of cardiac deaths result not from a blockage of coronary arteries, as in the case of a heart attack, but from a condition known as 'sudden cardiac death,' in which death is believed to result from sudden and serious cardiac rhythm disturbances. Current evidence directly linking work stress to sudden death is largely anecdotal, and retrospective studies of the relationship between life stresses and sudden death have been inconclusive (Binik, 1985). However, there are several studies demonstrating a significant relationship between potentially dangerous heart rhythm disturbances and psychological tasks (Lown, DeSilva and Lenson, 1978). Such work stresses as public speaking have been found to stimulate abnormal heartbeats in one-quarter of normal patients and prolific abnormal beats in nearly three-quarters of coronary artery disease patients (Taggart, Carruthers and Somerville, 1973).

The Type A behavior pattern is a controversial risk factor linking work stress to heart disease. Studies reviewed by Dorian and Taylor (1984) indicate that Type A individuals have higher blood pressure and cholesterol levels; are more frequently smokers; are more likely to be heavy drinkers; have less interest in exercise; and demonstrate other chemical and physiological alterations related to the development of arteriosclerosis. Compared to Type B individuals, Type A individuals show greater cardiovascular reactivity in daily activities, including greater elevations of serum norepinephrine, heart rate, and blood pressure under stressful circumstances. These effects have been found among Type A women as well as Type A men (Lawler, Rixse and Allen, 1983).

A more recent, large controlled study (Multiple Risk Factor Intervention Trial, 1982) found no significant relationship between Type A behavior and smoking, cholesterol, or the incidence of cardiovascular disease. In addition, recent studies of survival after acute heart attack have also failed to find an association between Type A behavior and long-term outcome (Case *et al.*, 1985).

It may be only specific components of the Type A behavior pattern such as hostility and cynicism which contribute to risk for heart attack. It has been suggested that it is the sisyphean pattern ('joyless striving') which leads Type A individuals to develop coronary heart disease (Jenkins, 1982). Physiologic evidence indicates that hostility and cynicism are associated with increased epinephrine levels, increased blood pressure, and increased blockage of coronary arteries. Perhaps most convincing is a study of 255 physicians who were followed from their student years at the University of North Carolina Medical School for the next 25 years (Barefoot, Dahlstrom and Williams, 1983). Physicians who had higher hostility scores on psychological tests taken during medical school experienced four times greater incidence of heart disease and six times the mortality of the low hostility group. It is the combination of work overload and sustained dissatisfaction or depression which appears to put the Type A at risk.

Cancer is another major source of disability and death in the US. The most common sites of fatal cancers in this country are lung, breast, colon and rectum, and prostate. An estimated three-quarters of lung cancers are attributable to smoking. To the extent that managerial stress increases smoking behavior, it will increase lung cancer and other tobacco-related cancers such as bladder cancer, stomach cancer, and cancer of the mouth, throat, and larynx. The impact of increased smoking among women is just beginning to be reflected in rising lung cancer among women.

Several books on the subject of stress and cancer review evidence suggesting that stressful life events are associated with the appearance of a variety of cancers, including breast cancer, uterine cancer, and lung cancer (Tache, Selye and Day, 1979; Cooper, 1984). Stress appears to have a direct effect on decreasing the immune response which might otherwise control a small cancer.

Pneumonia, influenza, and other acute respiratory infections are together the fifth leading cause of death in the US and a leading cause of lost workdays and work-related disability. Most of this death and disability is due to disease from specific bacterial, viral, chemical, or physical agents. However, evidence from some of the earliest studies of life events indicates that stress in personal, financial, social or work areas is associated with increased incidence of acute respiratory illness as well as chronic respiratory diseases such as tuberculosis (Holmes *et al.*, 1957).

Depressed immunity resulting from stress may be the common factor underlying both the relationship between stress and cancer and the relationship between stress and infections (pneumonia and influenza as well as nonrespiratory infections). For example, studies of undergraduates have found markedly decreased immune responses among those who cope poorly with stress, while students with high stress but good coping skills have shown the best immune responses (Locke *et al.*, 1984). Other studies have confirmed that chronic generation of stress hormones suppresses several components of the immune system (McClelland *et al.*, 1980).

Musculoskeletal conditions, including arthritis, low back pain, and displaced intervertebral discs ('slipped discs'), are another leading cause of lost workdays and disability. While much of this disability is related to work injuries and nonwork stress, increased work stress has o been associated with increases in acute and chronic musculoskeletal problems.

Finally, ulceration of the stomach and first part of the small intestine represents the classic psychosomatic illness. This description is due to the early work of H. G. Wolff (1953), a neurologist and pioneer in psychosomatic medicine. Wolff found that during times of prolonged emotional stress, the stomach lining became engorged with blood, acid production increased, and eventually bleeding erosions developed. Subsequent studies have documented a higher incidence of chronic stress in ulcer patients compared to control subjects, increased acid production triggered by stressful events, and a more prolonged course with poorer prognosis among patients with chronic severe anxiety.

Health Benefits of Stress

While stress is an inevitable part of living, it does not have to lead inevitably to the health problems just discussed. Milsum (1984) has explored the positive aspects of optimal or well-balanced stress. Recent evidence also indicates that stress can markedly increase blood levels of endorphins, naturally occurring morphine-like hormones associated with pain relief and feelings of well-being (McCubbin, Surwit and Williams, 1985).

There are several physically stressful activities found to be beneficial in either specific or general circumstances. The first of these is aerobic fitness. The benefits of aerobic fitness are primarily in improved cardiovascular functioning. These benefits include a lower heart rate, greater stroke volume, greater efficiency in returning to rest after stressful events, and decreased reactivity to stressful events. Roth and Holmes (1985) found that the physical health of aerobically fit individuals was not adversely affected by life stress while the physical health of less fit individuals was. Similar results were found concerning fitness and psychological depression.

Flexibility training is also beneficial. The process of improving flexibility, along with strength, in specific muscle groups leads to stresses on these muscle groups. However, this improved flexibility enables improved body posture, a key issue in considering the physical stresses imposed on the body during the normal course of living.

STAYING HEALTHY UNDER STRESS: THE HARDY EXECUTIVE

Though there are numerous potential negative consequences of stress, there is not a simple, direct relationship between high stress and ill-health. The executives which we have profiled report few serious health problems. Their stress symptoms are, in fact, relatively mild: general fatigue, preoccupation, and tension in back or neck muscles. Why do some people react to seemingly every stressful event, while others respond only rarely? Why do some individuals develop recurrent stomach ulcers, while other individuals never do? Selye (1976) theorized that individual moderating factors influence the body's response to stress. Factors suggested by Selye include 'internal conditioning factors' such as personality, family illness patterns, age, and sex, as well as 'external conditioning factors,' such as diet, drugs, and social setting.

Recently, research conducted by a team of behavioral scientists led by psychologists S. C. Ouellette Kobasa and Salvatore Maddi has shed considerable light on Selye's concept of conditioning factors by studying the personality characteristics of executives and other professionals who seemed to stay healthy under stress. Rather than studying executives who became sick under stress, the team took a different approach: they focused their attention on individuals who were under stress, but who showed few symptoms of stress. What made these individuals resistant to the negative consequences of stress?

In an early report (Kobasa, 1979) the team studied 200 Illinois Bell Telephone male middle- and upper-level executives who had experienced an unusually high number of stress events during the AT&T divestiture period. Of the officers and managers studied, 100 were chosen who reported significant numbers of stressful events and high levels of illness symptoms. The other 100 were chosen from among executives who had experienced similar levels of stress, but had few, if any, illness complaints. In comparing the two groups, the researchers found that the group of executives who remained healthy responded to stressful events differently than those who became ill. The healthy group expressed an 'optimistic cognitive appraisal' (Kobasa and Maddi, 1981), which included the view that change, good or bad, is an opportunity for growth and an inevitable part of life's experience. Rather than feeling threatened, these executives maintained a sense of control and an appreciation of challenge. Though they could not always control the changes which were occurring, they could and did control their responses to change. In addition to their belief in control and challenge, this group also showed a commitment to life, to their work and to their families. In short, the officers and managers in this group demonstrated 'hardy personalities.'

A similar study (Kobasa, 1982) looked at a group of 157 attorneys in general practice, many of whom had experienced significant changes at work and, in some instances, severe stresses at home. Again, there was no direct relationship between illness episodes and stressful life events. But there was a strong relationship between symptoms such as headaches, nervousness, and sleep disturbance and the lawyers' attitudes and responses to stress at work. Those who responded with anger, indifference, or withdrawal and those who drank or smoked more experienced more symptoms. Those who expressed a sense of purpose and belief in their work experienced the fewest symptoms.

The Illinois Bell study and the attorneys' study included only men. To determine whether the same relationship between one's outlook on stress and one's illness response holds for women, Kobasa and her colleagues studied 100 mostly white, middle-class, 25 to 35 year old women who reported a large number of recent stressful life events. Sixty of the women reported both significant amounts of stress and psychiatric symptoms, while the remaining 40 reported large numbers of stressful experiences, but few symptoms. The women in the latter group were characterized by a stronger sense of challenge, a greater feeling of control in their lives, and more commitment to work, family, and self.

Finally, in a prospective study, the psychologists followed 259 executives for up to five years. At the outset, each executive was rated according to 'hardiness,' as defined by a strong sense of control, commitment, and challenge. Over the next five years, under equal amounts of stress, those executives with hardy personalities experienced half the illness episodes of those with little hardiness (Maddi and Kobasa, 1984).

In sum, 'hardiness' appears to be an important determinant of an individual's response to stress and, therefore, the likelihood that one will experience any of the potential ill effects of stress. Kobasa (1988) identified the components of the hardy personality as being commitment, control, and challenge. She describes these concepts in the following way:

Commitment is the ability to believe in the truth, importance and interest value of who one is and what one is doing; and thereby, the tendency to involve oneself fully and in the many situations of life, including work, family, interpersonal relationships, and social institutions.

Control refers to the tendency to believe and act as if one can influence the course of events with an emphasis on their own responsibility and not simply in terms of others' actions or fate.

Challenge is based on the belief that change, rather than stability, is the normative mode of life. People with 'challenge' seek out change and new experiences and approach them with cognitive flexibility and tolerance for ambiguity. (Kobasa, 1988, p. 101).

Each of the executives profiled in Chapters 4 and 5 can be described as hardy personalities. For example, the oil engineering executive described the outlook of his ten vice presidents during a five year period of severe industrial upheavals in the following way:

All officers had an average of 25 or more years of service and were solid family men. To me it seemed they drew strength from their families— from children's educational endeavors, weddings, and the blessings of grandchildren. No problems were noted with health, alcohol or drugs, affairs or other distracting involvements. As a group, they seemed to have confidence in their leadership and our abilities to survive the storm. Strategic plans were developed, discussed, implemented and monitored against company performance.

He also observes that he spends little time worrying about the uncontrollable aspects of field operations. Similarly, the steel industry executive looks for challenge in adversity and concentrates on the learning opportunity posed by his company's commitment to growth.

Thus, the characteristics of the hardy personality facilitate effective coping with organizational and personal stressors. Other factors being equal, it is the hardy executive who can be expected to stay healthy under stressful circumstances. Hardy executives keep the stressors of worklife in perspective; they maintain a sense of meaning in life through their commitment to work and to family. Hardy executives also act with the confidence that they have the internal resources to deal with daily stressors; they recognize that they are in control of their responses to events, even if they cannot always control the events. Finally, hardy executives see stressors as potential opportunities for growth and change; they change positively as a source of challenge and excitement rather than threat.

PROMOTING EUSTRESS: OTHER MODIFIERS OF THE STRESS RESPONSE

Hardiness is not the only factor which explains differences in individual responses to stress. Other factors frequently identified as moderators of the response to stress are listed in Table 3.

One important part of the explanation for different patterns of stress response lies in the 'Achilles heel,' or 'organ inferiority' hypothesis developed through the work of Harold Wolff (1953). He hypothesized that an individual reacts to stress with a particular psychophysiologic pattern that is specific to that individual. Medical research provides support for this hypothesis. Studies have shown that individuals with stomach ulcers tend to respond to stress with greater gastric secretion (Wolff, 1953), that individuals with diabetes respond to stress with greater changes in blood glucose than do normal individuals (Hinkle and Wolff, 1952), that individuals with cardiovascular disease show greater variability in heart rate and respiration than do other people (Masuda, Perko and Johnston, 1972), and that individuals with a family history of hypertension but no personal history of high blood presure show greater rises in blood pressure in response to both psychological and physical stressors (Shapiro, 1961).

House (1981) has written extensively on the role of social suport in buffering the effect of stress. He identifies four forms of social support: emotional, instrumental, informational, and appraisal. Each person derives these types of social support from a variety of relationships at work, at home, and in the community. Emotional support may come from one's spouse, instrumental and informational support from

Table 3 Potential modifiers of the response to stress

Hardiness	Gender
	Role stress
Achilles heel phenomenon	Occupational stereotypes
	Sexuality
Social support	
	Age
Type A behavior pattern	
	Ethnicity
Personality	
Locus of control	Peer group
Self-esteem	
Other characteristics	Diet

immediate subordinates, and appraisal support from organizational or corporate leadership. Executives and managers should recognize not only the value of well-developed networks of social support for their own well-being, but also their potential role as sources of support for others in the organization.

Several personality dimensions appear to influence the impact of stressful events on the individual. In addition to the Type A behavior pattern and hardiness discussed earlier, locus of control is another personality dimension which may have a moderating influence, as demonstrated by Anderson (1977) in a study of 102 owner-managers of small businesses in a Pennsylvania community extensively damaged by a flood. Following the flood, managers with an internal locus of control responded in a more task-oriented way and demonstrated less stress.

Self-esteem may be another important moderator of the response to stress (Mueller, 1965). A study by Kasl and Cobb (1970) indicated that coronary heart disease risk factors rise as self-esteem declines. Other personality factors which have been associated with individual responses to organizational stress include tolerance for ambiguity, introversion/extroversion, and flexibility/rigidity (Brief, Schuler and Van Sell, 1981). Finally, a recent study by Flannery (1984) suggests that one's work ethic may be a moderator between life stress and physical illness.

Over the last two decades an increasing amount of attention has been paid to the impact of gender differences on relationships in the workplace. Much of the emphasis has been on the changing role of women. But in terms of stress-related illness, being male is much riskier than being female. This difference is related in part to the greater prevalence among men of smoking, alcohol consumption, and suicide. However, Quick and Quick (1984) review several studies suggesting that some of these risk factors may be on the rise among women and that this may be related to women's expanding work roles.

Aside from the relationship between gender and specific risk factors, there are several sources of stress at work which are unique to women. These include *role stress* resulting from conflict between the traditional role of the woman as mother–homemaker–wife and the contemporary role of the woman as a professional; the stress resulting from willingly going against or unwillingly adhering to *occupational stereotypes*; and *sexuality issues* reflected in sexual harassment or in the opposite— avoidance of otherwise desirable work arrangements because they might create 'the wrong impression' by putting men and women together in close working groups, on business trips, in office arrangements, or in informal business activities which might create 'the wrong idea' (Brief, Schuler and Van Sell, 1981; Nelson and Quick, 1985; Sorenson *et al.*, 1985).

Social scientists have identified several different relationships between ethnicity and stress, both individual and organizational (Ford, 1976; Brack, Staszak and Pati, 1972). There are certain stressors unique to particular minority groups, including blatant racial prejudice and lack of access to the 'informal organization.' In addition, the impact of commonly experienced forms of stress on minority groups may be magnified by cultural and social factors which result in less social support, lower self-esteem, or lack of familiarity with the business world.

Finally, other internal and external factors such as age, peer group, and diet have been suggested as possible moderators of the response to stress (Quick and Quick, 1984; Ivancevich and Ganster, 1987).

FIRST, TAKE YOUR OWN PULSE

Early in their training medical doctors are taught, somewhat facetiously, to first take their own pulse when faced with a life-threatening situation; the doctor who is not in control of himself or herself cannot take control of a medical emergency. So too, executives and managers should first become aware of their own stressors and their own responses to stress.

To identify and, in some cases, measure stressors at work and in other spheres of life, a variety of stress-related diagnostic instruments have been developed. These instruments, reviewed elsewhere (Quick and Quick, 1984; Quick *et al.*, 1985), include the Life Events Scale, Hassles and Uplifts Scale, Stress Diagnostic Survey, Michigan Stress Assessment, Quality of Employment Survey, Adams Stress Evaluation, Stressor Checklist and others. These instruments include questionnaires as well as structured interviews.

These formal approaches focus on one or more of the general categories of stressors described in Chapter 1 and listed in Figure 1. Some people will find these formal approaches to identifying their stressors quite useful. Others will undoubtedly find quiet reflection and self-monitoring to be most fruitful. Whichever approach is taken, the key to preventing the potential negative outcomes of stress is to ask the basic question, 'What are my stressors?' In seeking the answer to this question—either through formal methods or through informal reflection—bear in mind that one person's source of relaxation may be another person's source of stress.

Closely connected with the process of identifying one's stressors is that of identifying one's responses. Sometimes identifying one's stress responses and asking what routinely triggers the responses will lead to a more complete definition of an individual's stressors.

Again, there is a variety of structured assessment instruments relevant to identifying signs and symptoms of individual distress. These include the Daily Log of Stress Related Symptoms, SCL-90-R, Cornell Medical Index, Maslach Burnout Inventory, and other questionnaires, interviews, and observational measures. In addition, there are methods to assess individual modifiers of the response to stress, including Type A behavior pattern, workaholic propensity, social support, coping mechanisms, and so forth (Quick and Quick, 1984; Quick *et al.*, 1985).

As with the identification of stressors, the identification of one's responses to stress can also be attempted through quiet reflection and introspection. Consider behavioral, psychological, and physiological–medical responses. In the behavioral sphere, consider both work habits and personal habits. Stress symptoms at work may include tardiness, declining performance, or declining personal relationships at work. A change in or apparent inability to control personal habits such as smoking, alcohol consumption, use of prescription drugs, or eating patterns may also indicate increased amounts of inadequately managed stress.

In the psychological sphere, any of the problems listed earlier in this chapter—burnout, family problems, sleep disturbance, sexual dysfunction and so forth—may be indicators of individual distress.

Finally, in the physiological–medical sphere, the new onset of a major illness or frequent minor illnesses should be cause to at least *consider* work and personal stress as a contributing factor. In any case, it is wise to arrange a periodic medical evaluation which emphasizes identification of cardiovascular risk factors (cholesterol and related blood lipids, blood pressure, diabetes), cancer risk factors, and early signs of either type of illness.

SUMMARY

Stress—any demand placed on the individual by his or her work or personal environment—is an inevitable part of life. Without such demands life would be static, dull, and unproductive. The classic stress response includes familiar feelings such as pounding in the chest, heightened sense of alertness, and muscle tension. The stress response also includes more subtle, less noticeable physiological and hormonal changes. If the stress response is elicited too frequently or too intensely, it may contribute to a variety of behavioral, psychological, or medical consequences.

The individual and organizational consequences of stress represent the risk of executive success. But the negative outcomes of stress are not inevitable. The following chapter will consider the range of preventive and therapeutic strategies appropriate to coping with executive stress.

FURTHER READING

Asterita, M. F. (1985). *The Physiology of Stress*, Human Sciences Press, New York.
Cannon, W. B. (1932). *The Wisdom of the Body*, W. W. Norton, New York.
Cooper, C. L. (ed.) (1984). *Psychosocial Stress and Cancer*, John Wiley & Sons, New York.
Hurrell, J. J. Jr., Murphy, L. R., Sauter, S. L. and Cooper, C. L. (1988). *Occupational Stress: Issues and Developments in Research*, Taylor & Francis, New York.
Maddi, S. R. and Kobasa, S. C. O. (1984). *The Hardy Executive: Health under Stress*, Dow Jones-Irwin, Homewood, IL.
Nelson, D. L. and Quick, J. C. (1985). Professional women: Are distress and disease inevitable? *Academy of Management Review*, **10**(2), 206–18.
Quick, J. C. and Quick, J. D. (1984). *Organizational Stress and Preventive Management*, McGraw-Hill, New York.
Quick, J. D., Horn, R. S. and Quick, J. C. (1986). Health consequences of stress, *Journal of Organizational Behavior Management*, **8**(2), 19–36.
Rahe, R. A. (1979). Life change events and mental illness: An overview, *Journal of Human Stress*, **5**, 2–9.
Selye, H. (1976). *The Stress of Life*, 2nd Edition, McGraw-Hill, New York.

Chapter 3

Preventive Stress Management: What Works and What Doesn't!

Successful executives manage stress at an optimum level: enjoying enough eustress to be motivated, invigorated, and challenged, and preventively managing the distress which threatens them. The question is, how do they do it? In our idiographic profiles of executives, we discovered that each individual uses a unique combination of techniques to manage stress well. In addition, the executives we studied were quite forthright about the techniques they have used which proved to be of little help in the stress management process. This chapter will explore and review the range of preventive and therapeutic techniques appropriate to a top-level executive. The insights provided by our case studies will be supplemented with suggestions from other executives found in the literature and with techniques cited in the medical and psychological fields as being valuable to all individuals.

PREVENTIVE STRESS MANAGEMENT: A PRIMER

Human beings often attend to their health and well-being only when a problem arises. 'If it ain't broke, don't fix it' seems to be the axiom whereby many individuals ignore distress until it becomes of such magnitude that serious consequences occur. Such a reactive fire-fighting approach is counter to the attitudes and practices of the top executives we studied. In fact, the approach toward stress management adopted by these successful individuals is a *proactive and preventive* one; that is, they develop strategies for managing their stress levels on a daily basis. The behavioral literature details such proactive approaches as preventive management. While our executives did not directly refer to their practices as such, they were steadfast in their insistence that daily, proactive strategies for controlling stress contributed to their efficiency and effectiveness at work.

Preventive stress management is more than a set of techniques which individuals can use to manage their stress. It is a pervasive organizational philosophy that individuals and organizations together must take joint responsibility for promoting health and preventing distress. Five principles form the core guidelines of this philosophy (Quick and Quick, 1984).

1. Individual health and organizational health are interdependent.
2. Management has a responsibility for both individual and organizational health.
3. Individual and organizational distress are not inevitable.
4. Each individual and organization reacts uniquely to stress.
5. Organizations are ever-changing, dynamic entities.

The essence of the preventive management approach is that stress need not become evident through disease before intervention can take place; rather, preventive efforts should be instituted at the earliest stage possible. This way of thinking is derived from descriptions of disease progression in the medical and public health literature. Most diseases begin with a stage of risk, move on to early symptoms, and manifest in advanced or disabling disease. The idea is to begin preventive management efforts at the risk stage (primary prevention), continue through the asymptommatic stage (secondary prevention), and hopefully control the distress at these two early stages. If this is not possible, a range of techniques are available to treat stress-related diseases at the third stage (tertiary prevention).

Translating these medical notions into stress management applications, a three-tiered approach to preventive management evolves as presented in Figure 1. Primary prevention techniques focus on the source of stress (stressor). Such techniques modify or eliminate the stressors which individuals face. Secondary prevention techniques are directed toward the response to stress; that is, these techniques attempt to minimize strain. Tertiary prevention techniques are aimed at arresting distress—they are used when the first two prevention levels have not adequately controlled the stress problem.

Because preventive stress management is a joint individual–organizational effort, there are techniques at each of the three levels for both parties in the exchange to employ. Both individuals and organizations must work in concert to manage stress—this is a fundamental premise of

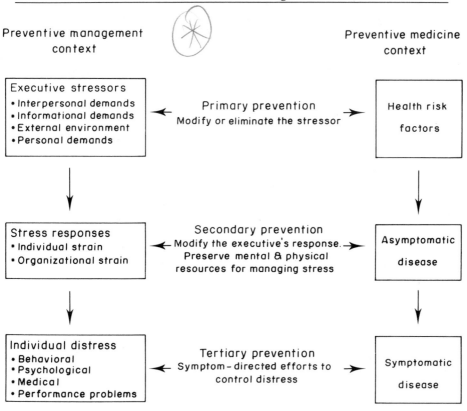

Figure 1   The preventive stress management approach for executives

preventive stress management. In this book we focus on the ways in which successful men and women at the top levels of organizations experience and handle stress; therefore, we will direct our discussion in this chapter toward individual-level prevention. The importance of organizational-level prevention must also be recognized. Participative management, flexible work schedules, and company goal setting are a few organizational preventive management techniques. Resources for further information on organizational techniques are presented at the end of this chapter.

WHAT TECHNIQUES WORK FOR TOP-LEVEL EXECUTIVES?

Our in-depth profiles suggest that executives rely far more heavily on

Table 1   Effective preventive management techniques cited by executives*

	Oil service company executive	Steel company executive	Banking executive	Real estate executive	District court judge	Fashion industry executive
Primary prevention						
Maintaining perspective	●			●	●	●
Psychological withdrawal						●
Leisure time	●	●	●	●	●	●
Time management			●			
Planning goal setting	●			●		
Social support	●	●	●	●	●	●
Secondary prevention						
Exercise		●	●	●	●	●
Relaxation					●	
Prayer and faith	●		●		●	●

* Note: This table includes only those executives profiled in Chapters 4 and 5. Other executives studied and included in the text of this and other chapters are not included in this table.

primary and secondary level preventive management techniques to facilitate their success than they do on tertiary level techniques. Table 1 identifies the strategies utilized by each of the executives profiled later in Chapters 4 and 5. In our extensive interviews and observations, the executives reported using several preventive management strategies in concert rather than relying on a single technique for managing their stress. The fact that medical or psychological help was rarely needed for stress-related problems demonstrates the effectiveness of these executives in controlling the potentially harmful effects of stress through primary and secondary level strategies.

Maintaining a Perspective

One common denominator among our executives is their insistence that work, while central to their lives, is not the single most important element of their lives. This notion was cogently stated by the oil company executive.

> . . . I can truthfully look you in the eye and say that my work is not the most important thing in my life. It is very important, but it's not the most important thing. To me, my family, my friends, my church, my personal enjoyment of life are actually more important to me than my job . . . I believe it will make you a more well-rounded person if you take this attitude.

Mary Kay Ash (1981) argues that corporate philosophy is a crucial ingredient for success. One cornerstone of her philosophy is 'God first, family second, career third' (p. 204).

This perspective is central to maintaining a balanced life essential to well-being, and avoiding such overinvestment in work activities as exhibited in the workaholic behavior pattern. Kiev (1974) in his prescriptive work on executive stress emphasizes the importance of maintaining continuity between work life and home life. Manuso (1979) argues that executives in particular must have such a philosophy for living a well-rounded purposeful life in order to manage stress effectively.

Another element of this shared perspective is the philosophy of the executives as regards stress. They recognize the inevitability of stress in their lives and accept the experience; not in a passive way, but rather to enable themselves to invest energy where it might better be spent. In discussing relocation programs as an innovation in the real estate industry, the chief executive officer (CEO) stated:

> Here is where your stress bunches up a little bit, because it is a large opportunity . . . so therefore it takes large effort, and there is going to be stress.

A health care executive we studied echoes this thought:

> I've learned very early that I'm always going to look for the toughest game I can find because I think that's where I contribute the most and that's what is going to satisfy me the most. I'm just aware that that's going to produce a lot of stress . . .

In his remarks about the volatility of the energy industry, the oil company executive shared this advice:

> I frankly don't worry too much about things over which I have no control. I think this aids my ability to concentrate on those areas where I do have some control.

Efforts such as maintaining a philosophy and managing one's perspective constitute attempts to manage the way the individual responds to stress. Previous literature has supported both maintaining a balance (Albrecht, 1979; Rountree, 1979) and recognizing the inevitable (Student, 1977). Selye (1974) was the early architect of the philosophical approach to preventive management in his discussions of the inevitability of stress at work and the ability of the individual to manage distress.

Leisure Time Use

Another key technique among our subjects was the effective use of leisure time. Several different uses for leisure time were noted. Both the real estate CEO and the banking executive use leisure time to read for pleasure. A naval officer we studied described spectator sports as his preferred form of leisure.

> I find that I'm a sports addict and will admit that I can watch an event

either in person or on T.V. and I can totally put my thoughts away from anything else. I become totally involved with the sporting event, and it's good for me because I get caught up in it and I'm not thinking about the problem of the day or the problem of the week, whatever it might be.

One leisure activity on which the executives did not agree was travel. One real estate CEO reported that business-related air travel was something she uses as a form of leisure, an 'enjoyable, exciting diversion.' A health care executive describes business travel as a source of stress. This underscores the notion that there are individual differences among executives which affect their perceptions of stress and their perceptions of the efficacy of various stress management activities.

Somewhat surprisingly, there is a relative scarcity of literature on the use of leisure as a stress management tool. Initial evidence supports the possible beneficial effects of this technique but additional empirical study is needed to ascertain effective uses of leisure time and specific benefits (Eliot, 1982).

The executives in our study also recommended preventive stress management strategies for organizing the personal work environment. Two of the most frequently mentioned techniques are time management and planning/goal setting.

Time Management

Lee Iacocca has contended that the starting point for good management is the effective use of time (Iacocca, 1984). He says that managers who use time well are self-motivated and results-oriented. Mary Kay Ash (1981) notes that the one quality essential for success in sales is good time management. She points out business lunches as real time wasters and prefers to lunch at her desk rather than spend two or three hours away, returning with little energy for work. Our subject executives each contributed unique strategies for using time effectively. From the banker:

I keep a calendar in my pocket and (my secretaries) keep one on their desks. We trade calendars, it seems, almost hourly. They really control my day to some extent. In terms of time allocation they keep me advised.

The naval officer said of time management:

I have found out that if you let your schedule get out of control, you function differently than you probably would normally. I found out that if I use the first hour or so of the morning I can think about what it is I'm going to do for the day. I always block off lunch and invariably take that time to sit back and read a paper. I block off the last hour every evening to take time to catch up. Usually right at the end of the morning I review what I've done for that morning. I think the middle of the day that I block out also lets me charge myself up again and get myself prepared to tackle anything that might come in the afternoon.

The health care executive:

I'd say my schedule is fairly flexible. Like last night I got back in at 10:00 from a trip out of town and I didn't go in to the office until 9:00 or 9:30 in the morning. And that's fairly typical. All things being equal, I probably have a fairly standard schedule, but I adjust it according to what opportunities I have. If somebody is available I want to visit with, I don't hesitate to take the afternoon off to visit with them.

Advice from the oil company president:

Avoid meeting deadlines at the last hour. Do your work early, so you have time to think about it before submission.

Other executives have noted their favorite time management tricks in the managerial literature. Stanley Pace, CEO of General Dynamics, does not schedule meetings early in the morning, preferring instead to use that early morning time to catch up on work. He also refrains from scheduling meetings late in the afternoon, so he can use that time to wrap up the day (Worthy, 1988). Time management helps prevent stress by reducing uncertainty, which is important for health and effectiveness (Schriber and Gutek, 1987).

Planning/Goal Setting

The empirical literature has long been focused on the value of goals in terms of motivation and stimulating performance (Locke, 1968; Locke *et al.*, 1981) and in reducing role stress (Quick, 1979). Similarly, planning has been accepted as a key to managerial success since the classical school of management thought (Fayol, 1929). Buck (1972) argues that individuals must plan ahead to avoid jobs which are overly stressful or which do not fit one's characteristics. Our executives go back to the basics on these preventive management tools, and place them in the context of crucial techniques for managing stress.

> Planning is effective for handling stress . . . it minimizes or eliminates surprises, the unknowns. When you can do that, you have less to worry about regarding what's going to happen down the road. And I have a list of goals for the company I keep in mind constantly in my daily working environment. As chief executive officer, the goals and plans for the corporation are foremost and my personal plans must coincide with those to achieve the most success. (Oil company executive.)

> What I have tried to do, first of all, is to be very sure that the people that work with me understand what we are trying to achieve. We do that in a formal way through a management plan every year. (Health care executive.)

> Throughout the growth of our company there have been goals . . . only in the last several months strategic plans, goals, and retreats have become formal in our association and company. While the goals seem to be short range as our business has grown, each short range goal fits into the larger goal which is to be the very best in the business, to try to make each transaction fair and happy so that it would in turn become a solid brick in the growth of our company. (Real estate CEO.)

Looking to the future through planning and goal setting allows the executive to focus energy, eliminate surprises, and therefore preventively manage stress.

While the executives we studied were happy to provide information on all of their preventive management techniques, one strategy seemed to dominate the others in terms of the vigor with which each executive argued for its effectiveness. The executives lauded the virtues of social support as a factor important to their success. They discussed with us the various forms of social support they use, the providers of the support to them, and ways they use this technique effectively.

Social Support

Chief executives who manage stress in a healthy manner are able to achieve a balance between separation and union. They accept their natural dependency feelings and use them as a driving force for developing professional and personal networks of social support. Of all the prevention techniques suggested by our executives, social support was the one strategy which they argued for vigorously and adamantly. They do not operate as loners at work; rather, they use a number of forms of social support to build important work and nonwork relationships. It is these relationships which allow them to draw on informational, emotional, appraisal, and instrumental types of support (House, 1981).

One way in which top-level executives utilize social support is in the cautious and careful development of psychological contracts with others. Focusing on informational exchange and emotional support, they work hard to achieve a fundamental integrity in these relationships. A psychological contract is an unwritten agreement between the individual and the organization which describes the exchange of inputs and outcomes between the two (Argyris, 1960; Levinson, 1962). Since for subordinates the CEO often represents the organization side of the contract, we find these psychological contracts evidenced between executives and their employees. Jack Welch, Chairman and CEO of General Electric, has spoken of the deal between GE and its employees, 'A company owes its people a fair, open atmosphere where they have the chance to do their best and win. Their job is to take advantage of this, to grow in it, change in it, and talk about tomorrow instead of yesterday' (Pare and Woods, 1988). Bennis and Nanus (1985), in analyzing the philosophies of today's leaders, say that a strict code of honesty and a demand that everyone in the organization gets a fair deal comprise the characteristics of a good psychological contract.

The contracting process used by the executives is a reciprocal exchange. The oil company executive described his approach, emphasizing the importance of honesty in the relationships.

> To me, a chief executive officer should be more than willing to seek out advice from several sources in helping to arrive at a solution. The first place he should go is the people who report to him. They're very often able to help solve the problem, and he is being a human being by asking for help. They appreciate it and respect him for it. I don't think you gain anything by trying to fool people into thinking that you know all the answers to every question.

The health care officer talked about his role as a source of support for subordinates.

> I want to listen to them if they're getting down. I want to be able to listen

to the tone of their voice or meet with them enough where I can see it in their eyes, so I know there's a problem. Also I just want to be available to have them bounce ideas off of, maybe give them some courage sometimes to do what they want to do. Probably 70% of the time it's just listening, agreeing with them. Or if they're reacting negatively from stress, I know about it.

The psychological contracts which are developed by successful executives also include their superiors. The health care officer also spoke about the importance of an open and honest relationship with superiors in terms of devoting time to these people, understanding their expectations, and keeping them informed of both opportunities and problems. The oil company executive discussed the importance of a good relationship with the board of directors.

The board of directors is very helpful in setting the long term direction path of the company—the major endeavors we should or should not go into. They really play a strategic support role.

Kotter (1985) indicates that, in terms of power and influence, development of good working relationships with superiors is crucial. An executive should assess the superior and himself, and create a relationship which meets the needs of both parties, developing dependability for both parties.

Psychological contracts are thus an important factor in the use of social support by the executives. They are comfortable in turning to others for support and in serving as a source of support for others.

An integral part of the ways in which the executives utilize social support effectively involves the selection of personnel. By surrounding themselves with competent individuals, the executives extend their own limits in terms of skills and abilities. The navy admiral discussed his thoughts on the importance of selection.

If you have the capability to do this, surround yourself with competent, capable people. I found that if I have people that are working for me of this caliber, that makes my job much easier . . . you try to get the best performer you can get—the best qualified, the best experienced. It gives you confidence in what they are doing and that it's going to be correct.

Kotter (1988) cites Iacocca's talent for selection of both top executives and entry level managers as being one factor contributing to his success at Chrysler. Former CEO of Banc One Corporation, John G. McCoy, credited with developing the largest banking organization in Ohio, has a stated philosophy of hiring people who are exceptional at something and giving them some rope (Wysocki, 1984). This articulation introduces another key use of social support for executives.

Delegation allows the CEO to take advantage of the abilities of these carefully selected subordinates. The executive must realize that he or she alone cannot be as effective as a team effort.

> When you've become the head of a large corporation, you cannot do everything yourself. One secret of making an operation a success is the proper selection of your subordinates, the delegation of responsibility and authority to those individuals expecting performance from them. (Oil company executive)

> In a time as complex as the one we're living in, I surely don't have all the answers or all the information. I've got a lot of very talented people working here with me. Not to take advantage of that talent at this particular time would be the grossest of oversights. (Theodore Brophy of General Telephone & Electronics) (Wysocki, 1984)

The real estate executive also talked at length about delegation, stating that the key in her organization is an emphasis on training and development. Tichy and DeVanna (1986) contend that a budding leader's growth is composed of 80% job experience, 20% training and study; thus freedom and responsibility early in the career are important, as is training.

John Akers, IBM's chief executive, has been described as 'superb at delegation' (Pare and Woods, 1988). 3M Company, named in many lists as 'best company to work for,' is headed by William L. McKnight who believes in his subordinates' potential. He gives young executives a great deal of freedom, including the freedom to make mistakes and learn (Manz and Sims, 1988).

The social support networks developed by executives involve personal investments as well as working relationships. The CEOs often have several close personal relationships in which they invest substantial emotional energy. Spouses play an important role here. Several of the executives we studied discussed the value of their spouse's feedback and appraisal. The banking executive described this relationship:

My wife is unique in that she takes an active interest in the business and the people involved in it. I truly believe that women have that second sense about people . . . she picks up the signals better than I do. She serves as my advisor, counselor, and consultant. If I want to bounce an idea off somebody nine times out of ten I'll bounce it off her first. And I will say she is more times right than wrong!

The health care CEO reported the value of his wife's appraisal of job candidates.

She has a good sense of the basic honesty of people and how genuine they are. If I'm going to hire someone, the best of all worlds is to have her go to dinner with us just to get her blessing on it. I would be very concerned if she simply did not trust someone.

Both the naval admiral and the oil company executive described their homes as important places to retreat from the demands of business. The role of home and family as sources of support was cited uniformly by our executives. The oil company president related a humorous incident regarding his family orientation, as was described in Chapter 1, page 14.

A final source of social support for the executives is the diversification of their involvements. They have investments and commitments to the commnities of which they are a part. The real estate CEO spends a great deal of time in speaking engagements and civic activities.

In real estate, the community is our inventory; therefore, it is not only a privilege but also an obligation to put something back into the community.

The banking executive's activities are the local chamber of commerce and the Young Presidents' Organization. The oil company executive remains a loyal alumnus to his undergraduate organization, investing substantial time and financial resources in its support. This diversity of involvements allows the executive to give social support to others and to develop a wider network outside the confines of the work organization.

Social support is thus an essential element of preventive stress management for top-level executives; perhaps the most crucial element. The sheer sense of attachment provided by supportive relationships allows the individual to feel needed by others and the need for others (Pearlin, 1985). Bowlby (1969) asserts that the behavioral propensity to seek closeness from others is a natural biological imperative important to well-being, and that the relationships we have come to refer to as social supports are clearly interactional in nature. The successful executive is not a loner; rather, he is comfortable in serving as a support source for others, and in turning to others for support in times of need. Levinson and Rosenthal (1984) studied six chief executive officers to ascertain their leadership styles. Some of their comments argue strikingly for the importance of social support.

> Each could change his mind based on that information, particularly from selected, trusted confidants . . . All were aware of the need to touch their own people and made a practice of it. This touching was also a device to pick up information. They were especially affectionate with people close to them, while still maintaining an appropriate distance . . . Although the leaders set a direction, changed significant personnel, and made heavy demands on their subordinates for exacting behavior and performance, they were also supportive . . . They did personal favors for those in distress.

Successful executives thus utilize a host of primary-level preventive management techniques to effectively manage the demands of their jobs. In addition, they utilize several secondary-level strategies, which allow them to better control and harness their responses to stress.

Exercise

Executives, like many individuals, find exercise a popular way to manage stress. Exercise has long been touted for its stress-relieving properties (Cooper, 1982; DeVries, 1981). The naval officer reported using running as his preferred form of exercise, because it allows time for free-form problem-solving.

> I find after thirty minutes of running I'm physically fatigued but I'm

mentally aware—in fact, I'm more alert. I think I've learned to use that to reduce the stress that might be built up inside me emotionally and physically. Sometimes when I'm through running I've thought of a solution to something, and I hadn't really been objectively, consciously thinking about the problem.

The health care company president, also a runner, concurs.

I'm a real believer in exercise. For the first time in my life a couple of years ago I began to develop some blood pressure problems and it coincided with stopping exercise. I've been a jogger for fifteen years, running four to five miles a day, and it seems to get the tensions out. When the tensions are out, you are not as fatigued; when you are fatigued, the problems seem so big and so difficult that you don't want to face them. So exercise has always been vital to me and gets the tensions out.

The banking executive, a competitive swimmer in college, credits athletics with preparing him mentally and physically for his demanding career.

I think exercise has played a very significant role in my life, not only in helping me maintain a good physical condition but good mental health as well. At a very early age, I believe, being involved in a sport that required that degree of discipline and competition taught me some very valuable lessons. In fact, I'm sure it did. It taught me hard work—it demonstrated very graphically, vividly, the payoff for hard work. When I entered my business career I tried to apply the same kind of discipline to my working habits that I did to my exercise in competitive sports.

The banking executive reported that he continues to swim and alternates this with a running program daily as a way of managing stress.

Boone Pickens (1987), in his autobiography, argues that fitness is essential to business success. His personal benefits from exercise, which for him means racquetball, are improved stamina and powers of concentration. The fitness center at his Mesa Petroleum has meant savings for the company in terms of reduced insurance claims, sick leave, and medical bills. Robert Crandall, CEO of American Airlines, runs four miles per day to stave off the stress of the volatile airline industry (Banks, 1988).

The literature regarding the beneficial effects of exercise has shown positive effects on both psychological factors and physiological factors (Baun, Bernacki and Herd, 1987; Winter, 1983). DeVries (1981) found that exercise can reduce muscle tension more effectively than tranquilizing drugs. Bruning and Frew (1987) found that exercise led to decreases in pulse rate and systolic blood pressure. Morgan (1979) reported exercise to be associated with decreased anxiety. In addition, exercise has been described as a palliative coping technique which is effective due to its function as a form of relaxation or diversion (Gal and Lazarus, 1975). No exercise program should be undertaken without consultation with a physician; however, exercise appears to have multiple benefits as a prevention strategy.

Relaxation, Prayer and Faith

Many of our executives used relaxation in combination with other techniques as a stress management strategy. The naval admiral used his lunch hour to read and relax; the real estate CEO reported air travel to be relaxing. In addition, she stated that when she experienced muscle tension, 'I sit down, close my eyes and think of something pleasant until it passes over.'

Many techniques from various religions such as prayer and meditation have been found to achieve the effects of relaxation through a common physiological reaction (Benson, Beary and Carol, 1974). Some of our executives cited their religious beliefs as central to their success. The oil company president insisted that, among other factors, his church was more important to him than work. The health care executive talked at length about his deep faith and its role in his life.

> To me, my religious faith has been always for as long as I can remember the motivating factor in my life. It has given me a great feeling of comfort. I know, for instance, if I fail at everything I am doing, the most important part of my life I will succeed in. So I do have an active prayer life, and that part of my life is just central. I can't overemphasize the importance to me—I'm sure because of it I don't get as uptight about winning or losing a certain event, even though I like to win.

RECOMMENDATIONS FROM THE STRESS LITERATURE

The results of our studies of executives and anecdotal evidence from well-known CEOs have provided a host of preventive techniques which are available for stress management. Figure 2 presents the individual-level preventive management strategies. Those strategies cited by our

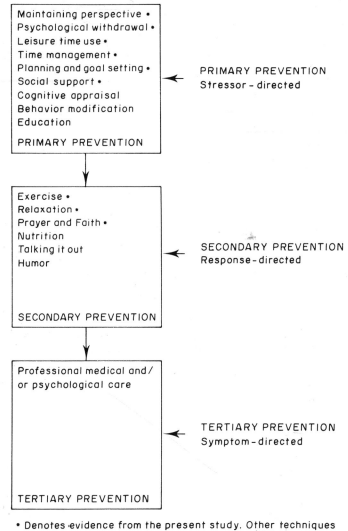

Maintaining perspective •
Psychological withdrawal •
Leisure time use •
Time management •
Planning and goal setting •
Social support •
Cognitive appraisal
Behavior modification
Education

PRIMARY PREVENTION

PRIMARY PREVENTION
Stressor - directed

Exercise •
Relaxation •
Prayer and Faith •
Nutrition
Talking it out
Humor

SECONDARY PREVENTION

SECONDARY PREVENTION
Response - directed

Professional medical and/
or psychological care

TERTIARY PREVENTION
Symptom - directed

TERTIARY PREVENTION

• Denotes evidence from the present study. Other techniques
suggested by the stress literature

Figure 2   Individual-level preventive management for executives

executives as being most helpful are emphasized. Our in-depth profiles suggest that executives rely on mainly primary- and secondary-level preventive management techniques to facilitate their success. Also included are other techniques which the empirical stress literature indicates might be beneficial to top-level managers.

At the primary or stressor-directed level, some cognitive techniques have been found to be effective. *Cognitive appraisal* involves examining the stressful situation in terms of its seriousness and possible outcomes. Many individuals become anxious about relatively minor job demands. Through appraisal, the situation is evaluated realistically so that action can be taken (Folkman *et al.*, 1986; Matteson and Ivancevich, 1987). A second cognitive technique which may prove of value to executives is *constructive self-talk* (Eliot, 1982). This technique involves a conscious effort to replace negative, irrational dialogue within the self with positive, self-efficacious, self-reinforcing talk. Some individuals, prior to an important event such as a corporate presentation, work themselves into a frenzy with thoughts of failure, embarrassment, or impending disaster. Constructive self-talk seeks to program into the thoughts positive messages such as 'I know I'll do this well,' or 'This is a real opportunity.'

Another primary-level technique is *behavior modification*. Often an individual's behavior exacerbates the stress experience. The most frequently cited culprit is Type A behavior, described in Chapter 2. Attempts to modify the behavior of Type A individuals have resulted in positive psychological and physiological changes (Friedman and Rosenman, 1974; Suinn, 1982; Suinn and Bloom, 1978). However, some researchers have argued that behavioral modification is of little use unless the attendant situational factors are altered as well (Howard, Cunningham and Rechnitzer, 1976). In addition, recent evidence indicates that the Type A pattern may in fact be facilitative for heart attack victims in that Type A individuals persist more diligently in recovery efforts and are more likely to closely follow doctors' orders in their recuperation (Ragland and Brand, 1988). Perhaps it is most reasonable to recommend that behavioral modification efforts should focus on minimizing the negative aspects of the Type A pattern (hostility, obsession with numbers, impatience, overzealous devotion to work) while encouraging the positive aspects (moderate competitiveness, drive for success, persistence).

At the secondary level, there are three techniques which executives might find of use in preventively managing stress. One technique is maintaining healthy *nutrition* habits. The argument for positive effects of nutrition on stress management is an intuitively appealing one, as it might be expected that a healthy diet minimizes the risk of heart disease. Presently the link between nutrition and stress in the literature seems to be for the most part conjecture, with little attention to empirical demonstration of an association between the two. One encouraging trend in the literature has been the recent surge of studies investigating the role of health habits (diet, exercise, sleep, substance use) in the stress–disease continuum (see Nowack, 1987). While this conceptualization makes it difficult to separate the effects of diet from the other factors, it does signal an interest in the preventive role of nutrition. A healthy diet, in terms of prevention, can be expected to arm the individual with the energy supply needed to manage the response to stress.

Another technique which may help executives in terms of secondary prevention is the emotional outlet of *talking it out* with others. This provides an acceptable way of expressing emotions associated with the experience of stress at work. By participating in activities where other top-level executives are involved, the CEO may find others who share similar problems and can then ventilate feelings and form networks of social support. Howard, Rechnitzer and Cunningham (1975) found this to be the second most frequently used coping strategy among a sample of 300 managers. In addition, they found that managers who reported fewer somatic symptoms of distress reported greater use of talking it out with others as a coping technique.

A third technique, seldom mentioned in the stress literature, is the use of *humor* as a way of coping with stress. Laughter is a great emotional release, and while we certainly do not advise laughing away the dilemmas of being a CEO, there is something to be said for being able to find mirth in a certain situation and in ourselves. Vaillant (1977) classifies humor as a mature defense mechanism which allows individuals to get through seemingly unbearable situations. A senior vice president of a major domestic oil company related that the most stressful period for his organization was when they found themselves in the throes of a takeover attempt by a larger international oil company. Lawyers advised the upper management to keep a closed-mouth approach with junior managers about the details of the takeover, lest there be a leak to the press. To relieve some of the stress of this situation, a junior research and development manager (and talented artist) produced cartoons which depicted the senior managers as the butt of jokes. Senior management, under great stress themselves, could have reacted harshly to these cartoons. Instead, they realized that this was a way the uninformed workers were coping with the uncertainty that was part of the takeover stress.

Anthony O'Reilly reportedly tells jokes to relieve tension when meeting with Heinz company's board of directors. William Popejoy of Financial Corporation of America takes time out to recall humorous incidents from his life when he feels pressure at work (Jefferson, 1987). Humor can thus provide a respite from the demands of executive life.

As previously noted, the aim of preventive management is to manage proactively the executive's experience of stress. The preferred means of accomplishing this are through altering the demands encountered and managing the individual's response to stress. These avenues of prevention should arrest stress-related problems before they develop into disease or disability. Should serious symptoms manifest, tertiary prevention techniques like counseling and medical care are steps which can be taken in order to control these symptoms. For executives who are unsuccessful at primary- or secondary-level prevention, a professional, therapeutic approach may be necessary in order to keep stress symptoms from developing into more serious illness.

An overall strategy which may prove key in helping executives manage stress effectively is *education.* Stress, with its very negative connotation in society, is the victim of many misconceptions, chief among them the notion that all stress is bad. Executives may be reluctant to discuss the stress of their jobs for fear of being labeled weak; however, this and other mistaken impressions must be rectified in order to encourage the executive and those who depend on him for guidance to take a proactive approach and manage stress rather than consider it something to be avoided altogether. An education in stress management should begin with the awareness that stress does exist in organizations and should enhance the executive's ability to cope with it. Executives must also be made aware that there are very real costs from mismanaged stress, both for themselves and for the companies they manage, in terms of performance, well-being, and satisfaction. Stress is a unique experience in that each executive experiences it differently. This makes diagnosis an important part of the educational process. An executive who has the ability to pinpoint the sources stemming from the job has taken an important step toward preventive stress management.

WHAT TECHNIQUES DON'T WORK FOR TOP-LEVEL EXECUTIVES?

The executives in our study also cautioned that they have found certain techniques for managing the demands of top-level management to be ineffective. The oil company CEO, early in his career, spent long hours at the office, as did many of his colleagues. Over the years, he has come to recognize that late nights at the office are indicative of a problem to him—that is, 'if you are working long hours at the office on a regular basis, chances are you are not delegating authority sufficiently.' Long hours, then, are not always a solution to job stress.

The health care executive, at one point in his career, put in the long hours too; but his overtime was spent at his home rather than at the office.

> I used to read every night or work every night and bring home a briefcase full, and really feel guilty if I didn't. I thought I owed that to myself and to the corporation. But I learned a number of years ago that I could be more effective if I didn't. I was more creative and purposely don't work now in the evenings.

One misconception of successful executives may be that they put in excessively long hours. The comments from these two CEOs definitely contradict this myth.

Kets de Vries and Miller (1984), in their work on neurotic organizations, describe a female CEO in apparel manufacturing who turned into a hermit after suffering personal tragedy. She retreated to her office, retained decision-making authority in all matters, and left her supervisors to run the show. As a result, power struggles ensued and supervisors appealed to the CEO to intervene. She merely instructed them to cooperate with each other, refusing to be involved and insisted on communication through written memoranda only. The result was a substantial delay in the firm's introduction of the fall fashion line and terrible sales performance for the season.

THE BOTTOM LINE: THE EXECUTIVE AS STRESS MANAGER

Why should organizations be concerned about the health and well-being of the chief executive officer? Besides the fact that replacement costs are tremendous, organizations must be concerned about how the executive deals with stress because he/she sets the tone for the way in which all individuals within the organization handle stress. Subordinates look to the CEO as a model to learn the acceptable norms of behavior and pattern their responses to stressful situations after this leader (Bandura, 1977). It follows that the figurehead role requires an effective demonstration of preventive stress management skills.

(2) A second reason for concern about the stress management style of the CEO is that poorly managed stress for this leader may lead to faulty decision making. The CEO who faces high demands may retreat into himself, failing to reach out for social support from others in the form of necessary informational input in the decision making process. Lost or incomplete information may therefore result in bad decisions. In addition, the executive who does not preventively manage the demands of the job may find that impaired judgment may result. The CEO who is overloaded and does little to manage this situation may not cautiously evaluate alternatives and may thus make a faulty decision. Janis and Mann (1977) refer to decision making under stress as 'hypervigilance.' Executives in this condition are prone to gross errors in judgment. The critical choices made by executives require a cool head and a rational mind; thus, preventive stress management plays a primary role in freeing the executive to operate effectively in decision making.

(3) A third reason why preventive stress management is important for top-level executives is that the CEO in fact may be a creator of stress for the members of the organization. Chapter 1 (see p. 7) described a banking executive (not in our study) who, with his directive management style and constant finger-pointing, involved himself in the detailed, everyday matters of the bank to such an extent that his very presence struck fear and anxiety inside the workers. He was uncomfortable in forming trusting relationships with others and was a source of stress to his organization, rather than an example to follow. Other examples of executives who pass stress down the line include Fred Friendly, former president of CBS news and an admitted stress 'carrier' (Bennis and Nanus, 1985) and Charles Revson, former head of Revlon, which is cited as one of the most stressful companies to work for in the US (Smith, 1975).

Much insight can be gleaned from examining the preventive management strategies which effective executives use to cope with their demanding jobs. As role models, they display appropriate coping methods to subordinates. Organizations depend on them for sound decision making. Perhaps most important, if they do not preventively manage stress, they may in fact be not only a recipient of stress but a major source of stress within their own organizations.

FURTHER READING

House, J. S. (1981). *Work Stress and Social Support*, Addison-Wesley, Reading, Mass.

Levinson, H. and Rosenthal, S. (1984). *CEO: Corporate Leadership in Action*, Basic Books, New York.

Quick, J. C. and Quick, J. D. (1984). *Organizational Stress and Preventive Management*, McGraw-Hill, New York.

Tichy, N. and DeVanna, M. A. (1986). *The Transformational Leader: Molding Tomorrow's Corporate Winners*, Wiley, New York.

Chapter 4

Profiles of Male Executives: Able Men in Trying Times

It is not stress that kills us; rather, it is effective adaptation to stress which enables us to live (Vaillant, 1977). Every executive encounters trying times at one point or another in professional or personal life. However, the way their lives turn out is not determined by the difficulties of those trying times but by the ways in which they *respond to* those difficulties. The implication of this is that individuals and/or management teams need to be studied longitudinally to observe their adaptation mechanisms and the successes or failures, as well as the modifications, of those mechanisms.

Since beginning our research on successful executives in 1983, we have interviewed, observed, audio- or videotaped men and women in a variety of industries and professions. While one of the purposes of nomothetic research is to draw general conclusions for universal application, one of the purposes of ideographic research is to profile individual cases for the purpose of better understanding the whole. Although we have employed some of the tools of nomothetic research, our approach in this and the next chapter is much more ideographic in nature.

In these two chapters we present profiles of three male and three female executives. We will profile them by looking at the biographical and developmental backgrounds; the organizations which they lead; their recent and current sources of challenge and/or stress; and their professional and personal preventive stress management strategies. We summarized in Table 1 in Chapter 3 the primary and secondary prevention strategies upon which each of these executives relies most. It is important to notice in that table that each relies upon a slightly different set of primary and secondary prevention strategies. The circumstances and experiences of each are unique. Thus, it should not be surprising that their prevention patterns are different as well. It is interesting to note that there *are* two common primary prevention strategies used by all three men. These are leisure time activities and social support systems.

Each of the men we have chosen to profile in this chapter is in an industry that has had trying and difficult times during the 1980s. The steel, oil field service, and banking industries in the US, and in particular Texas, have been traumatized by a number of factors. These include increasing foreign competition in their markets, both nationally and internationally; a dramatic decline in the price of oil in the international market during the 1980s; and a serious downturn in the Texas economy, largely as a result of the drop in the price of oil.

While the Texas marketplace is the third largest in the US and one of the ten largest in the world, it has been traumatized by the events of the 1980s. It is in this context and in the context of the difficulties in their individual industries that these men have succeeded. These industrial and state economic circumstances have placed great pressures on the organizations which these men lead, yet they have done well. Their organizations have enjoyed varying degrees of success during these difficult times and they have managed the circumstances well personally.

These three men are Purvis Thrash, President and Chief Executive Officer of Otis Engineering Corporation, a subsidiary of the Halliburton Company; Gordon Forward, President and Chief Executive Officer of Chaparral Steel; and Jody Grant, Chairman of the Board and Chief Executive Officer of Texas American Bancshares, Inc. Each man has been at the top of his organization for at least six years, which means they have led their organizations through this period of difficulty and economic diversity.

PURVIS J. THRASH, Sr

President and CEO
Otis Engineering Corporation

Biographical

Purvis J. Thrash Sr was born in 1927 in Nacogdoches, Texas, but grew up in Galveston, Texas, where he attended Ball High School. He graduated in June, 1950 from Texas A&M with a Bachelor of Science degree in Petroleum Engineering. In 1951 he married Betty Jo Johnston of Port Isabel, Texas. They have three children and two grandchildren.

After graduation from Texas A&M he held positions with Pan American Pipeline, Macco Oil Tool Company, and McEvoy Inc. In August, 1958 Thrash joined Otis Engineering Corporation as Sales Engineer in south Texas. This was the beginning of what was to become a career-long relationship between Otis Engineering and Purvis Thrash—a relationship which has spanned more than three decades and has seen Thrash rise through the ranks, through numerous positions in field operations management and headquarters staff and line management, to President and CEO.

While in south Texas, Thrash was involved in the development of artificial lift technology. Because of his expertise in the field of artificial lift, he served for a period as a consultant to the Texas A&M University Engineering Department and was a guest instructor for the Texas A&M and Louisiana State University Petroleum Engineering Departments. After three years in south Texas as Sales Engineer, he was made that area's Division Manager in 1961. In 1963 he was moved to Otis' headquarters in Dallas to become a Product Development Manager. During the next 13 years he held various jobs in the Sales and Service Operations. From 1968 to 1975, he was Regional Operations Manager for Otis' South Louisiana Region. In 1975, he became Vice President of Domestic Sales and Service Operations, and held that job until August, 1980, when he was made Senior Vice President of Manufacturing. Thirteen months later in November, 1981, he became President and Chief Executive Officer of Otis Engineering Corporation.

Thrash has been involved in both civic and professional community activities. He worked for several years as a volunteer with the Boy Scouts of America, has served as a board member for his church, and was a director of Dallas Junior Achievement. He has been a member of the Operating Committee of the Dallas Petroleum Club. He is a member of the Society of Petroleum Engineering, the American Petroleum Institute, and a registered professional engineer in the State of Texas. Currently, he is Chairman of the Board of Directors of Otis Engineering, a director of Halliburton Services, and a past director of Life Insurance Company of the Southwest. He sits on the Executive Committee of the Halliburton Company, the parent company of Otis Engineering.

Otis Engineering Corporation

Otis Engineering Corporation is a wholly-owned subsidiary of Halliburton Company. It specializes in the design and manufacturing of oil field
products used by oil and gas producers around the world to complete,
produce, and control wells. Many of the products are designed to be
utilized within the well or at the surface for purposes of providing safety
against disaster. Otis service personnel perform a wide range of specialized services on oil and gas wells for the producing companies,
including numerous remedial, testing, and analytical services. Services
are usually performed utilizing specialized service equipment also
designed and manufactured by Otis. These products and services are
provided in approximately 60 domestic sales and service locations and
in about the same number of foreign countries. Annual revenues for
Otis Engineering were in the $350 million bracket in 1988 and employ-
ment was approximately 4100.

Challenges Through a Career

In discussing his sources of stress over the years, Thrash touches on two
of four broad sources of organizational stress. The two are job demands
and physical demands. He touches only briefly on interpersonal demands and seems generally unaware of role stressors, such as conflict,
ambiguity, and overload, as sources of stress.

The fact that Thrash makes only passing mention of interpersonal
stressors shows the importance of individual differences as influences on
stress. Less than half of the executives we have interviewed note
interpersonal stressors. In Thrash's case, his emphasis upon directness,
honesty, and straightforwardness in all of his relationships may in part
account for the relative absence of interpersonal stressors.

Though he has not thought much about his leadership style, Thrash is
clearly comfortable in his role. He observes:

> I think every chief executive officer must be pretty much his own man.
> For me, neither [authoritarian nor democratic] style is the true case. I
> don't believe you can be purely democratic nor purely authoritative and
> be the best type of officer. I believe that it takes a melding of the two.
> Generally you would like to apply the democratic principles to your
> people as much as possible, but in doing so, you don't want to ever forget
> that it's your responsibility and yours alone in many cases and at

appropriate times to make the decision. This could, in effect, become authoritative. But if the case calls for authoritativeness, you must not hesitate to be so.

Whatever the style, there is no question in Thrash's mind that he is the boss: 'If I'm not the boss somebody else will be.'

Having served in both line and staff positions, Thrash sees the two types of roles as different, yet each important in its own right. Through his career, however, line management has generally been more stressful. Line management positions have had the responsibility for the supervision of people, where staff normally does not. At least in Otis Engineering, line management also has had the profit and loss responsibility. One must constantly work to make sure whatever unit one is responsible for as a line manager is a contributor to the overall good of the company in terms of how it is accounted for in black and white. Responsibilities associated with line authority are more diverse, including financial, personnel, and effective utilization of various technologies. The manager must combine these to successfully accomplish the job requirements. The responsibility for this can be stressful.

Oil field engineering has always posed to its executives and managers certain unique and unusual circumstances and demands. Otis Engineering Corporation designs and manufactures a wide variety of equipment which is used in the control of high pressure oil and gas wells all over the world. This includes both downhole and surface-type safety equipment. Otis employees also perform a wide variety of services on oil and gas wells. Invariably, they are working in a mechanical environment with high physical pressures and it makes the work inherently dangerous. There are always the elements of danger along with liability for Otis equipment and people. This goes on 24 hours a day all over the world. In this sense there is an extra burden that the executive for an oil field equipment and service company such as Otis must feel. Because of the worldwide activities, there are some very extreme sorts of physical environments to which individuals are subjected. Not only are there the conditions of the mechanical environment, but there is also the physical isolation. Frequently Otis employees can be found a long distance offshore on a platform, in a boat or helicopter, somewhere in a jungle or a desert in some type of conveyance, or at some type of work site where they must be very adaptable and there is a lot of exposure. There is a sense of responsibility then for the physical well-being of the 4100 Otis employees.

Challenges of Adversity

Shortly after Thrash took over as President and CEO, he entered the most challenging phase of his career to date. In 1982, after several years of the strongest demand for oil field equipment and services in history, Thrash faced a rapid, unprecedented, and highly unexpected worldwide decline in demand for oil field equipment and services. The major dislocation and uncertainty resulting from this downturn created a tremendous need for adjustment by Thrash, Otis Engineering, and the employees of Otis Engineering. As the leader and most visible personality in an organization, it is inevitable that the chief executive will experience stress from any environmental uncertainty through which he or she must guide the enterprise.

During the growth years, demand exceeded capacity and consequently heavy investment had been made to increase capacity. Most stressful conditions were incurred by management in making decisions on how to adjust successfully to smaller market demands for an industry that suddenly had an excess of capacity. The list of problems a corporation must quickly cope with under these circumstances is long and varied. Cost controls, manpower reductions, capital spending adjustments, inventory utilization, and debt servicing are only the most obvious areas to be addressed. The more subtle but equally important considerations include changing the operating philosophy of the company from growth to survival, protection of market share in a buyer's market, and evaluation of what programs to retain despite the obvious need to reduce expenses in all possible ways.

To illustrate this last point, Otis very soon decided not to eliminate or curtail research and development, employee training, manufacturing systems modernization, and CAD/CAM (Computer Aided Drafting and Computer Aided Manufacturing) implementation programs. Each of these programs are considered too important for Otis' future. They did not decrease Otis sales staff either, but for a different reason. Field sales efforts were considered even more important in a more competitive market to protect and increase Otis market share. The uncertainty of the overall situation, along with the urgency for effective measures to be taken, combined to cause unusual stress on management in general during this time.

After a most intense period of adjustment during the second quarter of 1982 and continued adjustment over the next several years, oil prices began to stabilize in 1985. This occurred at a time when many industry forecasters and spokesmen were predicting a 'bottom of the trough' condition which would be followed by an industry upswing. These predictions proved to be incorrect and oil price stabilization proved temporary. Saudi Arabia elected to flood the market with oil to teach the OPEC nations who were cheating on their production allocations a lesson. Consequently, about when the industry was expecting a positive reversal, the price of oil plunged to new lows. Conditions very quickly became worse during 1986 and early 1987 than at any previous time. Demand for products and services dropped further and discounting by suppliers reached new levels to the detriment of those still in business. For the weaker companies not already bankrupt, cash flow became the predominant strategy for survival and not necessarily profits. Those companies which had not effectively used 1982 through 1985 to improve efficiencies, repay debts, manage inventories and reduce operating expense were doomed.

The years of 1986 and early 1987 saw a renewed frenzy of bankruptcies, mergers, joint ventures, and acquisitions throughout the industry. It was during 1986 and early 1987 that industry conditions caused the most drastic survival actions and hence the stress of severe layoffs and stringent expense controls. Discounting pressures increased in intensity and coupled with this were new demands from key customers for the acceptance of new and potentially disastrous liabilities never before considered by the industry. Simultaneously, insurance rates skyrocketed and suitable insurance was difficult to obtain at any price.

Fortunately, at Otis sufficient control of problems such as debt reduction, inventory control, manufacturing cost reductions, and operating expense controls had been achieved during 1982 through 1985 to prepare it somewhat for these new and even more severe challenges. In spite of this and best continuing efforts, revenue and profit margins continued to taper down and by the second quarter of 1987 profit became very small. This performance bettered that of industry as a whole, but most oil field equipment and services companies sank even more deeply into the red at some point in 1986 even if they had successfully avoided doing so in prior years.

Managing the Challenges of Adversity

Mr Thrash, like any very healthy executive, manages stress effectively so that it does not become distress. What distinguishes Thrash from those who become ill or diseased as a result of stressful events is his incorporation of a variety of preventive stress management strategies in his normal lifestyle.

Throughout his career, and particularly during his thus far demanding tenure as President and CEO, Thrash has relied on both organizational and personal approaches to stress management. The broad benefits of combining both organizational and individual approaches to stress management are well illustrated in Thrash's reflections on the well-being of his immediate subordinates during the 1982 to 1987 oil industry upheaval:

> At Otis with 10 vice presidents and a CEO, there was not a single divorce to be counted. All officers had an average of 25 or more years of service and were solid family men. To me it seemed they drew strength from their families—from children's educational endeavors, weddings, and the blessings of grandchildren. No problems were noted with health, alcohol or drugs, affairs or other distracting involvements. As a group, they seemed to have confidence in their leadership and our abilities to survive the storm. Strategic plans were developed, discussed, implemented and monitored against company performance. Most health problems seemed to occur in middle management with several nonfatal heart attacks.

Organizational approaches to stress management

There are four organizational strategies which emerge from discussions with Thrash about his success as a leader and his effectiveness in stress management. These are a focused, analytic perspective toward his work; effective delegation; careful planning; and a broad-based social support system.

Focused, analytic perspective. Thrash tries to maintain his effectiveness during challenging, stressful times by focusing on those areas in which constructive action is possible and by maintaining an objectivity. He does not keep a regular list of goals for himself. Instead, he maintains a list of goals for the company. He keeps these in mind fairly constantly in his daily work and guides his actions according to these goals. His observation is that, 'As chief executive officer, the goals and plans for the corporation are foremost and my personal plans must coincide with those to achieve the most success.'

In Thrash's reflections on the perspective he has taken over the years in response to demanding situations, two recurrent, complementary themes emerge: 'concentrate on the problem' and 'do not worry too much about those things over which you have no control.' Concentrating on the problem begins with an objective analysis of the current situation. It means focusing on the problems which are most central to the goals of the organization. In times of crisis, concentrating on the problem may also mean severely limiting outside involvement in industry organization work or nonwork activities.

Factors which appear entirely outside of one's control should be taken into consideration, but time and effort should be directed toward those things over which one does have control. Otis operates in a variety of environments and often faces seemingly uncontrollable factors. Thrash is aware of these factors, yet he spends little time worrying about the uncontrollable aspects of field operations.

Thrash's focused, analytic perspective is illustrated by his approach to emergencies. When it comes to operation emergencies somewhere in the world (in contrast to, for example, an immediate physical emergency such as a fire in the building), Thrash has some fixed ideas that he feels have worked quite successfully for him. His approach is to be careful not to react, and particularly not to overreact, to first reports: 'You must exhibit some patience and seek information again from more than one source until you feel like you have a pretty representative picture of what's happened. Then it is time for you to take whatever action is necessary. It's too easy to react too fast in serious emergency situations.'

Effective delegation. Delegation of authority and responsibility is another key to this executive's success. Thrash puts the process of selecting subordinates and delegating responsibility 'very close to the top, maybe even at the top of the list' of methods he has used over the years to deal with the demands and the stress of leadership. As CEO and President he has found this to be even more important:

> When you've become head of a large corporation, you cannot do everything yourself. As a matter of fact, one secret of making an operation a success is the proper selection of your subordinates, the delegation of the responsibility and the authority to those individuals, expecting performance from them, and measuring performance.

Through effective delegation Thrash is free to concentrate on priority matters, and is able to control the number of hours he spends in 'direct'work. Further, he expects effective delegating skills of his managers. Thrash notes that an executive regularly working long hours may be an indication of ineffective or insufficient delegation.

Measuring performance is an important aspect of effective delegation. A line manager can be measured periodically on profit and loss, return on investment, revenues, cash flow—any number of measurements. Regardless of the discipline or the job, there are ways to measure. This should be done continuously on an informal basis with a formal review periodically.

The performance appraisal must consider the environmental circumstances. For example, when evaluating a line manager's profit–loss statement, the prevailing economic conditions must be considered. In business, a forecast is made to serve as a road map. It should be used as a measure, as long as things such as markets, conditions, etc., are those which are anticipated. But, warns Thrash, there should be flexibility.

> 'If there are curves in the road or chug holes, then you make allowances for those things that could not be anticipated. You must be fair in evaluating a person's performance, because he or she is a human being.'

At Otis Engineering there is a standardized performance evaluation system. But Thrash considers it to be,

> 'only one of several tools to evaluate a person . . . You cannot ever write down everything and every way to measure.'

In summing up his approach to delegation Thrash advises,

> Let others help—Practice the principle of delegation of responsibility *and* authority and live with it. Manage on a results basis with minimum interference.

Careful planning. The third strategy which Thrash draws on is careful planning. Thrash sees planning as playing an important part in the management of various stresses and demands of his role. He comments:

> In my estimation, planning is as effective for handling stress as delegation of authority and responsibility. Planning minimizes or eliminates surprises, the unknowns. When you can do that, you have less to worry about regarding what's going to happen down the road . . . I tell my people I don't like surprises. What that is saying is we need to plan.

It is the uncertainty that is often the source of stress for people in CEO and similar positions. The complexity and uncertainty of the oil field engineering industry demands careful forecasting, and Thrash draws upon a number of resources for information gathering. The board of directors plays a key role in long-term planning. Careful planning also characterizes Thrash's personal work projects and activities. He firmly believes in completing projects well in advance of deadlines. For example, he tries to complete papers, reports, speeches, and other such communications as early as possible. Waiting until the last minute creates stress in his view. Finishing work ahead of time also gives him a chance to review and revise it before it is actually due.

Planning also requires a willingness to make decisions. Thrash believes that timely decision making is important:

> Prompt, decisive decision making is needed and is respected of a chief executive officer, but this is not to say that every decision can be made this way. It's not uncommon for questions to come up that are so complex you need to get more than one source of information to evaluate before you make the decision.

In essence, he identifies a kind of an optimum point at which one has gathered enough information and now it's time to act.

Social support system. Related to the delegation of authority is Thrash's use of a broad support system. This includes his subordinates, superiors, and peers at work. He relies on key people for emotional, appraisal, and informational support. It is interesting to note that his wife is a key source of appraisal support, giving him evaluative feedback on himself. This is also characteristic of the other executives, although they differ somewhat in the ways in which they depend on their spouses.

Social support can arise in part from a common sense of purpose. A factor which Thrash identified as being key to Otis' successful management of the mid-1980s downturn was unity of direction and purpose among management ranks. He had formed a strong, effective, and open executive committee consisting of key officers. In addition to proposing programs himself, input was solicited from and considered by all members of the group. Decisions made by this group were regularly communicated to middle management by report. Thrash describes the two key elements of the process in the following way:

Share the load—Establish a competent staff and consult with them on selection of programs and goals deemed appropriate for conditions that exist. Thiokos should be done prior to and also during the implementation phase. Establish an atmosphere of open input from subordinates and middle management. Make a practice of allocating the necessary resources to accomplish a goal once it is accepted as worthy.

Do communicate with the company employees regularly through any available medium and in person. Appraise them as openly and honestly as possible about the real situation. They will help you. Be the same way with your superior, board of directors and stockholders.

In Thrash's judgment, the united efforts of the executive committee and the understanding of these decisions by lower management became a key factor of success. He concludes that

'Stress was minimized because of reliance on each other and confidence in ourselves as an effective management team.'

Thrash also relies on the board of directors for appraisal and informational support. The board of directors helps to set the long-term direction path of the company—the major endeavors into which it should go or not go. The board of directors really plays a strategic kind of role, as opposed to tactical. The board is also helpful in confronting complex situations which arise from time to time.

Finally, Thrash does not hesitate to look outside the organization for informational support. He advises executives to be open to learning from others:

Make practical use of outside information and experience in specific areas of expertise as is appropriate, yet recognize the application of all experience must be tailored to the peculiarities and culture of your own company.

Personal approaches to stress management

As important as organizational approaches to stress management has been Thrash's reliance on family, friends, and church relationships. His perspective on his job and life contributes to his successful management of stress.

Was work the most important thing in Purvis Thrash's life as he rose from sales representative to CEO and President? Thrash offers a definitive, 'No.'

> 'It is very important, but it's not the most important thing in my life. To me, my family, my friends, my church, my personal enjoyment of life are actually more important to me than my job.'

This is not to say that the job is not important to him, for it is indeed. But he places his work in perspective.

At the same time Thrash is very conscientious with respect to work and does see work-related benefits of his commitment to family, friends, and community. In his view, these relationships help him

> 'enjoy life outside of my job, which I think is essential to bringing a happy well-rounded man to a chair that must make decisions involving human beings. I should understand or have compassion for those people with whom I deal.'

Thrash does not believe in the 60, 70 or 80 hour weeks which typify the working lives of many key executives. He observes:

> 'Now there have been times in my career or the career of others where that [long hours] was required. But to my way of thinking that should be a temporary situation based on a peculiar set of circumstances at the time. As a rule, I believe that if an executive is regularly working those type of hours there is some kind of problem, probably with his management style. The first place I would look is to see if he is truly delegating authority and responsibility to those people under him.'

Considering the 1982 to 1987 oil industry upheaval, Thrash can identify no particular changes in lifestyle or stress management, except perhaps appreciating more weekends with his wife at a new lake home, built in 1984. He found that these weekends rested his mind and his body, while allowing him some perspective. He comments:

> It has been said that it is physically impossible to worry and fish at the same time. In my case, it must be true. Rather than worry, I could more leisurely analyze our business environment and position within it and come to grips with the problems in a logical manner.

These weekends also helped Thrash to think through a growing adversarial relationship with his corporate superior. The weekend respites helped him cope with this interpersonal stress until his superior's retirement in late 1987. The continuing successful financial performance of Otis as compared to other companies under his supervision and the industry as a whole may have served to neutralize the corporate superior.

Though family, friends, and church relationships tend to fortify and balance Thrash in his work, he rarely shares specific work concerns with them. He may carry issues home with him in his mind, but they stay in his mind. Only on rare occasions will he discuss work-related problems with his wife.

The long-standing depth of Thrash's commitment to family, friends, and community was illustrated by the incident which Thrash relates and was described in Chapter 1 (p. 14).

Curiously, shortly after Thrash became President and CEO, the president of the same industrial psychologist firm came to ask him for more business. After telling his visitor the story, Thrash learned from the embarrassed psychologist that the psychologist who had interviewed him fifteen years earlier had later been terminated because he had too many serious problems—particularly marital problems.

Postscript: From Adversity to Organizational Strength

Beginning at about mid-year 1987, world oil prices improved and Otis customers had for the most part completed their internal operating cost reduction programs. These two factors caused the market for Otis products and services to improve—finally after five and a half years. Subsequently, 1988 saw Otis revenues show strong increases over 1987 and profit ratios revive to levels rivaling those of pre-1982. There is evidence that Otis has emerged a stronger company with not only increasing market penetration but the ability to achieve improved margins. Those strategies implemented during the downmarket period to achieve these goals appear to be working. New products and services developed during those years now make significant contributions to both goals. Business management philosophies developed and implemented for hard times now serve them well in better times. There exist the ever possible adverse political events that may affect Otis markets again in the future. Meanwhile, Otis outlook for continued market improvement and Otis performance improvement is encouraging.

The successful emergence of Otis Engineering from the adversity of the 1980s and the good health of its leadership must be attributed in no small measure to the leadership style of its President and CEO. Thrash's perspective on his job and life contributes to his successful management of stress. He is clearly the boss in his organization; yet he realizes the need to rely on and utilize the support of others. He values prompt decision making, concentrating on those factors he can control rather than worrying over uncontrollable events. His family, his friends, and his church take priority in his life. While his work is important, it is not all-important. It is in these ways that Purvis Thrash has been able to sustain his health and success over an extended period of time.

GORDON FORWARD, PhD

President and CEO
Chaparral Steel

Biographical

Dr Forward was elected President and Chief Executive Officer of Chaparral Steel in 1982. Prior to assuming the office, he was Executive Vice President—Production at Chaparral. He assumed the additional duties as President and Chief Executive Officer of Texas Industries Cement/Concrete Division in April, 1988.

He earned a doctorate from the Massachusetts Institute of Technology (MIT) with a major in metallurgy and a Bachelor of Science degree from the University of British Columbia in Vancouver. Dr Forward was a Senior Research Engineer for the Steel Company of Canada and General Superintendent for the Lake Ontario Steel Company before joining Chaparral.

He is also a director of Co-Steel International of Toronto, Canada. (Co-Steel is the owner of Lake Ontario Steel Co., Toronto; Sheerness Steel Co., London, England; and Raritan River Steel Co., New Jersey.) In 1986, he became a director of the Steel Service Center Institute of the

US. Dr Forward is also President of the Gifted Students Institute In Texas. This is a nonprofit educational organization whose purpose is to develop a nationwide program to improve the educational opportunities of gifted and talented students of all ages.

In 1972, Dr Forward, together with Professor John Eliott of MIT, was the winner of the Distinguished John Chipman Medal for the American Association of Metallurgical Engineers for basic research relating to the solidification of steel. He received an honor from the same society when he was asked to present the Howe Memorial Lecture to their National Convention in Atlanta in 1985, and in 1988 they awarded Dr Forward the coveted Benjamin Fairless Award for innovation in the manufacture of iron and steel products. He was also recently recognized by MIT and added to their exclusive list as a distinguished alumnus when he received their 1987 Corporate Leadership Award.

In 1984, *Fortune* magazine selected Chaparral Steel as one of the ten best managed manufacturing companies in America and in December of 1987, author Tom Peters selected Dr Forward as Chief Executive Officer of the year.

Dr Forward's wife, Heather, is also a graduate of the University of British Columbia, and of the School of Law at Southern Methodist University in Dallas. Their sons, Mark and Paul, are presently students at the University of Texas at Austin.

Chaparral Steel

Chapparal Steel is the lowest priced steel producer on a delivered basis in the industry. They take 1.38 man-hours to produce a ton of steel where the industry average is 6 man-hours. This translates to over 1150 tons of steel per man-year, compared to a US average of 350 tons and a Japanese average of 600 tons. The mill currently produces approximately 1.5 million tons of competitively priced, high quality steel annually. The product line includes bars, structurals, rebar and Bantam Beams. Chaparral Steel currently employs approximately 900 people and has approximately $350 million annually in sales.

Stress and Challenge

The 1970s and 1980s have been a time of trial and turmoil for the US steel industry. Major producers have merged, gone bankrupt, or diversified. One illustration of the times has been the experience of US Steel who went from an employment of nearly 200000 to less than 100000 and in the process diversified into oil production by buying Marathon to create USX. Much of the challenge to the steel industry came from foreign competition and another part of the challenge came from within; that is, the escalating cost of steel production in part due to high wages. It was in the context of these turbulent times within the industry that Forward entered the business. As a Canadian employed by Co-Steel, he was operationally instrumental in taking a fresh approach to the whole notion of steel production. This led to the creation of Chaparral Steel as a generation of mini-mill steel producers who carved out a niche in the steel industry market.

Forward uses the word 'stress' in the pejorative, as do many in the culture. Under this rubric, there are at least three aspects of professional life which are stressful. One concerns the stifling effects of bureaucratic systems. As a creative and inquisitive individual, Forward finds it stressful to be constrained either psychologically or physically by the organizational system. As President and CEO of Chaparral Steel, that is really not a current source of stress. However, there have been times in the past when that has been an issue. The mechanical aspects of any organizational system would fall in this category, such as completing forms, vouchers, and those sorts of detailed work. While Forward well recognizes the necessity for the accurate completion of that sort of work, it does not fit his creative orientation. Demands that require him to operate in a detailed, mechanical way are very stressful.

A second source of stress for Forward is the experience of vulnerability and sense of lack of control. This is specifically related to an exposure to unmanaged risk or uncalculated risk. As a natural scientist, Forward is extremely interested in the exploration of the natural and social world with the realization that risk taking is involved in the exploration process. However, it is important to Forward that he or a close associate is monitoring and calculating the potential losses that are associated with a failure. The calculated failure is not particularly troubling to him, rather it is the uncalculated that does financial or physical damage of a catastrophic nature that is very disturbing.

A third source of stress for Forward is an excess of administrative layering or overhead within an organizational system. While he recognizes the need for both operational and managerial elements of an organization, he believes that an excessive amount of administration, for the purpose of control or any other reason, serves as a second stifling element to the growthful energy of the system. In any line of work, whether it is manufacturing, education, flying, or service, the operational aspects of the organization are the driving force. Forward's image of management is as the facilitating force which both encourages the natural operational energy of the system and channels that energy to successful conclusion. It is the flip side of his concern with the stifling aspects of administration that leads to his notions about the constructive aspects of stress, which he prefers to refer to as challenge or adrenaline (epinephrine).

According to Forward, bright people really need to be challenged in order to grow and develop their full potential. The challenge takes the form of a goal at which one either naturally or artificially arrives. For example, the rolling mill within Chaparral Steel was attempting to roll the steel using an entirely new process during November of 1988. The plant was like a maternity ward with everyone expectant about whether the new process worked or not. The steel makers had created this new challenge for themselves in the process of attempting to do a better job. Market-imposed challenges can serve the same function. However, in addition to the challenge or goal that causes individuals to go 'one step beyond,' Forward considers it vital that the individuals be given great freedom in the pursuit of the goals and challenges. That entails creating an environment which does not punish each failure. Failures are acceptable if a well thought out attempt was made for the purpose of achieving a success.

Forward's research background is vital to understanding this aspect of his perspective and behavior. He sees a constructive challenge in the search for how the world works, including its people, and he holds the belief that no one can fool Mother Nature. Rather, successful work involves the discovery of Mother Nature in all her splendor. Because he views the world and its people as mysteries to be discovered, he holds the underlying assumption that learning is not occurring if some mistakes are not being made.

We are all going to make mistakes.

Repeating the same mistakes will obviously indicate that learning has not occurred, but sequences of mistakes may still be instructive in understanding the various nonworkable pathways through the maze. One of the bigger growth challenges for Forward at this juncture is how to make Chaparral Steel into a bigger company without losing the creative, growthful dynamic. He was concerned about the growth from 450 to the current 900, yet that transition went smoothly. The central concern to the next level of growth is that there will be a bureaucratic hardening of the corporate arteries. He does believe that the potential for avoiding that does exist as illustrated in the current experiences of Hewlett-Packard and McDonalds. By growing as a mosaic with units of no greater size than perhaps 1000, similar to the current structure of Hewlett-Packard, there exists the potential for preserving the creative side of Chaparral Steel within the corporation.

Another aspect of the challenge which Forward sees as constructive stress is approaching the business in a holistic fashion. That is, by exchanging or teaming production and sales, or production and engineering people, each learns to appreciate the perspective of the other. This is illustrated in how Forward's vice president for engineering encourages his engineers to spend time in the rolling mills and foundry.

Challenging the Gifted

There are three ways in which Forward puts into practice his beliefs about education and its role in creating challenge for individual growth. The first is through his volunteer work as President of the Board of Directors of the Gifted Students Institute. Gifted and talented students are often lost in the traditional educational system because they are not adequately challenged by the system. Forward views this as an enormous waste of human resources and is committed to working with educators and psychologists to discover and nurture the talent of these able learners. There are benefits for the society, business, and the individuals themselves through such a commitment.

The Gifted Students Institute originally began with summer sessions in 1972 at Southern Methodist University designed to challenge gifted students. Within a short period, the summer programs were expanded to include visits to NASA, and the program gained a national footing. These summer programs continue today with two-week programmed activities of various kinds throughout the country.

These summer programs are no longer the main activity of the 14 person Board which Forward heads. With 10 staff members, the major activity of the Institute has more recently been the Pyramid Project. This has grown out of research done for the Richardson Foundation of

Fort Worth concerning able learners, or gifted students. The Pyramid Project is an alternative form of flexible pacing for gifted students which recognizes the possibility that the student may be gifted in only one area, such as in mathematics, while not in other areas *and* recognizes their need for social development along with intellectual development. Rather than skipping grades, the students are kept with their home social group while being accelerated to higher grade levels for a specific knowledge or skill area. The Pyramid Project was designed as a five year project and has worked well in a number of the independent school districts of the area, such as Richardson and Arlington. *Educating Able Learners* has also been one of the products of this effort which was designed to be a model for the nation.

The second way in which Forward puts his beliefs into practice is through the Vision Group of which he is a member. This Vision Group consists of senior corporate officers from Hewlett-Packard and Ford as well as academicians from Harvard and MIT. Through periodic meetings, this group brainstorms ideas for the improvement and advancement of industrial practice. It is in the context of this group that imagination and creativity can be exercised. While there are no formal objectives for this group, the orientation is the future and the process is one of cross-fertilization of ideas and thinking. The group will rotate meeting sites so that all have the opportunity to see what is being done in the others' system.

Part of Forward's belief is that the whole concept of manufacturing in America, and around the world, must undergo a transformation. The word manufacturing comes from the Latin roots which basically mean 'made by hand'. While this has been a historically accurate description of the process, Forward argues that the underlying process of manufacturing is changing with the incorporation of robotics and computer software engineering into the workplace. While we have an increasing need for manufactured goods, we are able increasingly to meet this need with a shrinking labor base supplemented by mechanical aids, such as robots. The trend is very similar to the trend in agriculture which has seen a decline in the proportion of the labor population devoted to producing our food.

Because of this trend, Forward argues that we need to start thinking in terms of 'mental-facturing,' a term he used for the first time at the Minerals, Metals and Materials Society Conference in Las Vegas during the spring of 1989. Forward does not mean by this that we truly make things with our minds. Rather, the intention is for us to use our imagination and creativity to design or 'make' what we need, then allowing the 'mechanical hands' we have produced in the latter part of this century to do the work.

The third and final way that Forward has put his educational beliefs into practice is through the Chaparral Steel Apprenticeship Program. This was developed in cooperation with the Bureau of Apprenticeship and Training, Manpower Administration, US Department of Labor.

> It is the intent of Chaparral Steel to provide the broadest possible growth experience for every person employed by the company. We believe that the company grows in excellence in direct proportion to the growth of its people. (Apprenticeship program, Chaparral Steel, December 21, 1987.)

This statement and the apprentice training program reflect the commitment of Forward to challenging people to grow and change, in the best interests of both themselves and their organizations. While there are distinctions to be made between education and training, the primary one possibly being the degree of immediate application of the knowledge, both are person change strategies. And both are ways to challenge the gifted, at work or at school, to which Forward is very much committed.

From Challenge to Curiosity

Connected to Forward's learning and research emphasis in the business is his curiosity about what others do and how they do it. At Chaparral Steel he has been committed to going himself and sending others in the company to the ends of the earth to see how things are done in making steel. Japan, West Germany, and the Scandinavian countries are frequent stops for the traveling Chaparral teams. These trips generate ideas and data to be used as input to Forward's own vivid imagination as well as the imaginations of the other members of his team.

Forward has been inquisitive through his whole life. He grew up on a university campus in Canada where his father was a professor of metallurgy and held a number of positions. As a real inventor, Forward's father also became involved in the basic research agenda for Canada, being the Scientific Advisor to the Prime Minister and setting up the Science Council at one point in his career. His father counseled his children to turn something upside-down to see how it worked if it was malfunctioning. In some ways, Forward views this as applicable to human as well as mechanical systems. He believes that it is in inquisitive and nonstifling atmospheres that bright people are able to innovate the best.

Managing the Challenges and Stresses

There are a number of professional and personal strategies which Forward uses to manage his challenges and stresses constructively. Probably the central strategy for him at work is the management team which he has constructed over time. He has built a very participative, collaborative team of vice presidents at Chaparral Steel (Forward, 1986). While he serves as the integrating core and distribution point within the team, there is much initiative taken by the next level down. When initially in top-level management, Forward's approach was to look for managers who were good in all areas. That has changed for him and he looks more now for complementary talents, realizing that few managers are good at everything. The senior team at Chaparral reflects this blend of talents.

Forward is frequently viewed by his vice presidents as the philosopher in the group. By that, the vice presidents mean that Forward is often a source of ideas and inspiration without necessarily having the details of his thoughts worked out. For them, this is a source of challenge and stimulation. One of the ways in which this plays out in practice is through the executive team's game of 'What if?' This is a game they may play at lunch or other times which is imaginative and future oriented. It often is engaged in as a response to possible problems or limitations in the production or sales process. Forward had one group of his managers play the game a bit more seriously in response to a New York banker's thought that there may be a market in Indonesia for a small (25 000 ton per year), efficient plant. Forward sent a group of his managers off on a retreat for a few days to plan a small steel operation. The team actually designed one small enough to place on a floating barge that could be run by 40 people or so.

While there is a strong emphasis on the management team at Chaparral Steel, it is clear that it is not a purely democratic organization. Forward considers the top level in any organization the critical core. He indicates that the orientals have a saying: 'If a fish begins to stink, look at its head.' The health and well-being of a company thus proceeds from the very top level. The net result is that Forward models what he expects out of his people and he also gets it.

A second way in which this concept is played out is through the selection of the next level of management below the vice presidential level. Specifically, Chaparral looks for individuals who will complement the boss. For example, if the boss is particularly talented technologically, then the complementing subordinate may well be a manager who is able to place more emphasis on the people oriented aspects of management. Teaming in this fashion creates greater structural strength within the organizational structure as they see it.

Another key ingredient for Forward in managing stresses and challenges is the concept of trust. He believes that trust is an essential ingredient of the work environment and is one of the reasons why Chaparral has gone to a salary system throughout the company. They have never used timeclocks. While he recognizes that some individuals are untrustworthy, he also believes that the 3% who are untrustworthy will be readily identified within a largely trusting environment. They will leave. This concept of trust leads to the sense of a safe working environment, psychologically, with its lower tension, conflict, and stress levels. This concept of trust also does not proceed from any deep religious or spiritual belief system since Forward is not a religious man.

The first time Forward had an opportunity to try out or draw upon his trusting nature was in his first production supervision job. He was frankly surprised that he was selected for the position given his strong interest and background in research. The production shop he became responsible for had a number of problems which were not all of a technical nature. He called all of his production people together for a meeting.

> I told them that we all recognized that we had problems and that the solutions did not rest in the front office. Rather, the solutions were right in the room. If we didn't have any solutions right away, we would just have to figure them out. I also told them that since I was not a production expert, I would have to rely on them.

Forward started leaving his office door open and talking to all the production people who came in to see him. This was his first experience where he could not think his way through work problems technically. He really had to rely upon others, and by doing that the whole atmosphere of the shop changed. He also added, 'Being reasonably calm under fire helped a lot.'

Forward's marriage is an important support system for him, not so much as a retreat or haven from the world but rather as an alternative source of growth opportunities. Heather is a civil attorney who deals with corporate legal issues. Her active mind provides challenge and excitement for Forward.

Forward also maintains a regular exercise program of sorts, though it is not highly regimented. He has a regular walking program which is supplemented with golf, racquetball or tennis with one or another of his sons, and he is contemplating the use of an exercycle. Therefore, while he does not have a rigidly structured exercise program, it is an essential ingredient of his personal stress management program.

Another element of his personal stress management program is a regular diet of reading, which includes historical works and detective mysteries. Churchill is one of his favorite historical figures. This appears to be because of the way Churchill rallied his nation during times of trial and tribulation. Tough times sometimes help people pull together and Forward considers that important. The other aspect of tough times that Forward considers important is the need for management and leadership to be supportive. Too often the reality is just the opposite; that is, when times get tough, management becomes more critical. Forward views this as particularly counterproductive.

A final element of his personal stress management program involves his ability to use his imagination in envisioning alternatives to his current circumstances. These include university teaching, managerial consulting activities, and writing activities, most probably in the form of a book. This reveals the sense of trust and confidence which Forward has in himself which is translated into the trust and confidence he exhibits in other people. Attitudinally stated, this may be expressed as a very optimistic view of the future.

The Inquisitive, Humorous Optimist

Probably the most distinguishing features of Forward as a person and as a leader are his genuine inquisitiveness about the world of nature and people around him; his subtle and light-hearted humor; and his pervasive optimism which leads him to believe that people really can do wonderful things. In Chaparral Steel, Forward and his management team have created a strongly mission-oriented specialty steel company in which people are a key ingredient to the final product. However, they have not created a monolithic structure nor do they want to do so. The sense of mission and purpose gives Chaparral the integrating mechanism to tie them together while at the same time allowing for autonomous flexibility among the individual managers and officers.

If there are hallmarks for Forward's style of leadership, there are probably two. First is the importance of challenging bright and capable people. He strongly believes that people need to be challenged to grow, develop, and to achieve their best results. Second is the importance of a creative, nonstifling psychological environment.

JOSEPH M. GRANT, PhD

Chairman of the Board and CEO
Texas American Bancshares Inc.

Biographical

Joseph M. (Jody) Grant is Chairman of the Board and Chief Executive Office of Texas American Bancshares Inc. In addition, he is Chairman of the Board and Chief Executive Officer of Texas American Bank/Fort Worth, the largest bank in Fort Worth and the seventh largest bank in Texas. Prior to his association with Texas American Bancshares, Grant was President of Capital National Bank in Austin, Texas from 1974 to 1975. From 1970 to 1973 he served as Senior Vice President and Economist for Texas Commerce Bancshares in Houston. He began his banking career at Citibank in New York in 1961 where he was a Commercial Banking Officer.

Grant received his BBA degree in 1960 from Southern Methodist University. As a member of the Varsity Swimming Team, he won four individual Southwest Conference championships from 1958 through 1960, individual high point honors in 1959, and was selected to the All-America team in that year. In 1973, he was inducted into the Texas Swimming Hall of Fame.

Grant received his MBA degree in 1961 and PhD degree, concentrating in finance and economics, in 1970 from the University of Texas at Austin. He was named a distinguished alumnus of the College of Business Administration in 1982. He is a member of the College of Business Administration Advisory Council of the University of Texas at

Austin. While working on his doctorate, Grant co-authored a book entitled *The Development of State-chartered Banking in Texas*.

Grant is a past chairman of the Fort Worth Chamber of Commerce (1983–1985) and a former chairman (1982–1983) of the North Texas Commission, which is a regional marketing organization for the Dallas/ Fort Worth Metroplex, and includes as its members approximately 24 Chambers of Commerce of the Metroplex. He serves on the Board of Directors of Texas American Bancshares; Texas American Bank/Forth Worth; The Modern Art Museum; Southwestern Exposition and Live Stock Show; and The Community Advisory Board of North Texas Public Broadcasting, Inc. (Channel 13/KERA). He is a member of the Exchange Club of Fort Worth.

For the year ended June 30 1988, Grant served as International President of the Young Presidents' Organization (YPO), which is a business organization of approximately 6000 members with 125 chapters in 65 countries throughout the Western world. YPO's membership is composed of individuals who became president or CEO of qualifying companies prior to their 40th birthday. In his capacity as International President, Grant was responsible for all YPO member activities during the year and the administration of a staff of approximately 70 individuals located at the New York City headquarters and officers in Geneva, Hong Kong, and Miami. He currently serves as a member of the President's Committee, consisting of the past President, President, the President-Elect, the Executive Committee, and the Board of Directors.

Formerly Grant was a Trustee of Southern Methodist University, All Saints Episcopal Hospital in Fort Worth, and Fort Worth Country Day School. He has served as a member of the Texas Christian University, M. J. Neeley School of Business Advisory Board, the University of Texas at Arlington—Business Advisory Council, the Economics Advisory Committee of the American Bankers Association and the Board of Directors of the Texas Bankers' Association, Snyder Oil Corporation, and the Fort Worth Club.

In 1983, Grant was one of several persons instrumental in forming The Fort Worth Corporation, an organization devoted to promoting economic development in Fort Worth. Eleven businesses pledged $3 million to support this effort and Grant currently serves as Chairman of the corporation. He is also a member of the American Bankers Association and the Association of Reserve City Bankers, whose membership is limited to 400.

In June 1988, he received the 'Man of the Year Award' from the Anti-

Defamation League of B'nai B'rith in 'recognition and appreciation of distinguished service and inspiring leadership' in Fort Worth.

Grant was born in San Antonio and is married to Sheila P. Grant. They have one daughter, Mary Elizabeth Grant, and one son, Steven Grant.

Texas American Bancshares, Inc.

Texas American Bancshares (TAB) Inc. is a bank holding company that provides a full range of financial services to consumers, businesses, institutions, and governmental agencies throughout Texas. Headquartered in Fort Worth, Texas, TAB owns 24 subsidiary banks with 36 banking offices. The majority of assets are located in Fort Worth, Dallas, Houston, and Austin.

The Demands of Commercial Banking

There are two major arenas which place demands on Grant professionally. These are the demands of the commercial banking industry and the community demands of being the leading banker in a major community. The industry demands during the early and mid-1980s came largely from the deregulation of the banking industry. While the banking industry was not deregulated overnight the way the American airline industry was during the early years of the Reagan administration, the piecemeal deregulation that affected the banking industry placed unique demands on commercial bankers like Grant. Certainly the boundaries and the barriers between different segments of the financial services industry were eroded so as to place commercial banks in competition with the investment banking houses and the major brokerage firms. Even major retailers and other nonbanking companies began invading the traditional fields of banking. Grant summed up the changing environment nicely in 1984 by saying: 'It's causing us to be very nimble.'

While the demands of an increasingly competitive financial environment are one source of professional stress for Grant, the other major arena that demands his attention is the community. 'I think that anyone who is in a position of responsibility in a banking organization or a utility has a commitment to the community and, as a matter of fact, the welfare

of the bank depends very much on the welfare of the community.' It is this perception that the interests and well-being of the bank and the community are inextricably bound together which creates Grant's sense of obligation to the Fort Worth community. During the mid-1980s he served as Chairman of the Fort Worth Chamber of Commerce and it was in this role that he was instrumental in creating an attractive climate for business. He was involved in negotiations which resulted in the relocation of corporate headquarters for companies such as Burlington Northern to the Fort Worth area.

In addition to the demands of attempting to bring business and industry into Fort Worth, Grant played an important role in a new effort to engage the Chamber in economic planning during the mid-1980s. There were two aspects of this initiative. One was the effort to develop an economic planning strategy which would build on all facets of the community in the process. In particular, this aspect of the economic planning strategy involved identifying and bringing together the major taxpayers for strategic planning purposes. The other aspect was an effort to sharpen the independent image of Fort Worth as a community. A commissioned Lou Harris survey had determined that a strong, independent image was lacking for the community.

While no longer Chairman of the Fort Worth Chamber of Commerce, Grant continues to play an active leadership role within the community. This comes from the continuing belief that, even in the late 1980s, those who hold a major leadership role in banking within their communities must also play important leadership roles in other aspects of the community's life.

Developmental Demands and Opportunities

'I think time pressure is the main pressure that I suffer from.' This was Grant's perspective during 1985 and it in part originated from the many demands that are generated by the two major arenas of Grant's professional life. However, he was also involved in what he labels extracurricular activities beyond these two arenas and outside the family. These activities place time demands on him and at the same time provide him with developmental opportunities that might not otherwise be available.

The most significant of these extracurricular activities was his involvement with the Young President's Organization (YPO). He has been involved with YPO since 1977. 'To qualify you have to have been president before you were forty years of age and in a qualifying company, as determined by size in assets and number of employees.' While able to relax and really enjoy himself in his activities with YPO, he has also found his involvement to have been one of the best business development activities in which he has engaged. For example, as a member of the Executive Committee for YPO in 1984, Grant organized a week long educational program in New York City that was attended by 1000 YPO members from around the world. The program involved making arrangements with 75 speakers who were distinguished members of diverse professions such as medicine, business, politics, and cultural affairs. His final speaker list included both presidents Ford and Nixon; Jean Kirkpatrick as US Ambassador to the United Nations; Tom Watson, Chairman Emeritus of IBM Corporation; Robert Jarvic, inventor of the Jarvic artificial heart; and others of this caliber.

In May of 1985, Grant was nominated to a sequence of offices with YPO which would lead him to the international presidency during 1987–1988. While the events in the banking industry made this sequence of responsibilities more difficult by late 1986, Grant was able to follow through with careful vacation planning from the bank and through circumstantial events within YPO. His predecessor as International President for the 1986–1987 term was a very activist individual who stimulated a number of initiatives. Thus, Grant's term was one of maintenance and stabilization rather than one of new initiatives and major undertakings. This fortunate circumstance made the demands of office somewhat less time-consuming and stressful.

While Grant's involvement with YPO has always been a source of stimulation and challenge as well as being developmentally important to him, the pursuit of his doctorate involved one of the more stressful periods in his life. He decided to return to graduate school for his doctorate after having spent five years in banking with Citibank and earning an MBA degree during that period. His decision was based on the belief that additional education would be useful in one or both of two ways. One the one hand, he thought that the additional education in finance, economics, and statistics would benefit him in his banking career. On the other hand, if and when he retired from his commercial banking career, he thought that the doctoral education might serve him well in possible subsequent careers, such as academia or government service. 'I guess there were moments when I wondered what I was doing in that program and whether or not I made the right decision. In retrospect, it was the smartest thing I ever did.'

One of the demands which made the doctoral program stressful for Grant was the fact that he had a wife and two small children at the time. Therefore, he was busy meeting their various needs and at the same time the program demanded he meet his own intellectual, developmental needs. A second feature of the doctoral program which made it stressful was the competitiveness and challenge within the environment.

While Grant does not talk about his competitiveness as a source of stress, he readily admits to the competitive element in his personality. This competitiveness has been evidenced through the years in his athletics (i.e., swimming) and his professional life. It is interesting to notice two facets of this part of his life. First, he has always been successfully competitive and secure in the levels of achievements he makes. The accomplishments are a source of pride though there is no ostentatiousness associated with their attainment. Second, his competitiveness is not other-directed. It is not oppositional. He largely competes with himself and with the intent of maximizing his abilities and accomplishments. This is illustrated in his athletics where he excelled in the individual sport of swimming as opposed to an oppositional sport such as basketball or baseball.

Financial Traumas and Uncertainty (1986–1989)

Grant became chairman of Texas American Bancshares at the end of the first quarter of 1986, just following a precipitous decline in oil prices. This collapse in oil prices contributed to a $20 million loss in the first quarter of the year and a $110 million loss for the year. While 1987 was a year that largely saw the new status quo continue with depressed oil prices, 1988 was a year in which the bottom fell out of the real estate market. It was the combination of these two industrial forces which had such a disastrous impact upon not only Grant's bank but the whole banking industry in Texas.

With the early realization of the impending economic storm to come and need for outside support to weather the storm, Grant and his senior management team went to the Federal Deposit Insurance Corporation (FDIC) in February of 1988. Their reasoning was to approach the problem as early as possible in order to head off real disaster. While the relationship between Grant's executive team and the FDIC has been a pervasively cordial one, the period of negotiation has been a protracted one for all concerned, extending into a year and a quarter. During this time there have been a number of investors invited in to work with the FCIC and Texas American Bancshares, the principal ones being Carl Pohlad and Richard Rainwater. Extensive negotiations, proposal reviews, and further negotiations have taken substantial amounts of Grant's time and attention during this period.

The uncertainty of this protracted process has placed a real strain on the bank whose challenge is to maintain its customer base and confidence in these trying times while also maintaining the strength of its employee team. While there has been some loss of customers, there has also been the necessity to write-down assets. The combination of these two activities has resulted in a 30% shrinkage of the corporation. At the same time, there has been a precipitous drop in stock price which has resulted in personal financial loss for Grant, his executive team, and other investors.

The combination of uncertainty for the bank, the financial strains due to decline in stock price, and the job insecurity associated with the eventual resolution of the bank's future with the FDIC and other investors have placed very unique pressures on Grant during the past year and a half. Prior to 1986, uncertainty was not the major source of stress for Grant, either professionally or personally. (As we will see later, uncertainty in his personal life arena is still not a major source of stress for Grant. Quite the contrary.)

Managing the Demands of a High Activity Level

There are a variety of prevention strategies which Grant has developed over the years which enable him to manage his high level of activity in a healthy manner. Some of these are of a professional nature and others are personal. One of the interesting professional stress management strategies he employs is a secretarial staff of two. He uses these two secretaries very effectively as a buffering device in that they play an important role in redirecting a large amount of the mail, telephone calls, and visitors who really do not need his personal attention. Therefore, the secretaries serve the triage function of directing people, information, and inquiries to the right departments and officers in the bank. While they serve a buffering function for Grant, they do not function to block access to him when necessary. In fact, for those who really need to get Grant's personal attention, they capably facilitate the process.

This buffering function of the secretaries is particularly critical in Grant's case because of the high activity level and time pressure that he experiences. Without this key social support, the high activity and demand level could easily be overwhelming for Grant. However, it is not only the secretarial buffers that enable him to achieve all that he does.

A personal, behavioral characteristic which Grant uses strategically is his well developed self-discipline. He attributes the development of this characteristic to the influence of his mother and the influence of swimming in his life. It was his involvement in swimming which required him to drill and practice on a regular basis to be successfully competitive. Not only did it teach him self-discipline, it also taught him the value of hard work while very graphically and very vividly demonstrating to him the payoffs that can accrue.

A second strategy which Grant uses at work is to delegate work as much as he can.

> I try to delegate all of the operational problems or tasks, as the case may be. With regard to decisions, my basic philosophy is that if a decision can begin or take form at the bottom of the organization, to use the extreme, and work its way up, it will be better received and be more easily adapted to the organization. This is especially true if the decision involves change. Decisions made from the top down, I think, are the hardest ever.

This does not mean that Grant does not have ideas of his own or make decisions himself. Rather, he will champion trial balloons with the hope that others will pick up the ball and run with it.

While delegation is his preferred strategy and one he generally follows, he does become involved operationally on various occasions to work through specific problems and/or issues.

> There are times when something cannot be delegated. For example, there are times when I have headed various task forces within the bank. A case in point occurred where we had an external vendor doing our data processing for us. We needed to disengage, or at least felt we did. I headed up the team to negotiate our way out of that contract. Well, that involved getting into a lot of detail.

Personal Strategies for Stress Management

In addition to the professional strategies which Grant uses to manage his work demands, there are personal ones with which he complements these. These include his regular exercise program, the support and counsel of his wife, his personal reading time, and his deeper spiritual beliefs.

While his early involvement in swimming taught him the value of hard work, the principle of self-discipline, and the payoffs that go with effortful behavior, he has also found there to be immediate and intrinsic value in his athletic pursuits. As an accomplished swimmer, Grant does maintain an involvement in his sport by engaging recreationally on a periodic basis. However, as he has matured, his athletic interests have broadened. He has developed as a runner as well, running several marathons and at times encouraging his bank to be supportive of the Cowtown 10K and Marathon Races originating in the stockyards of Fort Worth each February. Therefore, athletics have always had a very central place in Grant's life. 'They have played a very significant role in my life. Not only in helping me maintain good physical but good mental health as well.'

The relationship which Grant has with his wife is valuable and instrumental to him in managing both personal and work demands. The supportive role she plays is not only in terms of emotional nurturance, but also in terms of information and appraisal feedback. As he says: 'My wife is unique in that she takes a very active interest in the business and the people involved in the business. She can read people much better, by and large, than I can.' In a very real way, she complements him in her perceptions of key people with whom he must work. While not an insensitive person, Grant's focus does tend to concentrate on the task dimension of his environment more heavily than the relationship dimension. As a result, he believes that his wife has a slightly sharper antenna in understanding the complexity of other people in his life.

In addition to complementing him in the interpersonal arena, Grant trusts his wife implicitly as advisor, counselor, and consultant. 'If I want to bounce an idea off somebody, 9 times out of 10 I'll bounce it off her first.' It is in this relationship that he does much, though not all, of his brainstorming and imaginative thinking.

Grant's personal reading program consists of both educational and escapist elements. He reads novels for the purpose of escaping for a period of time. This is a retreat world for him much as a ranch, hunting lodge, or other physical location might be for another executive. He can give himself to the novel psychologically, becoming absorbed in the world of the novel for a brief period of time.

In addition to reading novels, which serves a useful withdrawal function, Grant finds reading books that he can learn from important. For example, he thinks James Michener is a great writer and while he may be verbose and hard to read for some, Grant learns a great deal from his works. *Poland* gave him some interesting insights to the history of Europe in general and Poland in particular.

While Grant is not an institutionally religious man, he does hold some deep beliefs about God. His deep spiritual beliefs enable him to place life and many of the demands and stresses of life in a larger perspective. This takes some of the intensity and energy out of the moment while providing a larger sense of peace and order in the world. This has been especially true during the trials and tribulations of the 1986–1989 period.

Changing Styles in Trials and Tribulations?

The 1986–1989 period has been unquestionably the most trying and stressful time during Grant's professional life and the forces within the banking industry have been instrumental in creating this stress. There are two important observations concerning Grant under these circumstances. First, he had in place a number of preventive stress management practices during the earlier period of his professional and personal life which were only tested, not altered, in his most difficult period. That is, his regular exercise and athletic activities, his strong family and marital support system, his peer support relationships through his profession and YPO, and his strong sense of self-discipline have been key assets upon which he has been able to draw in the crunch. Without those assets in place prior to the period of trial and tribulation, the story might well have been different.

Second, Grant has developed two new guidelines and modified two of his prevention practices during this critical period. His guidelines have been: (1) make no major decisions alone during a period of extremely high stress and uncertainty and (2) maintain an active and regular schedule during the difficult period. The first guideline hedges against errors of judgment and the second against wasted time devoted to worry. The two changes he has made concern his network of professional relationships and his reading program. He has been active in extending his network of relationships while at the same time drawing upon his already established relationships. In addition, he has refocused his reading when not at the bank to include less heavy and professional topics while incorporating more light and recreational reading.

An Orderly Achiever in the Midst of Chaos

The 1980s have been a particularly demanding and difficult time in the Texas banking industry. The early 1980s saw the piecemeal deregulation of the industry nationwide under the Reagan administration. This was followed by a collapse in specific sectors of the Texas economy, including oil and real estate. These collapses had dramatic effects on the banking as well as saving and loan industries across the state and region.

In the midst of this chaos and disorder, Grant has been able to maintain a positive and achievement oriented perspective which has been therapeutic not only for himself but also for many with whom he works. His professional relationships around the country and around the world as well as his strong personal, family support system provide part of the stabilizing effect that is valuable to him. His internal self-discipline and his regular exercise programs are also important elements that contribute to his healthy attitude and condition.

Chapter 5

Profiles of Female Executives: The Ladies at the Top

In our studies of executives, perhaps the most interesting and most rewarding activity has been developing profiles of those individuals who have succeeded in their pursuit of success while maintaining their health and well-being and in spite of the various trials and tribulations they have encountered. These executives have allowed us to get to know them through close and personal examination of their professional and personal experiences. In interviewing them, observing their behavior, and gathering insights from those who work closely with them, our eyes have been opened to the many different paths to success and yet the many common features which successful individuals share. Each profile has a distinct tone of its own—some rather heavily reflective, others light-hearted—yet they all reflect the executives' candor and willingness to examine their own experiences with careful introspection. We presented the salient elements of three male executives' personalities and behavior, the many stresses each experienced, and the ways in which they coped with stress, in Chapter 4. In this chapter we present three profiles of ladies who have succeeded in the patriarchical culture of the US.

A careful review of the annual reports of leading American corporations in a wide range of industries, from forest products and oil field to health care and automotive, reveals that there are few female directors of major industrial concerns and fewer still officers of these corporations. While American females may hold great wealth in terms of stock ownership in American industry, their operational control has not been comparable. This situation has changed somewhat over the past two decades with the increasing influx of women into the workforce, but evolutionary change is a slow process.

An alternative to rising through the ranks of the corporate hierarchy is to seek prominence in the professions, or to found and build your own organizational system. That is what the ladies we will look at have done. Two have founded and sustained companies which have been forces within their respective industries, real estate and fashion design/modeling. The third is a civil court judge, often resolving corporate conflicts.

Success is evident in the women you are about to meet: Ebby Halliday, the 'first lady' of Dallas residential real estate; Catherine Crier, Judge of the 162nd Judicial District Court; and Kim Dawson, founder of the internationally known Kim Dawson Agency. These are three women who are assertive, articulate, and outspoken. Each has her own unique style of managing, outlook on life, and approach to the stresses of the executive suite. Perhaps the feature of their profiles which stands out most directly is that their lives truly dispel some of the conventional myths about female executives.

It is important to point out that both Ebby Halliday's and Kim Dawson's businesses have enjoyed success for over a quarter of a century each. Such sustained, long-term success is both admirable and remarkable. The other remarkable aspect of all three women is their health and well-being which have been sustained through the challenges of building and maintaining their businesses and, in Catherine Crier's case, the challenges of political campaigning. Public officials at all governmental levels and in all branches of government or military service have come under careful scrutiny during the 1980s.

Each of these ladies experiences the natural stress response which we detailed in Chapter 2. It is clear that they do not interpret this as negative nor has their experience of stress led to any of the variety of forms of distress we discussed earlier. In Chapter 3 we reviewed the primary, secondary, and tertiary strategies used in the context of preventive stress management. In that chapter in Table 1, we also summarized the primary and secondary prevention strategies employed by the executives we will profile here. In this chapter we will develop in more detail the challenges, stresses, and strategies of the women so as to better understand the completeness of their experience.

EBBY HALLIDAY

Founder and President
Ebby Halliday REALTORS

Biographical

Ebby Halliday is recognized as one of the country's most outstanding women in business. She founded Ebby Halliday REALTORS in 1945, and has served as President of the company since that time. Her entry into the real estate industry is an unusual one. She worked for a major retailer in the millinery field and decided to open her own shop. Successful in this entrepreneurship, she was approached by a customer's husband to decorate and sell several homes he had built. Ebby decorated and sold them, and became sold herself on the real estate business. The challenge and excitement motivated her to found her own company. She now holds the designations of Certified Real Estate Broker, Certified Real Estate Specialist, and DSA, which signifies that she is a recipient of the Distinguished Service Award from the National Association of Realtors (NAR). The DSA designation is given to individuals for outstanding service. Ebby is one of only three women to have received this honor.

The real estate profession has honored Ebby in many ways. In addition to the DSA, she received the Medal of Honor for Distinguished Service from the International Real Estate Federation (FIABCI) in 1985. She has been named Texas Realtor of the year and has received the Dallas Board of Realtors Easterwood Cup. The local business community has recognized her efforts as well; she was named one of Dallas Chamber of Commerce's Outstanding Women in Business in 1985, and received the Outstanding Salesman Award from the Sales and Marketing Executives of Dallas.

Ebby has served as a leader in real estate organizations at all levels, including board memberships in the Texas Association of Realtors, Greater Dallas Board of Realtors, and has also served as an advisory board member of the Federal National Mortgate Association. Among her most outstanding achievements is being a founder of the RELO, a nationwide network of relocation services. Ebby is also Past President of the Women's Council of the NAR, and has served on the Executive Committee of the NAR.

Community service is a passion for Ebby Halliday. A leader in community affairs, she has served as President of several organizations including the North Dallas Chamber of Commerce and the Greater Dallas Planning Council. Her involvements in community service are too numerous to mention; evidence of this commitment is her recognition as 1986 Fund Raiser of the year by the National Society of Fund Raising Executives, and the Dallas Historical Society's Award for Excellence in Professional Community Service.

Beautification is a theme in Ebby's community service. As President of Keep Texas Beautiful in 1986–1987, she led her state to the top achievement in the Keep America Beautiful effort. For her service, she was awarded the Lady Bird Johnson individual honor for beautification. In addition, she is a founder of Clean Dallas, Inc., directed toward prevention of littering at the local level.

Another theme in her community service is education. She is a member of the foundation board of the Dallas County Community College District, and has served on the Dallas Independent School District's (DISD) Facilities Task Force. Ebby Halliday REALTORS sponsors a local elementary school in DISD's Adopt-A-School program. Ebby attends school functions and focuses her attention on helping young people succeed in school.

Ebby Halliday is a woman who has heavily invested in her community, not only in real estate, but in beautification, education, and other efforts to improve the lifestyle of her city. She believes strongly in giving back to the community which has been a key factor in her success.

Ebby Halliday REALTORS

Founded in 1945 in Dallas, Ebby Halliday REALTORS is one of the largest privately owned residential real estate companies in the US. The company has grown to consist of 23 offices and 902 associates. In 1987, the company recorded 8090 home sales.

Stress and Challenge

In Dallas, the name 'Ebby Halliday' means real estate. And to Ebby Halliday, the female executive, the real estate industry means service. She has built a successful 45 year career around that theme, ensuring that each residential real estate transaction ends in a happy conclusion. When asked to describe the nature of the stress she experiences, Ebby spoke of the dynamic nature of the real estate business and the need not only to respond to change but to forecast it. One example of such a challenge came in the form of technological change. Her company was a leader in the computerization of real estate services, with marketing, analysis, and appraisal information all included. She noted with pride her company's state-of-the-art system—named 'Merlin'—aptly coinciding with her company's culture, which encourages informal, first-name-basis communication. Ebby's organization was one of the first to become automated, largely due to her involvement as a member of NAR's computer committee some 30 years ago. Even then, when computerization was a rarity, she envisioned the future benefits of this innovation for her industry.

Another example of the need to respond to change came in the form of the novel trends regarding home ownership in the 1980s. One of Ebby's many service commitments to her profession is serving on task forces for the international realtors' association. One trend which was noted by the task force early in the 1980s was the fact that home ownership was no longer static, but people were becoming more mobile and job transfers were increasing. Along with other realtors, Ebby organized a relocation network (RELO) to assist the transfers. Prior to the development of the network, the realtors operated by an informal service which was outgrown by the proliferation of customer need. Now the company is fitted to serve an entire customer relocation. Ebby acknowledged that this transition was a stressful one; not a bad stress, but a positive one brought about by the large opportunity the task force recognized and the tremendous effort required to respond to the need.

The positive stress posed by the dynamic real estate environment is a constant challenge for Ebby. Keeping current on legislation, business practices, economic issues, and the political climate, both at the national and local level, is critical. She lists as her most current sources of distress the increasing traffic in Dallas, particularly in the growing North Dallas corridor, and the banking and real estate debacle in Texas.

Part of Ebby Halliday's success in handling the stress of her career can be attributed to her perspective; that is, she views as opportunities many situations which would be perceived by others as threats. Another key to her ability to manage work stress is that her game plan is not a responsive, reactive one; rather, it is a *proactive* approach to the many opportunities provided by the dynamic industry in which she operates.

In our interviews, she revealed two trends on the horizon. The first trend or potential source of stress revolves around the tax laws. She referred to the current tax laws as 'an investor's nightmare' and cited the high level of real estate development as a positive contribution to the economy in terms of employment. Looming on the horizon, however, she forecasts changes in the tax laws in conjunction with efforts to reduce the massive federal deficit.

The realtors' association which Ebby is actively involved in is lobbying for a constitutional amendment which will limit government spending in accordance with revenue levels. She plays a very active role in political activity, noting that approximately 85% of all legislation has some bearing upon the real estate industry. Keeping current with regard to legislative activity is but one part of her political role. The other part of that role is an emphasis on education of the real estate industry. Ebby has been quite vocal about the responsibility of realtors as business people and citizens to guard the profession and vote against the legislation which restricts home ownership and freedom of ownership of property. The trends in the economy and political arena are thus a current and future source of stress which she continually monitors and works to manage in the best interests of her industry.

A second source of future stress which Ebby discussed is the influx of gigantic corporations into the real estate industry, with substantial movement currently occurring and no end in sight to their entry. The net effect of this change, she says, has been to make industry leaders more efficient, a definite positive sign. She fears, however, that the intrusion of these giants into the industry may lead to an erosion of service and local responsibility, which she feels is the cornerstone of Ebby Halliday REALTORS.

The volatility of the real estate industry is thus a major source of stress for this executive. We asked her to describe the most stressful time of her career, and she responded quickly with the example of escalating interest rates in the early 1980s. Home ownership rises and falls in accordance with interest rates, and the period in which interest rates rose above 17% left realtors under tremendous stress, jockeying to sustain sales volume while providing good service for the struggling first home buyers. While consumers were willing to scrape and sacrifice to make monthly mortgage payments, most first-time buyers found that they could not qualify for the loan. Ever service-minded, Ebby and her colleagues devised many forms of creative financing to assist buyers. This stressful time saw the advent of all sorts of short-term renegotiable mortgages, with the secondary market opening new mortgage horizons for the industry.

In reflection, it can be seen that many of the stresses Ebby Halliday faces are the result of economic circumstances, seemingly beyond her control. Her style, and an effective one for her, is not to give in to uncontrollable situations; rather, she makes a concerted, well-planned effort to make whatever impact is possible upon these stressful situations, ever mindful of the goals of her business. She is able to acknowledge the stressful nature of her work, yet she views the stressors as challenges to be tackled and energetically focuses on meeting those challenges.

All of us experience signals of the stress response. Each individual possesses a unique pattern of indicators which signal us that we are under too much stress. For some, the signals are psychological: irritability, listlessness, inability to concentrate. For others, the symptoms are of a physical or medical nature: headaches, nausea, high blood pressure. For Ebby Halliday, the signals are physical ones. She readily admits that her personal signal of too much stress is tension in the shoulder muscles and the neck. This is her personal cue to take time out from the strains of daily real estate hassles. Her response is normally to sit down, close her eyes, and let her mind wander until the relaxation of the neck and shoulder muscles occurs in response to the mind's relaxation.

Managing Personal and Professional Stress

Coping with stress is something successful executives do well. Each executive has a personal repertoire of ways to cope; and Ebby Halliday shares with other successful professionals a particularly well-developed repertoire of coping methods. Some of her coping techniques are personal ones. The aforementioned moment of mental and physical relaxation is one way she copes. Another method Ebby commonly utilizes at work is changing the activity she is involved in. The stimulating nature of her job allows her to move into another interesting activity, and she relishes this variety because it allows her to relieve tension by moving into another challenge. Ebby finds reading a form of relaxation. She has a penchant for historical novels, and in addition her leisure reading includes real estate periodicals, economic reports, and the *Wall Street Journal*. Michener's *The Covenant* about Africa is a recently read favorite. Not all coping is positive, and Ebby candidly admitted that her negative coping device, as is the case with many people, is a tendency to eat too much. This is encouraged because of her husband's enjoyment of fine food—Maurice knows famous chefs throughout the world—and Ebby claims the couple visit these gourmets too often!

One of Ebby's most distinguishing traits is her quick wit, and it follows naturally that she uses humor as a way of relieving stress. After delivering a rather serious address to professional colleagues, she has been known to bring out her ukulele and break up the audience with her versions of well-known songs. When the real estate industry in Texas was beginning to show signs of recovery, she delivered such a performance to a group of realtors, to the tune of 'Happy Days Are Here Again.'

Happy days are here again,
Interest rates are down again
Builders build and realtors wear a grin
Happy days are here again.

Even though oil price is down
Other business can always be found
Roll up your sleeves—there's always work to do
Sell pre-owned homes as well as new
Then there's land and lots and commercial, too
Happy days are here again!

This quick wit and sense of humor allow Ebby to keep her perspective and her trademark positive outlook even in the troubled times realtors have faced in the Southwestern United States.

Other coping techniques which Ebby Halliday uses to manage the stress in her life are work-related methods. Business travel serves as an exciting, enjoyable diversion for her. Active in the international Real Estate Federation as well as the national association, Ebby and Maurice serve on multiple boards and committees, and the travel which goes along with these responsibilities is often quite glamorous . . . and often adventure filled. On one trip, the couple attended a board meeting in Cyprus a mere four weeks after 20000 Turkish troops had invaded the northern half of the island and claimed it as their territory. The effects of the invasion and the tension-filled excitement provided more than sufficient adventure and diversion. This travel allows Ebby the opportunity to render service in the international arena. She notes that the economic system and property rights in the US which Americans often take for granted are not in place in other countries. The associations of which she is a member and leader work with leaders in other parts of the world to change the property rights from the government-dominated form to private citizens' rights. While travel is stressful for some executives, Ebby Halliday finds it a natural stress management technique which gives her adventure and an opportunity to contribute to international causes, which she finds an extremely satisfying experience.

A staunch advocate of goal-setting, Ebby states that only recently have such words as strategic plans, goals, and planning retreats been introduced into the realtors' associations. In the international congress, a full-day seminar was devoted to strategic planning in the real estate operation business. Setting company goals, both short-term and long-term, allows Ebby and her associates to function from a plan which takes into account the volatile nature of the industry. She articulates her overall company goal as 'to be the very best in the business . . . to try and make each transaction fair and happy so that it, in turn, would become a solid brick in the growth of our company.' Her objective has always been to be number one. 'Oh yes, of course! Is there any other place to be?' The goals which are set within the company vary by the segment of business addressed. In the acquisition of offices, for example, the planning horizon of necessity is at least three years in the future. Building new office space requires at minimum a five year horizon, typically stretching to ten years because of the heavy investments required in opening up new territories. Ebby notes that as her business has expanded and developed, the goals have become increasingly long term. Short-range goals are set as well, and these short-range goals are carefully integrated into the larger goals. The coping method of organizational goal setting allows Ebby to function proactively and meet the opportunities presented in her challenging industry.

The reputation of Ebby Halliday REALTORS for service is linked with another image among those in the real estate business. The company is known for its leadership in providing training to personnel. Ongoing training is an integral part of the business, not only in terms of ever-changing financing methods but also on standards of the real estate practice, business ethics, and the mechanics of good business practice. The proliferation of computers in the industry and the addition of

'Merlin' to the company have also made computer-related training a necessity. Training and developing personnel is one of the keys to Ebby's success. By surrounding herself with well-trained professionals, Ebby can function with confidence that the representatives of her company are delivering the service which has made her successful. A competent staff has allowed Ebby to achieve a comfortable level of dependence on others. She is the furthest thing from a loner, and builds networks both within her company and throughout the industry which have allowed her to sustain this success over her 40 year career. Training and development efforts provide her with confidence in personnel through which she can extend her own limits.

Another work-related coping mechanism for Ebby Halliday is the active political role she plays. Besides fulfilling what she sees as her responsibility as an American citizen, her political activity may be seen as a form of stress management. The key to political activity as a form of coping is that it serves to increase Ebby's perception of control over environmental stressors. The uncertainty posed by the economic environment can be unnerving; however, by the active political commitment she makes, Ebby Halliday exercises the control available to her and thus manages this uncertainty and uncontrollability to the fullest extent possible.

To understand how Ebby has achieved her level of success, it is necessary to examine the social support she relies on. One form of social support is her dependence on a well-trained, competent staff. Another, and perhaps more important, form of social support stems from the relationship between Ebby and her husband, Maurice Acers. Their relationship, that of a dual-career couple, revolves around a comfortable balance between separateness and dependency. Maurice has his own corporations, of which Ebby is Board Chairman. Maurice, in turn, serves as General Counsel and Chairman of the Board of Ebby Halliday REALTORS. Managing the sheer number of time conflicts between the two executives' schedules requires a great deal of effort, but this effort is facilitated by careful planning. Their ability to travel together provides important time for support, and this support is reciprocal. In addition, the couple have an active religious commitment which provides important support for both partners. The unique interdependence between Ebby and Maurice is thus an important support for each, and the fact that they have careers in the same industry allows them to provide multiple sources of support to each other.

In stepping back to look at her experience of both personal and professional life stress, Ebby regards her positive attitude as the most helpful stress management tool she uses. She views what many of us would consider stressful circumstances as challenges and opportunities, and attacks them with confidence and vigor. In her recent past, she claims she has become more philosophical in her approach to stress, and has found this to be of great benefit.

A Personal and Professional Theme: Service

Ebby Halliday allowed us to intrude on her personal and professional life so that we could better understand the ways in which successful executives manage the stress of a highly demanding career. Our perceptions and impressions of her can be summarized in one common theme, and that theme is personal service. The theme is reflected in two major ways. One is her company itself. Its structure is a highly personalized one, and the company which bears her name has a culture which can best be described as a 'family.' The artifacts of this culture, the first-name basis for communication, including a name for the computer, remembering employee birthdays and special occasions with personal visits and cards, a positive attitude and 'we' feeling, represent the attitude of personal concern and closeness immediately discernible to outsiders. This theme has resulted in a cohesive, closely-knit staff which Ebby can depend on.

A second way in which the personal service theme is manifested is in the value Ebby places on giving back service to the community. Her many service-oriented commitments to her profession and multiple philanthropic pursuits characterize her as a 'giver.' Her giving is not limited to the local level; it extends to the national and international arenas.

When we asked Ebby to describe her own definition of success, she responded as follows.

> Reaching a balance between business and personal life achievement . . . reaching one's potential in both categories is the epitome of success. My real estate business success is based on knowledge of product and people and high priority. My personal life success is based on luck!

Ebby listed her heroes as Thomas Jefferson, Davy Crockett, Jonas Salk, and Madame Curie. All of these individuals were path-breakers and explorers who made great contributions to the life we enjoy today. And Ebby Halliday is a pioneer in her own right.

As we mentioned in the introduction to this chapter, our interactions with the female executives we profiled have served to dispel some of the myths surrounding women in the workplace. Perhaps the myth which Ebby Halliday dispels best is the commonly cited notion that females who wish to be successful must abandon feminine-oriented traits in their personalities in favor of the more masculine-oriented ones such as aggressiveness, competitiveness, and emotional detachment. One is struck, upon meeting Ebby Halliday, with the warmth of her personality, her quick wit, and the feeling that she is not one who takes herself too seriously. One outstanding impression of her is her tendency for nurturing others, borne out by the personal attention she devotes to her employees. Yet, in sharp contrast, her competitive streak bares itself when she talks about the industry and her company's position within it. Ebby Halliday is a woman who has *not* forsaken those feminine aspects of her personality; rather, she has cultivated them as an integral part of her private and public persona. But the masculine aspects of her personality are in place as well. She is driven, decisive, and assertive, Perhaps she can best be described as a truly androgynous person, knowing when to rely on her feminine traits, and when to call up the masculine ones, and achieving a rare blending of these characteristics within her personality.

CATHERINE J. CRIER

Judge
162nd Judicial District Court

Biographical

Catherine Crier's career in the field of law has been on a trajectory with a steep ascent. She earned her bachelor's degree in political science and government from the University of Texas in 1975. Immediately following graduation, she entered Southern Methodist University (SMU) and graduated with her law degree in 1977.

Her employment experience began in the Dallas County District Attorney's office upon graduation from SMU. She was engaged in criminal prosecution trials from 1978 to 1981, and during this time was appointed Felony Chief Prosecutor by District Attorney, Henry Wade. She left the District Attorney's office to join the law firm of Riddle & Brown, and served as a civil trial attorney for that firm, involved in corporate, business, real estate, and personal injury litigation.

Catherine was elected State District Court Judge in 1984. In that capacity, she was elected Local Presiding Judge for the Civil District Courts in 1987 and 1988. She also chaired the Civil Court Rules Committee. Legislative committees have been the focus of her involvement as well; she has held memberships on the Executive Committee of the Dallas County Juvenile Board, the Judicial Legislative Committee, and the Central Jury Room Committee.

Judge Crier has been admitted to practice in all Texas State and US District Courts, and the US Supreme Court. She was elected to membership in the Texas Bar Foundation in 1985, and is a member of the College of the State Bar of Texas and the Texas College of the Judiciary. Much of her time is devoted to service in legal organizations, including the American Bar Association, the Texas Bar Association, the Dallas Bar Association, and Dallas Women Lawyers' Association. She serves on numerous committees, councils, and task forces for all four organizations.

As a member of Executive Women of Dallas, Catherine is a frequent speaker for business, professional, women's, and students' organizations. Politics is a passion with her; she chaired the Hospitality Committee at the 1984 Republican National Convention, and participates in the National Center for Policy Analysis, the Texas Women's Alliance, Dallas County Republican Women's Caucus, and Dallas County Republican Forum.

A host of civic activities reveal Catherine's creative side and love for the arts. She is involved in the Dallas Museum of Arts, Dallas Symphony League, Dallas Women's Foundation, and Friends of the Kennedy Center. She lists as hobbies archaeology and painting, and would like to develop these creative outlets further.

Volunteer work allows Catherine to contribute to the community in a significant way. She serves on the women's board for the Northwood Institute and Therapeutic Riding of Texas. In her work with Swiss Avenue Counseling Center, she chaired the Children and Adolescents Advisory Committee. Catherine also served on the steering committees for Volunteers of America and Midas Touch for Dallas.

Several organizations have honored Catherine for her success. The Dallas Chamber of Commerce selected her for its prestigious Leadership Dallas program for 1986/1987. Catherine is listed as Texas' youngest elected district judge. She received the American Success Award in 1985, the Share in Success Women of the Year Award in 1984, and was named an Outstanding Young Woman of America in 1981.

Catherine's high level of achievement has been met with considerable attention by both local and national media. She has been featured twice in *Glamour* magazine. The television program 'NBC Today' interviewed her in conjunction with her selection by *Glamour* magazine as one of '10 Outstanding Working Women in America 1987.' *Vogue* magazine selected her as Dallas' 'fast track' career woman for 1987, and she was honored at a program conducted by the magazine as well. Several local publications have featured her, highlighting her success and executive style. Among these publications are *Dallas Downtown News, D Magazine, Ultra,* and the Dallas Morning News' *High Profile. Landscapes of Texas Women*, a photography exhibit and book which is to be a part of the permanent collection in the Women's Museum in Washington, DC, features Catherine.

Scholarly activities including seminars and publications are part of Catherine's multifaceted career. She has been a Trial Advocacy Instructor for SMU's School of Law and for the National Institute for Trial Advocacy. She has also taught at SMU's Edwin Cox School of Business in the Costa Institute of Real Estate Finance. Catherine has authored multiple legal publications on the subjects of impeachment, sanctions for discovery (pretrial) abuse, and Texas rules of evidence.

The 162nd Judicial District Court

As State District Judge, Catherine presides over civil litigation including business and corporate disputes, personal injury and malpractice cases, real estate, aviation, and banking matters. When she inherited the docket for the 162nd District Court, there were some 1700 active cases pending—the second highest caseload among these courts. After four years, she now possesses the second lowest caseload and carries an active docket of approximately 975 cases. Thus, she and her staff have been able to dispose of quite a few more cases each year than are assigned to them.

Early Life Experiences and Career Preparation

Texas State District Judge Catherine J. Crier is in the process of becoming a 'Renaissance woman.' The Dallas native credits her early years as the formation of this ambition. Her hobby of raising and showing horses since the age of eight developed her love of competition, and taught her the value of individual effort and responsibility. The positively stressful aspect of this hobby and the rewards she has reaped have made this a lifelong avocation for her. Catherine says her desire to have wide-ranging interests was also encouraged by her parents, who taught her that there was no such word as 'can't.' She developed a personal philosophy that individals have the power to make things happen in their lives. They are *not* victims of the external world.

A self-professed high school 'jock,' Catherine says that self-competition has been an enduring theme in her interests. She likes most sports, having recently taken up snow-skiing, scuba, and golf ('I like it because it's just you and the ball'). She doesn't relate her performance to others, but to her own expectations.

Catherine claims to have known since early childhood that she would pursue a career in the law. Her mother contends that she would 'argue with a fencepost,' and Catherine agrees. Government, politics, and the law have always fascinated her, although she has been known to bend a few rules herself. In college at the University of Texas in Austin as an undergraduate, she changed majors several times just to be able to take interesting courses. Flamboyant trial lawyers such as Clarence Darrow, Edward Bennett Williams, and F. Lee Bailey were her early heroes and spurred her pursuit of a law degree.

Her transition into law school at SMU was a smooth one which required only a minor adjustment in her method of study. Education has been a constant in her life; currently she is pursuing a Master of Liberal Arts degree at SMU. Her continuing education gives her an outlet quite different from the law and satisfies her high need for challenge and personal growth.

Career Challenges and Stresses

In the early law career, Catherine served as Assistant District Attorney and Felony Chief Prosecutor. This period in her career provided her with intense trial practice, but she found that criminal law did not hold her interest as well as the intellectual challenge and variety she enjoyed in civil law.

Catherine became Texas' youngest elected district judge in 1984. As State District Judge, she presides over civil legislation of many types including business and corporate disputes, personal injury and malpractice cases, and real estate, banking, and aviation matters. She describes the running of her firsttime, hotly-contested political campaign during the demise of her marriage as 'quite a rollercoaster' and definitely the most stressful period in her life.

When asked to describe her major source of daily stress, she quickly replied that time pressure for pursuing her many personal and professional interests is a constant demand. Each case has its individual nuances, and the delicate balance between running a court of equity and a court of law requires intense study and preparation. The issues she deals with are never black-and-white, only gray. Catherine believes justice is not done when the guardians of the law adopt a strict, black-and-white perspective. She says the lawyers she works with spend hours upon end preparing briefs, and if they spend this time preparing them she in turn feels it her duty to read them. Catherine works without the luxury of a briefing assistant or research assistant, and agrees that the addition of such individuals to her staff would help her combat part of her time-pressure stress.

Catherine faces several major civil court challenges over the next five years. Continuing effective docket management is a priority, recognizing the old axiom 'justice delayed is often justice denied.' Another issue she sees as paramount is reducing discovery (pretrial) disputes between lawyers and encouraging a return to more professional conduct in the courtroom. This would free the court to spend more time with legitimate disputes and less time simply babysitting the preparation of cases for trial. Catherine intends to focus future efforts on promoting the use of Alternative Dispute Resolution (ADR) among lawyers and clients. ADR provides an effective means of narrowing disputes as well as resolving them in lieu of costly, time-consuming courthouse litigation.

Aside from the challenges of managing the court, Catherine is active in the Dallas Bar Association, the Texas Bar Association, and the American Bar Association. Her professional and political activities contribute to the demands on her time. She is an active member of Executive Women of Dallas, the National Center for Policy Analysis, and Texas Women's Alliance, having traveled to Spain on a trade mission with the last group in 1987. In addition Catherine is involved with Republican party politics as the local and national levels.

Her civic activities are varied, including the Dallas Museum of Arts, Dallas Symphony League, and Dallas Women's Foundation. Catherine serves on the governing boards of several charities and volunteer organizations. Therapeutic Riding of Texas (TROT) is one such charity with an unusual emphasis. TROT emphasizes horseback riding as rehabilitative activity for physically or psychologically impaired individuals. When she became involved with the group, Catherine was very active in serving as an officer on the board, attending classes for the children and working in a 'hands-on' capacity. She now serves on the Advisory Board for the organization.

Such a high level of achievement and involvement at a relatively young age has not escaped the notice of others. Among her many honors and awards are her selection by *Glamour* magazine as one of Ten Outstanding Working Women in America, 1987, her receipt of the American Success Award in 1985, and her selection for the 1986–1987 Dallas Chamber of Commerce Leadership Dallas program.

Management of Personal and Professional Stress

Learning to make time for herself has been a major effort for Catherine in coping with the hectic pace of her career. Exercise plays a major role, as does horseback riding, both activities providing her 'fresh air.' Pleasure reading helps her get away from it all. She exists in a house full of books and periodicals. One secret to coping which she shared with us is that she is a firm believer in the benefits of naps. She averages six to seven hours of sleep per night, but when possible takes a 45 minute nap in the early evening which leaves her refreshed for additional business reading or for leisure activities.

Catherine is a voracious reader; she claims she 'tithes' to book clubs and orders three or four books per month on topics as diverse as Impressionist art, history of opera, speaking Chinese, and mysterious places around the world. When asked to list her favorites, she found it difficult to select a favorite category of books, much less favorite individual books. Nevertheless, she names as recent favorites *Everything I Ever Really Needed to Know I Learned in Kindergarten, The Tao of Pooh*, and *A Brief History of Time*. Three favorite categories of books are history (particulary 20th century), such as *The Last Lion* by

William Manchester, Russian literature (especially *Crime and Punishment*), and John Le Carré and Robert Ludlum spy thrillers. Reading for both professional enrichment and for pleasure is a major stress management activity for Catherine.

Social support plays an important role in this judge's life. Her clerks, bailiff, court reporter, and administrative assistant are 'priceless jewels' on whom she relies a great deal. Support from others is something Catherine has learned to be aware of. Togetherness for her has been a learned process rather than a natural one. She admits to being a bit of a loner, finding it easy to entertain herself and comfortable in solitude. Time with friends, for example, is something she enjoys when she takes the time and she finds it extremely beneficial to nurture these relationships. Her social support network consists much more of friends than family. While she is confident that her family is supportive, they are not her 'active' support network. Her friends are few, close, and very caring. She does not 'bare her soul' often, but values special people with whom she can 'let her hair down' and relax. There is a group of five women she gets together with for lunch or dinner on occasion, which she says is a new and delightful experience for her. She wants to be a better friend and to devote more energy toward the maintenance of friendships.

Pets have been a constant in Catherine's life—large, small, and in between. Her dog, a Great Dane, died recently. Since moving to a high rise, she has not acquired another pet and misses this terribly; yet she admits that her living space and travel schedule is not conducive to having a pet. She does have a source for interacting with pets, however, in retreating the 30 minute drive to the farm, where there are 35 horses, four family dogs, five cats, two birds, and assorted other creatures.

The spiritual aspect of Catherine's life is an important one for her. Raised in the Methodist church, she is not currently involved in organized religion per se, but says a sense of unity with the world is important to her well-being.

Interestingly, Catherine is not a specific goal-setter. She has no specialized long-term goals, preferring instead to 'keep the radar open' and look for opportunities. This allows her to be prepared, be perceptive, and therefore be at the right place at the right time to take advantage of potential opportunities. Rather than the high structure of self-set goals, she prefers to flow with her environment and scan for the possibilities which arise.

Her outlook on life facilitates her well-being and adjustment.

Catherine claims to be a 'Mary Sunshine optimist' whose career in public service gives her life an importance beyond person and position. Her personal life includes a recent divorce which she discusses candidly as 'the right thing to do.' Personality differences led up to the decoupling, among them her strong career orientation and love for travel. She is pleased with her amicable relationship with her former partner and seems certain of the positive outcome from the change in the nature of the relationship.

The Process of Becoming

Catherine Crier has achieved phenomenal career success at a rapid rate and a young age. At sixteen, she began her university career. At 23, after completing her law degree, she joined the Dallas County District Attorney's office. At 26, she was appointed Felony Chief Prosecutor. At 30, she became Texas' youngest district judge, and the first woman elected (as opposed to appointed) to such a position.

Many of the aspects of this woman's life show that she is in 'the process of becoming.' Her recent interest in taking up new sports such as golf and scuba shows this need to grow. She seeks to be a better friend. Catherine also chastises herself for not being more impulsive. Her life to date has been guided by logic and left-brained concepts. She has right-brained creative desires as well, such as painting, which she would like to develop further.

When asked about her priorities in life, work was not paramount to her. Family, friends, and personal growth are her first priorities. Her philosophy is that jobs and careers come and go, but those other elements are a constant. Katharine Hepburn is one of the judge's personal heroines, and is admired for her independence, her brilliance, and her ability to retain her femininity. The image of competitiveness and adventure portrayed by Hepburn and yet her ability to convey that she is not invincible are the traits Catherine cites as one she aspires to. Other heroines include Jeanne Kirkpatrick and Margaret Thatcher. The Prime Minister's ability to assertively run the Parliament while exhibiting grace and femininity are admired qualities.

We note that Catherine Crier shares these qualities which she admires in her heroes. She is well on the way to becoming a Renaissance woman. Along the way she faces continued stress and challenges both personally and professionally. The stress management mechanisms she has developed and her forward-looking focus on 'becoming' should allow her to sustain this high level of achievement and continued success.

KIM DAWSON

President, The Kim Dawson Agency
Fashion Director, Dallas Apparel Mart

Biographical

Kim Dawson was born and grew up in Center, Texas. Her family consisted of her mother, her grandmother, a sister and a brother. After high school graduation, she moved from the small East Texas town to Dallas to attend business school; she resided at the YWCA. After completing her six-month secretarial course, she worked at several different jobs in several organizations, but quickly learned that she craved greater adventure and challenge.

During World War II, a high school friend moved to Washington, D.C., and Kim followed. She approached Senator Tom Connally's office for a job, and while she didn't meet the senator, she won over his secretary and landed a job taking dictation. True to form, she became restless and started to sell war bonds, soon winning a sales contest. The prize was a trip to New York City, and Kim found the place 'fabulous.' During her week-long stay, she met Harry Conover, owner of a top modeling agency, and was offered a job as a model.

Kim never had a modeling lesson, but learned by putting on the clothes and watching the other models. She quickly became a busy runway model for Seventh Avenue designers. To supplement her income, she taught modeling at the Barbizon School. It was then that Kim discovered her gift for teaching modeling, and the extra earnings were sent home to help her younger sister with college.

After the war ended, she headed for Europe with a friend via the Queen Mary and modeled in Paris. Kim was a standout with her Texas drawl and short hair. She left Paris to visit St Tropez and Spain for relaxation and fun. Money ran out, and her mother wired her the fare to return to New York.

Back in Dallas, Kim modeled for Neiman-Marcus and taught modeling at the Patricia Stevens school. During this time, two important people entered her life. She met Evelyn Lambert, whom she credits with helping her begin her career as a show commentator. Also, she met George Dawson, a string bass player with the Dallas Symphony Orchestra, who became her husband.

Kim opened her first business in 1960 with a friend in the advertising business. Their partnership centered on advertising, public relations, and modeling. Kim claims there was little business, so the two 'played like' they were in the modeling business, laughed, had lunch, and returned home to their families.

Dallas developer Trammell Crow hired Kim to become Fashion Director of the Dallas Apparel Mart in 1964. Her partner left the business, and Kim moved her agency to the Apparel Mart and expanded her staff. The Dallas Apparel Mart has grown to become the largest in the nation with Kim as its fashion industry spokesperson and producer of all the market shows. Similarly, the Kim Dawson Agency has developed national and international importance. Kim is now regarded as the queen of fashion in the Southwest.

Kim's family also grew during this period. She and George have a son who is a Young Life (a non-denominational Christian youth organization) leader, a daughter who is an obstetric physician, and another daughter who is a former model and now a counselor for new models at Kim's agency.

Kim Dawson has an active role in many civic and professional organizations. She has served on the Board of Directors of the Dallas Chamber of Commerce, Dallas Theatre Center, Goodwill Industries, and Fashion Group of Dallas. She is also a past president of the Dallas Communications Council. Her many contributions have been recognized as she was recently inducted into the Texas Women's Hall of Fame.

The Kim Dawson Agency

Kim began her agency with six models when there was essentially no fashion business in Dallas. Her six million dollar agency now represents over 800 individuals. Kim Dawson Agency encompasses fashion, print, children's, men's, radio and television, and talent divisions. In addition, the speakers and programs division provides entertainers and celebrity speakers for all occasions, and the Pro/Motion division represents athletes for television commercials and public appearances. The Kim Dawson Studio offers a complete support system of classes and seminars for models and casting and videotaping facilities for clients. The studio was recently accredited by the Southern Association of Colleges and Schools.

Dallas Apparel Mart

The Dallas Apparel/Menswear Mart is one component of the Dallas Market Center. The other components are the World Trade Center, the Trade Mart, the HomeFurnishings Mart, the InfoMart, and Market Hall. The Dallas Apparel Mart is known as The National Gallery for Fashion Genius and constitutes the largest collection of women's apparel, childrenswear and accessories under one roof. More than 1200 permanent showrooms display women's apparel, menswear, bridal apparel, maternity apparel, uniforms, childrenswear, shoes, accessories, and intimate apparel. There are an additional 350 Market-Time showrooms which display additional apparel. In addition to representing manufacturers from coast to coast in the US, the Dallas Apparel Mart represents manufacturers from the International Fashion Centers around the world.

Early Life Influences

Kim Dawson is an executive who can look back on her early years and easily identify the individuals and experiences that shaped her later life and contributed to her success. Two contrasting personalities that had profound effects on her outlook were her mother and her grandmother. From her mother, Kim adopted an optimistic attitude. This was programmed very early in her life, and has endured. Her mother also encouraged her to grow beyond her East Texas roots and explore the world. Kim says that her brother, sister, and herself are good credits for her mother's hard work and positive outlook. Sending three productive individuals into the world was her mother's great accomplishment. Kim's sister established the first public relations agency in Honolulu, is now semi-retired, and writes and publishes travel books along with her husband. Kim's brother is a petroleum engineer. She speaks with pride of both siblings.

The other dominant influence in Kim's early life was her grand-mother. In strong contrast to her mother, Kim's grandmother was a strong-willed, principled reader of the *Bible* and *True Confessions*; her attitude was more 'doom and gloom' than optimism. It was her grand-mother who set the ground rules for Kim, heavily influenced by the Church. Kim credits her grandmother with giving her a clear sense of right and wrong. In a sense, Kim's grandmother fulfilled much of a father-like role in that she was the disciplinarian of the household. As the first born child, Kim refuted Grandmother's rules and challenged them—she fondly recalls resisting afternoon naps vigorously and with rebellion. She always lost the argument, and thus learned to cope with frustration and discipline.

The clash of wills between Kim and her grandmother was often reported to her mother upon her return from work at the end of the day. This reporting of confict was, according to Kim, one of the best things she learned as a child. 'You have to verbalize, not just think, about what specifically it is that makes you unhappy, or happy. And you have to learn to tell someone these things. So Grandmother and I told Mother both sides of the story . . . and I learned coexistence.' Now a grand-mother herself, Kim believes that rules are a necessary and vital part of childhood. They provide a structure which children need in order to grow and develop.

Kim gained a flair for the dramatic by watching the same Ruby Keeler and William Powell movie time after time, and then staging neighbor-hood productions with her brother and his friends. Her brother was her childhood 'great buddy' and she ran the show, always in charge of the theatrics and dances.

The art of conversation and socializing with others was refined by riding to school with neighbors. When someone was kind enough to give her a ride, Kim felt the obligation to be entertaining. Described by an early colleague as 'lippy,' her ability to converse has served her in good stead throughout her career as a fashion commentator.

Education has played a central role in Kim's life, although her educational process has not been the traditional, formal learning one might assume. She considers her modeling and fashion training throughout her early career, especially at Neiman-Marcus, a 'college degree.' To this executive, learning is both formal and informal. While she never completed college, she did enroll in literature courses at New York University while modeling in New York. She says her inquiring mind has been a major asset in the fashion business. 'I'm always thinking, what can I do next? Is there another direction I/the agency can go in? It's all about the "what ifs" in life—they keep it alive and interesting.'

Career and Life Stress

Kim Dawson readily acknowledged that her career has been and continues to be full of stresses. The most stressful period in her career, she says, was the early growth of the agency and the fashion industry in Dallas. When she began, virtually nothing was going on in Dallas, so she and her associates had to create everything. There was no clear road-map at the very start, so there was substantial ambiguity and uncertainty. She remembers this period as exciting, but also as stressful.

The major source of stress for her now stems from the multiplicity of opportunties which present themselves each day. The diversity of her agency and its clients creates many demands for Kim. Her husband claims that Kim says 'yes' too often, even when she is overcommitted. Crises arise on a daily basis for her agency and the Apparel Mart. This is another source of stress for Kim, although she says she now manages crises much more effectively than she did in the past. In fact, she claims to look forward to them on slower days because they provide challenges and break up her day. A third source of stress for Kim involves the rejection often experienced by the talented individuals she represents. Because of the nature of the fashion and talent business, rejection is a reality. Kim feels the disappointment of these individuals deeply and shares their pain when an opportunity does not work out.

For Kim Dawson, multiple opportunities, daily crises, and the pain of rejection comprise the major stressors in her career. Over the years, she has learned to manage these demands through developing effective stress management strategies.

Managing Personal and Professional Stress

The stress of directing a major fashion mart and heading a diversified fashion conglomerate requires well-developed coping skills. Kim Dawson depends on a healthy repertoire of preventive management strategies for dealing with the stressors which arise from her personal and professional lives and their overlap.

She cites as a primary source of coping the many relationships she has cultivated over the years, specifically mentioning Trammell Crow, who asked her to head the Dallas Apparel Mart. He has been a constant source of support and a critical force in her career and development. 'My whole business is relationships,' she has said. In addition, Kim surrounds herself with strong, capable people. Her ability to comfortably rely on people has been learned with 25 years of experience. Market times, which in the past were quite stressful because of their hectic nature and the multiple shows which Kim is responsible for, are not as stressful now, due to her talented staff. Her attitude about market now is 'We've done this now for 25 years and have done it well . . . we can do this!'

Another relationship-oriented way of coping that Kim uses is the network she has built and perpetuated within the fashion industry. 'Competitors,' she notes, 'are not the enemy. Without them, you get sloppy.' Since she was, in essence, the first of her industry in Dallas, she is familiar with the other agencies and their respective CEOs. This group of agency heads counsels within the group and is marked by a sense of friendly dialogue and community. Kim notes that this group is a stimulus for her, a positive challenge and source of support.

Outside the city, there also exists an international network of people within the fashion industry. Kim is particularly pleased with the relationship which has grown with the Eileen Ford Agency of New York. The diversity of the fashion business today, with national ads, billboards, video, as well as traditional catalog work and point of purchase work, requires good negotiation skills, and Kim contends that Jerry Ford is the best negotiator in the business. He has shared his knowledge with Kim, who says the international industry, in general, is 'generous . . . not cutthroat.'

A major preventive management mechanism for Kim Dawson is therefore the support network she relies on. She extends herself remarkably well through other people. Her family, local business associates, and members of the international fashion industry provide her with the informational and emotional support to deal with the admittedly stressful nature of her business and the many commitments in her daily life. She uses this support system with a great deal of comfort, and does not hesitate to reach out for whatever type of support is required at the time. No one would accuse Kim Dawson of being a loner. She could accurately be described as a 'people person,' and the ease with which she gives support to others and alternately reaches out for support from others has facilitated her ascent to the top of the fashion industry.

The perspective which characterizes Kim's approach to life is also an asset in terms of dealing with stress. She is an eternal optimist, an outlook adopted early in life and encouraged by her mother. She is fundamentally an action-oriented person, and believes it effective to 'DO something' rather than merely ponder on it. Kim describes her work as play. Each morning, she is 'ready to go to the playpen for eight to ten hours a day . . . then afterward, I'm tired, ready to rejuvenate, and return the next day.' Her definition of success reflects this perspective. 'The bottom line is how much fun did I have?'

The value system Kim learned from her grandmother is another plus in coping with stress. Thus, in situations requiring decisions which might cause anguish for another person, she never feels any doubts about what is the right thing to do. Her values dictate the answers in many cases. Kim related to us a recent example in which an employee of the child talent division of another agency was threatening to leave and use valuable information (which children had particular talent) to get back at the agency owner. Kim's attitude was 'that's not our business.' She feels strongly about not taking advantage of a fellow businessperson. A strong intuitive knowledge of what is right allows her to take decisive action when situations demand it and make tough decisions with confidence.

Ventilating her anger and frustrations sometimes has been effective for Kim. During market, when as many as ten to fourteen shows in three days are produced, things can get tense. Kim claims that in the past, before market became more of a routine, she used ventilating as a 'performance, to try to be effective.' Her frustration was usually a situation, not a person, and the ventilation was never targeted at a particular individual. Kim relies on this mechanism to a lesser degree now, preferring to expend the energy it requires in other ways.

Exercise plays a minor role in this busy executive's collection of coping techniques. Kim likes exercise, and attends a water aerobics class once a week. In addition, she bicycles at home when time permits, and wishes she had more time for exercise and its benefits. Although her approach to exercise is an unstructured one, she remains convinced of its positive effects in terms of energy produced.

Withdrawal and recovery time is very important for coping with the stress of the fashion industry. After a busy market, she returns home to 'crash and burn,' to spend time with her husband, children, and grandchildren. This escape allows Kim to disconnect from the world momentarily and renew her energy.

Faith and spirituality also play a role in Kim's life. In her childhood, she was at church at least twice a week, and her grandmother saw to it that religion was always present. Church also served an important social function for her during her early life. Although her attendance at church has declined of necessity because of the business (markets at the Dallas Fashion Mart are on Sunday), she still attends when she can and relies on her strong faith to support her in stressful periods. Her reliance on faith was established in early childhood, and the habits she developed have continued on in her adult life.

Part Priest, Part Psychiatrist, Part Parent

'We all need each other . . . we're mutually beneficial.' Perhaps the most striking feature of Kim Dawson's personality is her ability to function as a source of support for other people. She proudly claims to be 'part priest, part psychiatrist, and part parent' to a host of individuals, particularly the models with whom she works. The fact that they turn to her as a sort of mother figure sometimes strikes Kim as amazing. 'Why do they imagine I know anything? I try to be accommodating . . . to be really objective and tell them what it's [the business] like.'

In this regard, Kim related a story about a young model who left her agency to join the Ford agency in New York. The model went on to Paris and Milan, but returned to the US with her marriage on the rocks and spiritually wiped out. Kim counseled her, worked with her, and the model is now resuming a successful career in Dallas.

Kim is convinced that it is her 'old-fashioned values' which allow her to be effective in supporting others. In fact, when asked what career she would have selected had it not been in fashion, she said she would be a psychiatrist. When we pressed as to why she did not pursue this interest, she was quick with her answer. 'I got to know a student of psychiatry once . . . she wasn't happy. I want to have a good time!'

A Source of Stability in a Changing Industry

The fashion industry has the potential to be a fickle, unpredictable, glamorous, and usury business. From that perspective, it focuses on the exterior appearance and the moment. Models may be treated as chattels, and today's winners can become tomorrow's losers. Models are sometimes sent to Europe, only to return burned out, drug addicted, and disillusioned. This dark side of the industry is not the dominant side yet it is the side which all too often will get the publicity and the attention because of its sensationalism.

It is in this context that Kim Dawson is unusual for the stabilizing traditional values she brings to the industry. She treats her models and talent with respect, caring for their souls as well as their facades. She is a personal force in a very impersonal industry. In many ways, good values have made for good business for Kim. Finally, she has found in her competition the oppositional allies who stimulate her own growth, development, and improvement as opposed to enemies who must be sought out and destroyed. Rather than kill the competition, Kim would prefer to convert the competition into collaborative allies who will advance the entire industry.

Chapter 6

Meeting the Challenge: Messages From the Top

Executives and professionals face a variety of professional and personal challenges, as we have seen in the experiences of the men and women profiled in Chapters 4 and 5. All too often executives interpret the confrontation of a challenge in the boardroom, the courtroom, or the marketplace as an enemy attack. This converts the dynamics of work into a war game and the validity of that conversion must be examined. We will examine that issue in the first section of this chapter. We will then turn to the messages that emerge from an examination of the profiles and our experience with other executives who have helped us to understand the healthy dynamics of stress at work.

IS IT WORK OR IS IT WAR?

We examined in detail the psychophysiology of the stress response in Chapter 2 where we looked at the risk of the pursuit of success. The underlying dynamic of the stress response may be best understood in the context of confrontation and war. Walter Cannon argued that the urge to kill and to avoid death were firmly rooted in 'the fighting emotions' of human nature, which give rise to what he originally called the emergency response. Only later did this response become known as 'the stress response' and the 'fight-or-flight' response. It is not surprising that challenges of various kinds place us on a war footing.

> The militarist contention that the fighting instinct is firmly fixed in human nature receives strong confirmation in the results of our researches. Survival has been decided by the grim law of mortal conflict, and the mechanism for rendering the body more competent in conflict has been

Table 1   The principles of war

1. *Objective*: what the military action intends to accomplish
2. *Offensive action*: act and take initiative; don't react
3. *Surprise*: attack at an unexpected time, place, manner
4. *Security*: protect friendly operations from the enemy
5. *Mass and economy of force*: balance between these two
6. *Maneuver*: friendly force movement in relation to the enemy
7. *Timing and tempo*: optimize the use of friendly forces; inhibit the enemy forces
8. *Unity of command*: use a single battlefield commander
9. *Simplicity*: promotes understanding, reduces confusion, and permits ease of execution
10. *Logistics*: sustain man and machine in the battlefield
11. *Cohesion*: establish and maintain an integrated, war fighting spirit

revealed in early chapters as extraordinarily perfect and complete. (Cannon, 1929, p. 379).

In the context of territorial conflict, geographical aggression, and military warfare, the stress response is a valuable source of energy for victory. Military commanders have used the 'principles of war' for decades to conduct military campaigns, channel resources effectively, and win battlefield victory. These principles have been attributed to British Major General J.F.C. Fuller of World War I. The principles, as modified over the years, are outlined in Table 1.

Corporate warfare is rooted in the same human fighting emotions and arises out of economic conflict and industrial aggression (Nelson, Quick and Quick, 1989). Corporate commanders frequently use the same principles of war employed by their military counterparts, as illustrated by Lee Iacocca.

I was the general in the war to save Chrysler. But I sure didn't do it alone. What I'm most proud of is the coalition I was able to put together. It shows what cooperation can do for you in hard times. (Iacocca, 1984)

This quote illustrates the use of three of the principles of war in Table 1: Principle 1 (*Objective*)—'. . . to save Chrysler'; Principle 8 (*Unity of command*)—'I was the general . . .'; and Principle 11 (*Cohesion*)—'. . . the coalition I was able to put together.'

The War Game

For the war game framework to be used, it requires that a set of allies and enemies be clearly identified. Without a set of opposing players of this sort, the game will not work. In cases where a specific enemy or opponent can be identified who exhibits economic and industrial aggression, then a war game framework may be very valuable for conducting operations. And the enemy need not be human, as illustrated in the Iacocca quote. Here the enemy was the death of Chrysler Corporation.

The usefulness of the war game framework as a basis of action breaks down when there is not an identifiable enemy or opponent, *or* if the costs of destroying the enemy are too great. For example, it is conceivable that IBM Corporation could eliminate its competition from the marketplace, given its size and power. However, the US legal system has established constraints on the conduct of corporate warfare operations which would preclude this course of action as a viable option for IBM. A more fundamental question here is: Does the war game need to be the basis for providing the experience of challenge at work?

Inevitable Challenge

As we noted at the beginning of Chapter 1, based upon Vaillant's (1977) research, life does pose a variety of challenges by way of trial and tribulation. He found no life he studied free of some trial or tribulation and the same held true in our research, these trials or tribulations frequently forming the basis for the challenges of professional and personal life. In some cases, the challenge was strictly professional, such as the collapse of the oil industry or the banking failures of the mid-1980s. Purvis Thrash's humorous observation that the collapse in the oil market that had occurred only six months after he became president and CEO of Otis had not been his fault is a powerful image. It reflects both his recognition of the reality of the collapse and his personal powerlessness to alter it.

In other cases, the challenges were of a more personal and possibly painful nature. The end of Catherine Crier's marriage is a case in point, occurring during a period of feverish political campaign activity. The continuation of the relationship as a friendship reflects her realization of the value of both herself and her former husband while at the same time accepting the death of the marital aspects of the relationship.

Work and personal life *do* create inevitable challenges. However, this does not mean that we need to go on a war footing in the face of the challenge. To do so may actually lead to a set of self-destructive behaviors which are counterproductive. Two alternative ways in which we may respond to the inevitable challenges of life are identified by Siegel (1986). He argues that there are no incurable diseases, only incurable people. For Siegel, the disease becomes the challenge to which an individual may respond with hope, optimism, and self-responsibility. *Or*, the individual may respond with despair, pessimism, and denial of responsibility. Individuals who respond in the former way to disease, or the other challenges of life, become transformational in nature. That is, they transform situations or events in which they are involved, rather than simply allowing events to overtake them. And they transform themselves in the process. Specifically, they become therapeutic forces through their inner peace and greater tranquility. This does not mean that they are necessarily less passive or less achievement oriented.

Executives who fit this category may be called change makers, as Cooper and Hingley (1985) have labeled them. In their study of leading British industrialists who were forceful in their transformation of their industries, the authors found that the distinguishing feature of these powerful leaders was some trial, tribulation, or difficulty during childhood. Rather than being overwhelmed by the event, they responded with a compensatory drive which enabled them to overcome that and other adversity.

Work as Creation

When work is experienced as a civilized form of warfare, it requires that a specific enemy be identified, attacked, and destroyed or neutralized. The alternative to a war game framework for work is to see the inevitable challenges of the environment as problems to be solved in the process of creating valuable products and services. Competitors are no longer enemies. Rather, as Kim Dawson has shown us, they become prospective allies or collaborators whose actions challenge you to better yourself.

The physical and psychological risks of corporate warfare may be different in kind than the risks of military warfare. The consequences in terms of combat stress and battle fatigue are frequently the same. Both forms of warfare are risky business. Certainly the men and women we have interviewed do not see the war game framework as either the healthiest or most constructive basis for corporate or courtroom action. What do these men and women say?

Table 2   Messages from the top

1. *Be intellectually curious*
   Intellectual curiosity and education (formal or informal) expand a person's understanding of the world, providing perspective as well as knowledge for problem solving.
2. *Be physically active*
   People who are physically active dissipate stress-induced energy while at the same time developing a stronger, more efficient cardiovascular system.
3. *Balance work with nonwork*
   People who balance work with nonwork activities place their work in a larger, broader context of life which gives perspective and reduces psychological dependence.
4. *Seek social support*
   Supportive relationships provide people with a variety of informational, evaluative, and emotional need gratification essential to healthy functioning.
5. *Create systemic change*
   The people at the top need to be able to create a work environment that is challenging, productive, and creative and at the same time emotionally healthy.

MESSAGES FROM THE TOP

There are five messages that emerge from the profiles and our research with executives. They are:

1. Be intellectually curious.
2. Be physically active.
3. Balance work with nonwork.
4. Seek social support.
5. Create systemic change.

These five messages are summarized in Table 2. We will address each one separately.

Be Intellectually Curious

The importance of intellectual curiosity, learning, and education emerges in one way or another in each of the profiles. This may be in either a formal educational sense or in a more informal one. From a formal educational perspective, three of the six individuals hold advanced degrees; one in metallurgy, one in finance, and one in jurisprudence. The advanced degrees are in none of the cases a requirement for the position they hold, even in Catherine Crier's case where the law degree is a logical characteristic of the judicial position yet not a requirement for it. For Purvis Thrash, formal education is important enough for him to contribute to the teaching function at his undergraduate school and to the authorship of articles in the field of his expertise. Drs Forward and Grant are both distinguished by the scholarly and research contributions which they have made to their particular fields.

However, formal education is not the central characteristic in this message. The central issue is that of *intellectual curiosity*. This means the inquisitiveness of exploring the world and engaging in the process of learning new things. The people we have interviewed all engage in reading programs which go *beyond the requirements of their immediate positions*. That is, they read and learn more than what is essential to their immediate functioning. While some of this reading falls outside the realm of the educational, as illustrated by Grant's novels and Forward's detective stories, much does fall in the realm of the educational.

The fourth principle of preventive stress management (see page 46 in Chapter 3) concerning the uniqueness of the individual suggests that those we studied engage in a process of expanding their pool of knowledge of how different individuals, organizations, and cultures have responded to the various experiences and events of their lives. This knowledge provides some input to the range of possible response and coping behaviors then available to our men and women when cast in trial or tribulation. This places them beyond the level of learning from direct experience and places their learning activities beyond the level of training.

Training activities may be beneficial in response to specific demands or specific symptoms. The value of this is illustrated in Chaparral Steel's Apprenticeship Program. However, the one-for-one applicability of learning achieved in the training process has narrow applicability. Educational activities are much less efficient when it comes to direct applicability yet they contribute to the individual's increasing pool of knowledge which becomes a valuable resource for responding to changing circumstances and events. This is why Beau Sheil (1987) argues that artificial intelligence has such limited applicability in the solution of simple, general problems. To be useful in such cases, the artificial intelligence system would have to have an overwhelming pool of data. Like training, artificial intelligence is useful for limited, specific tasks that require a limited range of response choices.

The ongoing intellectual and educational activities of the executives in our profiles, while not always highly systematic, contribute importantly to their ability to change, cope, and adjust in response to the changing demands of their lives. While reading activities are one vehicle through which this ongoing educational process occurs, it is important to point out that there are other educational formats through which our executives learn.

A second major format is through direct, personal interactions, often enhanced by travel though not always. For example, Gordon Forward not only travels frequently nationally and internationally to learn how other people are doing things, he encourages the same for his people. Ebby Halliday does the same by traveling extensively in several professional contexts, often by way of doing service for her profession. However, she is ever alert to the possibility of learning from those with whom she is interacting. Finally, Kim Dawson's early domestic experiences in New York and international experience in Paris provided invaluable input for her in creating and building her business.

A variation on learning by traveling is to import the information or people who have specialized knowledge or expertise. Purvis Thrash talks about the importance of this when it comes to bringing in consultants who know more than he does about specialized areas. The learning which he and Otis Engineering did from Deming (1986) in this regard is a case in point. Therefore, bringing in others becomes an alternative to seeking out others by traveling.

Regardless of the pathway of the intellectual curiosity or the mechanism through which learning and education occurs, be it by reading, travel, or the recruitment of experts, the underlying process that is important here is the expansion of the executive's general pool of knowledge. It is this knowledge pool that serves as a vital resource in choosing specific response patterns for the demands to which the executive is subject.

Be Physically Active

While the men and women whom we have interviewed and studied may have a very common thread in their intellectual curiosity and learning behaviors, they are very different with regard to their pursuit of exercise and athletics. It is in this area that the principle of uniqueness probably is the most pronounced. And the difference cannot be seen as a difference in the ages or the sexes either. Quite specifically, exercise and physical activity are not important stress management strategies for either Purvis Thrash or Ebby Halliday.

The antithesis of this position is reflected in the experiences of Jody Grant and Catherine Crier. Both are avid and accomplished athletes, though it is Jody Grant who is the standout of the group in terms of athletic achievement. However, is that the real issue when it comes to exercise as a preventive stress management strategy? Probably not.

It is probably important to distinguish between two underlying motivations for the engagement in exercise and athletics. One is activity-based and concerns the engagement of competitive, social, and activity needs. It is therefore a forum for activity, and golf may be the most classic illustration of athletics that fall into this category. The other motivation is function-based and concerns the effort to protect the system by improved cardiovascular activity (Baun, Bernacki and Herd, 1987; Kahn, 1987). Both these motivations for, and ways of engaging in, exercise and athletics may contribute to preventive stress management, though differently.

Activity-based athletics provide not only some physical activity but at the same time serve as a psychological distraction for the individual. Gordon Forward talks of golf, racquetball, and tennis played with his sons, while Catherine Crier talks about the host of animals she plays with, especially her love of horseback riding. The more solitary activity, such as lone horseback riding, swimming and individual running, may also serve as periods of psychological withdrawal and reflection which border on the rest and restorative theme we will discuss next.

Function-based athletics are the basis for health maintenance programs which have become increasingly popular in American corporations. While some of these programs, like the ones developed by Xerox Corporation and Kimberly-Clark, emphasize the exercise component of the wellness program, not all such corporate programs do. An illustration of the alternative is Johnson & Johnson's 'Live for Life' program, which provides a cafeteria of activities including exercise, nutrition (often done in collaboration with local American Heart Association units), yoga, and stress management education. Not all of the executives we profiled believe in corporate wellness programs. And, of the executives we talked to, probably Gordon Forward comes the closest to having a functional attitude with regard to exercise and athletics. He does it because he feels better, physically and mentally, for having done it. However, it is not a central issue for him.

For Jody Grant and Catherine Crier, their exercise and athletics are central issues in how they organize their time nearly every week. Jody Grant looks at the weekly calendar with an eye to when he can plan in his swimming and/or running activities, as the case may be. Kim Dawson falls somewhere between these two alternatives with her modest, regular involvement in physical activities.

While there are some good research data to support the benefits that are to be had through regular exercise and athletic programs, the exceptions probably prove the rule. This is illustrated in our executive profiles of Purvis Thrash and Ebby Halliday, but more dramatically so by the case of Professor Emeritus of Pediatrics, Dr Otto A. Faust (Quick and Quick, 1990). In part due to a tuberculosis damaged right hip from childhood, Dr Faust was inhibited in ever engaging in exercise and/or athletic activity. However, the absence of these activities in his life in no way interfered with his reaching the advanced age of 100 years in 1987.

Balance Work with Nonwork

While there was much variance among those we profiled with regard to involvement with physical and exercise activities, there was variance also with regard to activities aimed at balancing their work investment. In no case did we find the work all consuming. Probably Purvis Thrash's comment in this regard is the most telling when asked directly if work was the most important thing in his life. The answer was a clear 'No' with a clarification of the role and importance it did have. The executives we profiled all have significant alternative investments to their main occupation activities. These fell into two major categories, which were active and passive activities. Either set of activities leads to the establishment of a counterbalance to the executive's main occupational investment.

The active counterbalances to their main occupational investment also fell into two categories, those of a more professional nature and those of a more personal nature. A good example of the former is Jody Grant's involvement with the Young Presidents' Organization. This contributed to his professional development, as he points out, yet does not fall directly into his main occupational arena of banking. Another example in this regard is Gordon Forward's involvement in the Vision Group.

Active counterbalances of a more personal nature would include

Catherine Crier's involvement in TROT, which builds on her love of horses and riding. While these activities for her may be psychologically restful and rejuvenating, they certainly would not be construed as physically restful or passive activities. Another example is Ebby Halliday's personal traveling, which is frequently connected to her professional travel. Seeing different peoples and different cultures is again not a physically restful activity but can be psychologically rejuvenating.

Not all of the activities of those we profiled fell into the active counterbalance category. There were also passive counterbalances to the main occupational investment. The best example of these activities may be Purvis Thrash's fishing activities and relaxing trips to his east Texas retreat. These trips for him were not only psychologically relaxing but also physically rejuvenating. For Kim Dawson, her withdrawals following a major market to play with grandchildren or to simply be left entirely alone fall into the more passive category.

Whether of an active or passive nature, each of the executives had one or more counterbalancing activities to their main work investment. We should point out that these counterbalances are over and above their personal relationship investments in family and friends which we will turn to next.

Seek Social Support

While there was much variance in the presence or absence of exercise and athletic activities among the executives we profiled and there was some variance with regard to the types of counterbalancing activities that they had to their major work investment, there was little variance in the area of social support. Each of these executives had well-developed professional and personal support systems in place. These people are not loners, though there are executives who are loners. We will turn to risk and problems of the loner in the next chapter.

While the content and nature of their professional support systems did vary, they each had a set of supportive relationships in the work organization and also had a developed network of professional contacts. Good examples within the work environment include Gordon Forward's team of vice presidents who have been with him for over ten years; Jody Grant's two-secretary team who buffer him so effectively; Catherine Crier's administrative court clerk who does much the same for her; and Ebby Halliday's staff. These working relationships function as sources of information, feedback, and stability. Their long-term nature is an important distinguishing feature of many of these relationships, signaling an important capacity in both parties to the relationship.

The larger professional network which each of these executives has is also an important feature of their professional lives. These relationships serve less of a stabilizing function than as sources of information and environmental screening. The absence of these relationships would leave any one of them quite isolated. This might be best illustrated in the case of Kim Dawson who has a strong national and international network of professional resources.

As well as long-term professional relationships, these executives also have long-term personal relationships. Ebby Halliday's interlocking work and personal relationships with her husband Maurice illustrate that the relationships in these two arenas are not necessarily mutually exclusive. In fact, they are frequently complementary because the functions of the personal relationships are usually quite different than the professional ones. However, there may be overlap.

The deeper emotional needs of these executives are met in their personal support system. Each of the executives we profiled had some recognition, even if at a semi-conscious level, of the importance of this set of needs to their long-term well-being. Their families are a cornerstone in this regard, whether that family be of a more nuclear nature, as with Ebby Halliday, or a more extended nature, as with Purvis Thrash and Kim Dawson. These family relationships are supplemented in varying degrees with friendships, as both Catherine Crier and Purvis Thrash discuss.

When there is loss or interruption in any of the relationships, we do not see a distancing response; rather, we see a response of accommodation and adjustment to meet the need in a new way. This is illustrated with the adjustment activities of Catherine Crier in response to her divorce. Two aspects of this adjustment are important, one being affirmation of her ex-husband through friendship, as opposed to total rejection, and the other being the emerging importance of her friendships to fill the void left by the absence of a marriage. The alternative for her might have been to throw herself in an unbalanced way into her work.

While each of these executives has a rather well-developed set of personal and professional relationships, they vary with regard to the extent of their involvement in civic relationships. Both Jody Grant and

Ebby Hallilday see their organizations as heavily dependent upon the community and therefore they feel some obligation to become invested in community and civic activities. Gordon Forward's major civic investment is the Gifted Students Institute which is highly compatible with his educational, developmental agenda as it concerns people. Purvis Thrash maintains a low profile when it comes to civic and community activities, this being an area of very modest investment for him. Therefore, the occupations and interests of the executives play an important role in shaping the ways in which they become involved in civic and community relationships.

In Chapter 8 we will explore in detail the dynamics and the processes for forming healthy attachments. These are the basis of a person's social support system which is critical to individual health, well-being, and functioning.

Create Systemic Change

According to Kerr's (1988) understanding of the family systems literature, individuals will vary with regard to the degree of personality differentiation and the extent to which they experience chronic anxiety. It is this latter characteristic which infuses stress, strain, and tension into a system of relationships within a family or other form of organization. Chronic anxiety has an ongoing, long-term quality which interferes with the adaptive capabilities of those in the relationships system. Kerr (1988) argues that where chronic anxiety is low and individuals have well-established, comfortable relationships, they are more likely to adapt successfully to stressful events.

From a systemic perspective, as opposed to an authority structure perspective, the executives we have profiled are in an ideal position to create systemic change that will result in healthy stress levels in the organization. This ties in with the principle of the interdependence of individual and organizational health. As healthy members of the system with comparatively lower stress and anxiety levels, they function socially to draw stress out of the system. This is especially true given their hierarchical position.

By assuming responsibility for their own health and well-being, they are in effect assuming some responsiblity for the health and well-being of their organizations. As Purvis Thrash points out, his work goals and objectives are convergent with those of Otis Engineering because of his responsibility as President and CEO. This creates a trickle down effect of their behavior patterns, either good or bad, within the system.

While they *have* a responsibility for individual and organizational health, they *are not* fully responsible for it. The distinction here reflects the limitations which even they have for creating or initiating change. Again, Purvis Thrash reflects an understanding of this distinction when he talks about letting go of inevitable events which cannot be controlled.

While these executives create systemic change through the effect and impact of their personality–behaviour patterns, they also create systemic change through a social process of self-selection. Gordon Forward talks about the social effects of creating a trusting work environment in which those who are untrustworthy will either self-select out of the system or leave through peer pressure. This process creates a homeostatic system which, if it did not interact effectively with the environment, would run the risk of becoming pathological. However, the effective interaction with the environment, which Gordon Forward and other members of Chaparral's management achieve, imparts sufficient information, energy, and other resources to keep the system open enough to be healthy.

Each of the men and women we profiled is an initiator of change, shaping the systems of which they are a part, as seen with Purvis Thrash, Catherine Crier, and Jody Grant, *or* creating their own systems as is the case for Ebby Halliday, Kim Dawson, and Gordon Forward. At the same time, they each understand that there are limitations in terms of the effects they can achieve and they do not over-reach, though they do stretch. Gordon Forward talks about the balance of going beyond where you are in a growthful way without taking unreasonable risk in the process.

CONCLUDING COMMENTS

Some people confuse work and war, engaging in sophisticated war games designed to destroy real or imagined enemies on the corporate battlefield. While there are times to utilize elements of a war game framework in corporate operations, the challenges of work need not come from this sort of confrontation. And, one need not assume a war game framework or the presence of corporate enemies to develop strong allies and alliances in the pursuit of success at work.

Executives cannot achieve success without drawing upon their talents and abilities as well as their drive and ambition. It is not the pursuit of success alone which leads to various trials and tribulations, for Vaillant (1977) found some trauma or struggle in each of the lives he studied, regardless of the extent of their success. And some executives experience short-lived success for a variety of reasons. The more problematic task is one of *achieving and sustaining* one's success over an extended period of time. That has been the case for the executives we have examined in these profiles. They have sustained their success through trying industrial and economic times through a combination of professional and personal strategies.

Each emphasizes intellectual curiosity in one way or another, having an interest in learning and growing. Each has balanced his occupational investment with one or another professional or personal investments in time and energy. Each has a complex yet well-established set of professional and personal relationships through which information, emotional nurturance, appraisal feedback, and instrumental support are received. Each is a force for systemic change within the systems he has created and/or led.

However, they differ notably with regard to their investment in physical activities and exercise. In addition, they differ notably in how they pursue their learning, how they balance their occupational investment, how they create supportive relationships, and how they effect systemic change. Thus, while there may be some marked similarities at the general level, there are real individual differences at the specific level.

FURTHER READING

Cooper, C. L. and Hingley, P. (1985). *The Change Makers*, Harper and Row, London.
Cooper, K. (1982). *The Aerobics Program for Total Well-Being*, M. Evans and Company, New York.
Epstein, J. (1981). *Ambition: The Secret Passion*, E. P. Dutton, New York.
Levinson, H. and Rosenthal, S. (1984). *CEO: Corporate Leadership in Action*, Basic Books, New York.
Nelson, D. L., Quick, J. C. and Quick, J. D. (1989). 'Corporate warfare: preventing combat stress and battle fatigue,' *Organizational Dynamics*, **18**(1), 65–79.
Vaillant, G. (1977). *Adaptation to Life*, Little Brown & Company, Boston.
Zaleznik, A. (1977). 'Leaders and managers: Are they different?' *Harvard Business Review*, **55**(3), 67–78.

Chapter 7

Loneliness: A Lethal Problem

In Chapter 1 we reported the case of a commercial bank chairman who experienced substantial problems with separation anxiety as evidenced by his overly individualistic behavior (see page 7). Some people would label his behavior pattern *counter-dependent* because of the extent to which he avoids interdependent involvement with others in the workplace. A more pernicious example of the problems associated with emotional isolation and loneliness in the workplace was illustrated by a corporate division comptroller several years earlier.

As in the case of the bank chairman, this individual had rather severe problems developing emotional comfort and effective interdependence in his working relationships. This was most evident in the working relationships he had with his three immediate subordinates, who were respectively responsible for accounting, information systems, and management analysis functions of the division. His anxiety and insecurity were largely directed into conflicts with the managers of the accounting and information systems functions, possibly because these were the functions about which he knew the most. He exhibited a pattern of harassment and intimidation to which the two managers responded quite differently. The accounting manager became acutely anxious himself over the comptroller's tactics, eventually experiencing difficulty eating in the morning and actually trembling on the way to work. The information systems manager simply ignored all but essential interactions with the comptroller. As a result of his ineffectiveness in these relationships, the comptroller was relieved after one year.

In this chapter, we will deal with the problem of loneliness associated with the psychological and/or social isolation of executives such as the bank chairman and the division comptroller. First, we will discuss the cultural, organizational, and personal–behavioral forces that contribute

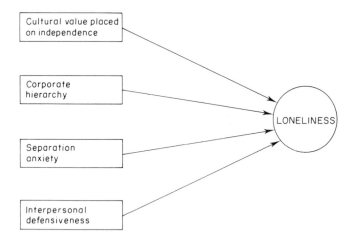

Figure 1   Forces leading to loneliness

to the experience of loneliness for executives, especially chief executives. Second, we will examine loneliness in the context of being alone and the two alternative experiences of being separated from other people. Finally, we will look at the health risks associated with chronic loneliness.

FORCES LEADING TO LONELINESS

The cases of the corporate comptroller and bank chairman illustrate some of the problems and dilemmas that go along with the experience of loneliness and isolation in the workplace. Within 20th century American corporate culture, there are four potential driving forces that may contribute to the problem of loneliness for those who arrive at the top—the chief executives. These are: (1) the value placed on independence and individualism within the American culture; (2) the sociological process of organizing through a corporate, pyramidal structure which creates role distinctions by hierarchical level; (3) the problem of separation anxiety for individuals who have not successfully developed through secure attachments; and (4) the interpersonal defensiveness which is often reflected in communication and interaction patterns. These forces are identified in Figure 1 and we will discuss each in turn.

The Myth of Independence

An important element within American folklore and myth is the value placed upon the independence of the individual. We may call it the 'John Wayne' myth or the story of the Lone Ranger or Superman. These heroic figures within the culture are, to a large degree, solitary figures who appear rather self-sufficient. The underlying psychodynamics or fantasy for this myth is that a well-developed individual really does not need other people. This myth is captured in Harold Geneen's famous statement while Chairman of the Board of International Telephone & Telegraph: 'If I had enough arms and legs and time, I would do it all myself.'

We call this a myth because it is a key underlying belief within American culture and the truth or falsehood of the belief is not important. What *is* important is the extent to which individuals believe that it is true. Not all executives do believe in the myth, yet they are all part of a culture which, in varying degrees, fosters it. Not all cultures foster this value, belief, or myth. Hofstede's (1980a, 1980b) large scale study of 160 000 people working in 60 countries found significant differences between cultures concerning the value placed on individualism and independence. The US was among the most individualistic cultures while Taiwan, Japan, and Hong Kong were among the most collectivistic.

We have seen much attention given during the 1970s and 1980s to the differences between American and Japanese management styles concerning individual versus collective values. The Japanese place much greater value on group and collaborative efforts, in part by negatively sanctioning too much individual effort. This appears to be a pervasive characteristic of Oriental cultures. Rosalie Tung spent a summer studying work sites in China and found that peer group pressures for conformity in work performance were ever present and visible (Tung, 1981). For example, workers who did not meet group standards for a week had their names placed on a blackboard at the end of the week. If the individual did not meet standards the next week, his name remained and the supervisor would counsel the individual. By the end of the third week, if things had not changed, then the whole work group would counsel with the individual.

In contrast to the value placed on individualism within American culture, Chinese and Japanese cultures appear to place greater value on

Table 1   Cultural comparisons

	American	Oriental
Value	Independence	Collectivism
Focus	Individual	Family, group
Process	Separation	Attachment
Consequence	Loneliness	Bonding

conformity to collective standards of behavior. These differences in behavior patterns between the cultures were evident during a behavioral medicine scientific exchange to China in the fall of 1988. While the collectivism of the Oriental culture insures that the individual is not isolated or separated from the group, it at the same time curtails individualistic and/or exploratory behavior. The individual values in American culture have very different consequences from the collective values in Oriental culture. These alternative value schemes are compared in Table 1.

For Americans, the value placed on individualism serves as a disconnecting force in human relationships and contributes to a sense of loneliness. That is not to say that all Americans are lonely people, but that the underlying current of the culture pushes individuals to be solitary beings outside the context of human relationship. For Chinese, the value placed on collectivism serves as a binding force in human relationship and contributes to a sense of connectedness. Thus, by contrast, the Chinese cultural force pushes the individual into a social network.

In both cultural contexts, there will be variance around these norms and they should not be taken as absolute. Nor should they be taken as the primary determining force contributing to the problem of loneliness. The myth of independence in America is the broadest undercurrent force to consider in looking at this problem of loneliness for corporate executives. The second broadest force is that of organization hierarchy and social role discrimination.

The Corporate Hierarchy

Through the centuries human beings have organized themselves in a variety of ways. Military organizations are among the oldest forms of human organization because of the need for defense and survival. The clans of the Scottish Highlands and the tribes of Israel are illustrations of this form of organization. The advent of the Industrial Revolution and the evolution of industrial organizations led to the construction of corporations, bureaucracies, and other forms of hierarchy which discriminated among people based upon social role responsibilities.

The social process of discriminating among people based upon role authority and responsibility is an underlying force for the separation and isolation of the individual. This process can be countered for the individual by identifying peers in social roles with whom he may identify. In traditional hierarchical forms of corporate structures, the process of identification and sharing with peers is not a particularly acute problem for those in the middle or bottom of the hierarchy because of the availability of peers. However, for the top level executives there is an increasing sense of isolation and peers of common experience are not as readily available in the corporation.

For alternative forms of corporate organization, such as the professional bureaucracy or the 'adhocracy' discussed by Mintzberg (1979), this sociological force is not as dominant in pressing the chief executive into a lonely position. This force appears most notably in the tall hierarchy which places heavy emphasis upon vertical distinctions between responsibilities and authority.

Schein (1989) has argued that our notion of an organizational hierarchy is an ingrained element of how we think about work in corporations. He argues that the whole way we conceptualize work is being challenged by the computer revolution. This revolution will necessitate a comparable revolution in the structure of organization. The future will demand a more nonhierarchical structure in the workplace and an executive will be less able to rely upon hierarchical authority to influence people's work behavior. The potential benefit of this for senior executives is that they will be less pushed out of human relationship by an authority hierarchy that will no longer be there.

Both the corporate hierarchy and the cultural myth of independence are forces which affect all executives and individuals. These cultural and organizational forces are not the only determinants of whether a chief executive will experience loneliness or not. A third key force which affects some executives is that of separation anxiety. This is a characteristic which evolves in the early stages of the individual's development and to which we will turn our attention next.

Separation Anxiety

Normal human development requires that the individual attach himself to secure attachment figures at various times of threat or need. The underlying process whereby this occurs will be discussed in the next chapter. According to Bowlby (1982), this is an instinctual, behavioral process which is exhibited by all humans. If there are interfering events that block this instinct, the normal and healthy development of the individual is delayed or stopped, resulting in separation anxiety which leads to isolation and loneliness. Bowlby (1973) has examined in detail the problem of separation anxiety and the resulting insecurity, anger, and distress.

Separation anxiety first appears for the individual when he or she reaches out for an attachment figure only to discover that the person is not there, for whatever reason. The anxiety and fear concern the inability to achieve need gratification. All individuals experience some degree of separation anxiety and there is functional value in learning to respond constructively to short periods of separation anxiety because it contributes to learning to respond to other frustrations in life. Separation anxiety becomes an important factor in adult loneliness, as we saw with the corporate comptroller in the opening vignette, only when it becomes a relatively permanent feature of the personality; that is, if separation anxiety becomes a learned response to legitimate needs.

There are basically two ways in which this developmental problem may occur. The first is if the primary attachment figure(s) for the individual is not sufficiently available. This leaves the child physically and psychologically isolated. In times of need for attachment, the child will experience fear, separation anxiety, anger, and a sense of helplessness. It is possible for the individual to eventually learn compensating behaviors and/or responses, but the underlying dynamic of the isolation will always be there.

The second way separation anxiety may develop into a problem is if the attachment figure(s) is unpredictable in terms of availability. That is, if the attachment figure is not predictably available at the time of the child's need. For example, the attachment figure may be relatively available over a given period of time but makes contact with the child many times when the child is not in need and does not make contact in times of need.

Either pathway leads to the experience of anxious attachment or 'overdependence.' Anxious attachments have a 'clinging' characteristic because the individual does not feel safe in letting go of the attachment figure for fear that a permanent separation is going to result. Individuals who grow up in the context of anxious attachments do not become self-reliant or sufficiently autonomous because they are neither able to form secure attachments, as need and circumstance dictate, nor are they able to separate appropriately with an internalized sense of peace and security.

Because secure attachments and anxious attachments are polar extremes on a continuum, individuals may fall anywhere along the spectrum. All individuals have experienced separation anxiety and the associated anger, fear, and distress that are associated with it. There are varying degrees to which separation anxiety becomes a permanent feature of the personality and therefore an adulthood problem, as for the bank chairman discussed in Chapter 1 (p. 7).

Interpersonal Defensiveness

Vaillant's (1977) 35-year study of life adjustment among men focused on the nature of their defenses as the discriminating factor in determining their degree of success. He argued that those with more mature defense mechanisms, such as sublimation and humor, had better long-term outcomes than those who had less mature defense mechanisms. Wells (1984) has taken a slightly different perspective on defensiveness by examining how defensive communication and interaction patterns in organizations may lead to isolation, loneliness, powerlessness, and other negative outcomes. Hers is a more behavioral and less psychodynamic approach. Both perspectives have a bearing upon this volume but it is her work that directly relates to the experience of loneliness.

While there are times when it may be appropriate to be defensive, such as in the face of severe physical or psychological attack, we all too frequently engage in defensive interactions when nondefensive responses would be more effective. The consequence of defensive interactions is the establishment of barriers between the individuals involved and the social distancing of one person from the other. This may be done either actively or passively. The various forms of active defense include aggressive attacks, dictatorialness, arbitrariness, and forceful controlling. The various forms of passive defense include physical and psychological withdrawal, submissions, apologies (when not appropriate to the circumstances), and self-deprecation.

Either active or passive forms of defense establish distance in the relationship between two people and create a dynamic of alienation. The opposite of interpersonal defensiveness is nondefensiveness. Nondefensive interaction may be characterized by openness, choice, self-control, powerfulness, and nonreactivity. It does not necessarily lead to psychological intimacy nor is it necessarily comfortable at all times. While two people engaged in nondefensive interaction may not always agree, there is not a psychological barrier to the meeting of their minds. It is the psychological barrier accompanying defensiveness which contributes to the experience of loneliness.

An example of nondefensive interaction was exhibited by a professor of religion shortly following the release of a new theological book he had written. During a faculty meeting, the new book was critiqued by his faculty colleagues. Many of them had very critical, and at times caustic, comments concerning the quality of the work. Rather than become defensive, the author maintained a nondefensive attitude and interaction with his colleagues. He listened patiently to their criticism and comment, hearing fully what was said without taking a position of agreement or disagreement with the points. While it was neither easy nor always comfortable for him to maintain his nondefensiveness, he was successful in doing so. In the longer run, the author found the session educational and informative, if not always enjoyable. In addition, he found he was better able to understand some of his colleagues following that faculty meeting.

LONELINESS VERSUS ALONENESS

We will examine loneliness and aloneness from two perspectives. One will be from that of the executive's personality. Is he a leader or is he a manager? The other way we will look at it concerns the categories of social provisions available in group settings which aid individuals in overcoming loneliness.

Leaders and Managers

Not everyone who is separate and alone is lonely. While individuals vary in the degree to which they have problems with separation anxiety, they also vary with regard to their capacity to be self-sufficient, autonomous, and separated from other people. Zaleznik (1977) has argued that leaders and managers are fundamentally different personalities in this regard. He argues that managers are socialized beings who have a strong need for the presence of other people, though not in emotionally close or highly charged relationships. In contrast, leaders are solitary beings who have a genuine capacity to work and function autonomously, forming emotionally close and intense relationships with a few other people in the world.

The leader is the individual who operates alone much of the time without being lonely, while the manager becomes very lonely if there are not other people in close proximity. The distinction between being alone and being lonely is an important one because it is the experience of loneliness, not aloneness, which is an important health risk for the executive. Zaleznik (1977) argues that the two personalities are fundamentally different. Bowlby's (1973) work on separation anxiety will help us understand the difference in expectations concerning other people and which leaders and managers have support needs. Specifically, a self-sufficent leader will have a basic expectation that other people will be available if he needs them *or* he can reach out and get to them in time of real need. On the other hand, the socialized manager will not have as much self-sufficient expectation concerning the availability of other people to meet his fundamental needs.

It is this difference which enables the leader to work contentedly in a relatively solitary fashion without experiencing loneliness—only a sense of aloneness. The internalized sense of self, autonomy, and the integrity of the personality enable the leader to function autonomously at times while at other times to function intensely with others in issues, dilemmas, and plans surrounding the work. Herein lies the paradox of the leader and the self-reliant person. The converse of this personality is the insecure manager with separation anxiety problems who is neither fully capable of autonomous functioning nor fully capable of intense interpersonal connection.

Loneliness and Group Life

It is through interpersonal connection that an executive overcomes the problem of loneliness. According to Shaver and Buhrmester (1985), there are two ways in which we can overcome loneliness through group life. One way is through psychological intimacy and the other is through integrated involvement. Individuals who achieve connection through psychological intimacy receive a number of benefits or social provisions from their involvement. These include:

—Affection and warmth.
—Unconditional positive regard.
—Opportunity for emotional expression.
—Lack of defensiveness.
—Security and emotional support.
—Giving and receiving nurturance.

This form of connectedness is frequently achieved through group life in family settings; hence the need for a balance between an executive's work and personal life.

Achieving connectedness and overcoming loneliness in work settings, while it may be done in part through psychological intimacy, is frequently done through integrated involvement. Individuals who achieve connectedness through this form of involvement receive a different set of benefits or social provisions. These include:

—Enjoyable and involving activities.
—Social identity and self-definition
—Being valued for one's skills and abilities.
—Opportunity for power and influence.
—Conditional positive regard.
—Support for one's beliefs and values.

Because connectedness through integrated involvement is frequently achieved through occupational and work-related activities, retirement becomes a high risk transition for the loss of this sort of involvement. Individuals who do not plan well for this transition may well encounter loneliness problems (McGoldrick and Cooper, 1990; J.F. Quick, 1990). The alternative is illustrated by the case of an executive of a large oil company who retired from work and then began volunteer work activities for his city. He works three days each week patrolling the city streets looking for obstructions to traffic signals and signs. Based upon his reports to the city, the municipal government gets property owners to clear the obstructions. Through this form of integrated involvement, the retired employee is able to have a new social identity and contribute a valued service to his community.

Further, Shaver and Buhrmester (1985) argue that loneliness itself is not a singular experience. Rather, it is possible to distinguish between *emotional* loneliness, which results from the inability to achieve psychological intimacy, and *social* loneliness, which results from the inability to achieve integrated involvement. An individual may encounter problems in one or the other or both of these areas. In either case, the problem results from a discrepancy between the individual's needs and expectations concerning the various social provisions *and* the availability of social provisions to meet the individual's needs.

The central theme of this chapter is that loneliness poses a health risk for individuals which may, in the extreme, be lethal by contributing to premature death. What is the underlying theoretical support for this theme? And what are the health risks to which we refer other than premature death? It is to these two questions that we will turn next.

LONELINESS AND HEALTH RISK

An Infomedical Model

Much of Western medicine has been founded upon a biomedical model which argues that health, well-being, and disease patterns are best understood by examining the biological processes of the body, the genetics of human nature, and the environmental risk factors. The extreme of this model or framework excludes psychological, social, and cultural factors as causal variables in the evolution of a disease process. The biomedical model adheres to a rational, logical perspective which is fundamentally reductionistic; that is, diseases may be traced in a deterministic fashion to one or more specific causal health risks. In the extreme, the amount of contribution of each risk to the disease may also be determined.

An alternative to the biomedical model has been proposed by Foss and Rothenberg (1987), which they call the infomedical model. It proceeds in part from the psychosomatic theorizing of Freud and others. Within this medical framework, a larger number of classes of health risks are considered in attempting to understand a disease. For example, cultural and human relationship variables become important considerations in understanding why a person becomes ill. The infomedical model does not assume that all diseases can be reduced to a simplistic set of causes nor is the framework a deterministic one.

It is the infomedical model, not the biomedical model, which we view as more useful in enabling people to understand both health and disease. It is difficult to argue within this framework that loneliness is a direct causal factor in any disease process. However, it is not at all difficult to understand how loneliness can establish the fertile ground for a number of health problems. It is in this sense that it is a health risk of significant importance.

Loneliness and Health Problems

The first order health problems that proceed from loneliness are of a psychological and behavioral nature. It is these first order outcomes which, together with loneliness, may lead to a variety of diseases. The four health problems to be addressed here are emotional deprivation, depression, social misadjustment, and physical illnesses. These are shown in Figure 2.

Emotional deprivation is a direct result of loneliness. Research with infants had demonstrated that normal development does not occur for those who experience emotional deprivation and who encounter loneliness through physical isolation. These adverse developmental effects occur within relatively short periods of time in the case of infants. Parallel effects in the adult stages of life take longer to evidence themselves for two reasons. First, it is rare that an individual will experience total isolation and loneliness. Rather, it is more commonly the case that the individual will operate 'a quart low' for extended periods of time. These conditions of low to moderate levels of emotional deprivation take their wear and tear gradually as opposed to dramatically.

Second, most adults have a larger emotional reservoir to draw upon than do children and infants. As a result, they may operate in a deficit position for extended periods of time without totally depleting their emotional reserves. Good illustrations of how that may work come from the experience of American prisoners of war in North Vietnam during the 1970s. The ones with deep emotional reserves were able to survive the years of internment without total collapse. However, this condition could not have gone on forever even for the strongest.

Depression is a second health problem that will grow out of loneliness and overlaps to some degree with emotional deprivation. As in the case

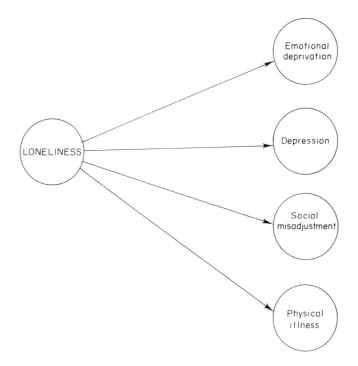

Figure 2 Loneliness and health problems

of emotional deprivation, there are varying degrees of depression to which an executive will be subject. Mild depressions may continue untreated for extended periods of time because they only minimally interfere with other aspects of the executive's personal and work life. Interference with decision making, judgment, and other key cognitive processing is relevant for the depressed executive.

Social misadjustment is a third health problem for the executive subject to loneliness. People at work take a wide range of social cues and role-related information from the network of relationships in which they are involved. When a person experiences loneliness and the associated disconnection from these key relationships, he also loses contact with the information and expectation flow that comes through the network. Mild forms of social misadjustment may appear humorous, such as missed responses or slightly inappropriate initiatives. However, in more severe cases of social misadjustment, the executive appears to be disconnected altogether. This occurred in the case of the division comptroller discussed at the outset of the chapter.

Over a twelve month period, his superiors realized how inappropriate his interpersonal adjustment was and removed him from his position.

Physical illness may also result from extended or intense experiences of loneliness. In his 25 year study of the Pennsylvania community of Roseto, Stewart Wolf found a more than doubling of the coronary heart disease rate and a tripling of the hypertension rate associated with increased loneliness caused by dislocations and disruptions in the tight network of community relationships (Rosch, 1989). Lynch (1977) found similar dysfunctional effects in cardiovascular functioning caused by loneliness in laboratory, clinical, and field settings. This evidence would suggest that it is the cardiovascular system that is most likely to be affected by the experience of loneliness.

SUMMARY

There are both cultural and personality forces that contribute to the loneliness experienced by executives, especially chief executives. These are the cultural value placed on independence and individualism in American culture; the discrimination of individuals across the corporate hierarchy; defensiveness in communication and interaction patterns; and the problem of separation anxiety attributable to insecure or anxious attachments in the early developmental years of life. These forces lead to the experience of loneliness, though not everyone who is alone is lonely. A distinction needs to be made between the experience of loneliness and aloneness, the latter occurring during periods of autonomous, appropriately independent, and self-sufficient functioning.

The emotional and/or social isolation associated with loneliness is problematic for an executive's health, especially as understood from an infomedical model perspective. There are at least four health problems which may proceed from the experience of prolonged or intense loneliness. These are emotional deprivation, depression, social misadjustment, and physical illness. Barring unusual circumstances, such as the temporary internment of Ross Perot's executives in Iran (Follett, 1983), the experience of loneliness is not inevitable. In Chapter 8 we will examine the importance of secure attachments, well-developed social support networks, and the ways in which these networks and secure attachments may be cultivated.

FURTHER READING

Bowlby, J. (1973). *Attachment and Loss, Volume II: Separation Anxiety and Anger*, Basic Books, New York.
Foss, L. and Rothenberg, K. (1987). *The Second Medical Revolution: From Biomedical to Infomedical*, New Science Library, Boston.
Hofstede, G. (1980a). *Culture's Consequences: International Differences in Work Related Values*, Sage Publications, Beverly Hills, CA.
Hofstede, G. (1980b). Motivation, leadership, and organization: do American theories apply abroad? *Organizational Dynamics*, Summer, 42–63.
Lynch, J. (1977). *The Broken Heart: The Medical Consequences of Loneliness*, Basic Books, New York.
Schein, E. H. (1989). Reassessing the 'Divine Rights' of managers. *Sloan Management Review*, **30**(2), 63–8.
Zaleznik, A. (1977). Leaders and managers: Are they different? *Harvard Business Review*, **55**(May–June), 67–78.

Chapter 8

Forming Healthy Attachments: Key to the Paradox

In our work with executives, we have observed that they have unique talents for forming relationships with others which are strong, reciprocal, and supportive. It is our contention that the formation and maintenance of these relationships is a key factor in the executive's sustained health and success. Each executive we have studied possesses a well-developed network of individuals on whom he depends for many different types of support. And each executive's network is unique in that it consists of sources of support from different arenas, both personal and professional. Thus, while there are individual differences in the exact composition of attachment relationships and in the functions which the various relationships serve, there is a commonality. Each executive is comfortably dependent on others, and does not hesitate to turn to others for support when needed.

In this chapter, we analyze the issue of relationships from the executive's point of view. First, we examine one of the most widely held myths in American culture and how it contributes to some basic misunderstandings and inaccurate perceptions about executive life. Second, we analyze the process of establishing relationships with others, the drive to bond, and the hows and whys of supportive relationships. Our third section examines the various functions of support, and the ways in which each type of support contributes to the executive's need satisfaction and productivity. Fourth, we develop a network of supportive others which executives can use as a model for forming their own social support systems. Our fifth section turns the focus outward; that is, it examines the executive's role as a source of social support for others, and the importance of this role for the executive. Finally, we present some tools for self-assessment which executives can use to address their own attachment behavior and the social support networks they currently have in place. Our thesis is that successful executives have mastered the art of developing healthy attachments with others, and all of us can learn from their experiences as they have related them to us in our research.

THE JOHN WAYNE MYTH OF THE SUCCESSFUL EXECUTIVE

Many of the heroes in American culture are to be found in the Western 'cowboy' culture of the movies and television: John Wayne characters, the Lone Ranger, Roy Rogers, and so the list goes on. These are the hard-riding, tough, independent, take-charge kind of individuals who are admired by many. But what if these famous figures were executives? What kind of success would they have achieved?

These questions are interesting to address and somewhat amusing, yet they have profound implications because they apply directly to the stereotype of the successful executive in American culture. What happens when we apply this 'John Wayne' stereotype to the successful executives? What emerges is a portrait of a larger-than-life hero, individualistic and independent; a hard-driving loner who lives for work. To the casual observer, admired executives like Boone Pickens and Lee Iacocca might well appear to fit this mold. In many executive development seminars, when we have asked managers to describe the successful executive, the word 'independent' is a recurring trait. A closer examination of the lives of successful executives, however, reveals that our stereotype of the successful executive as a rugged individualist must be called into question.

Perhaps it is most appropriate to address the issue of executive independence by beginning with examples of executives who have failed to develop healthy relationships with other people. Theirs are the stories of suicide, such as Eli Black of United Brands in 1975, who jumped to his death after smashing through his 44th story office window with his briefcase. Another suicide was that of Alvin Feldman of Continental Airlines, who in 1981 had experienced a traumatic takeover battle, a hijack attempt, and his wife's death from cancer. Many management scholars attribute the lack of success and subsequent deaths of such executives to the inability and/or unwillingness to develop supportive attachments with others. They have been described as alone with their misery and the failures of their organizations, as having tried to do it all themselves, and as independent.

While these may seem extreme examples of executives who have not coped with the stresses of the executive suite, there are countless everyday instances in which executives become liabilities to their organizations for their failure to relate in healthy ways to others. How many times have executives made solitary decisions which have been failures, only to have their subordinates remark behind their backs, 'if only he had asked us, we could have told him that it wouldn't work'? One executive who comes to mind as a contrasting example is the director of a large research laboratory who manages a staff of some 20 highly trained professionals. He works an average of eighteen hours per day, and is constantly seen looking over the shoulder of a researcher or sitting beside a researcher asking questions (while the researcher patiently answers questions with a pained facial expression). His staff shudder as he enters a room, wondering whose project he will interfere in next. The turnover rate in his operation is extremely high, as could be expected. This executive is one who has a host of talent in his staff, but cannot unleash it because of his own need to control each and every activity in the lab. In addition, when research project results are reported in public seminars, he insists on presenting the speech himself and garnering the credit for the work. On face value, it would appear that this executive is dependent; rather, he is independent—he cannot comfortably depend on others (e.g. his capable staff) to perform the work for which they were hired. The preceding behaviors are indicators that executives have not resolved the issues of separation and union in their lives. Failing to reach out for support from others and failing to trust others are signs that healthy attachments are not in place.

The issue of paramount importance here is that we may be deluding ourselves in thinking that successful executives are independent, and that it is indeed lonely at the top. Instead, we find that successful executives have resolved their own internal conflicts regarding separateness within the world and union with other people, and that they are not independent; rather, they are self-reliant.

The self-reliant executive is one who is able to rely comfortably on other individuals when the demands of the situation warrant such reliance. In addition, the self-reliant executive is able to identify the appropriate circumstances for relying on others. In general, we can say that it is appropriate for an executive to reach out to others when his own limitations in terms of time, energy, knowledge, or abilities are reached. By relying on others, the executive is able to extend his own limits, thereby increasing effectiveness. Self-reliance is a process of developing relationships which are characterized by confidence, trust, and mutual respect. This does not mean that self-reliant executives are hesitant to act alone or to make decisions alone; rather, it means that the executives diagnose the situation, rely on themselves when appropriate, and rely on others when they need support.

Thus, self-reliance characterizes the successful executive. It is a form of responsible behavior which means accepting responsibility for one's own well-being, and knowing with confidence that someone will be available and willing to help in times of need. This self-reliance develops over a period of years as other personality attributes develop. In general, those individuals who have not yet developed this self-reliance and self-confidence may be facing separation anxiety problems; that is, they have not yet come to terms with the issue of their separateness in the world and their union with other people. A comfortable balance between the needs for separation and union is something that facilitates and encourages self-reliance.

The idea that successful executives are independent is thus a myth— these successful individuals are *dependent*, and are not hesitant to admit that they rely on a host of other individuals for support. Had the John Wayne type of cowboy hero been an executive, chances are he would not be successful unless he was willing to forsake his independence in favor of self-reliance. Even the Lone Ranger had Tonto, and Roy Rogers had the Sons of the Pioneers. Whether these two cowboys relied on them may be the real issue here. Witness the account of Lee Iacocca (1984) of his rebuilding of the Chrysler Corporation in his autobiography. He very candidly admits that while he was the leader, he did not achieve the transition alone. He extols with pride the team he was able to assemble, and credits them with the success.

Healthy executives achieve success in the face of great stress and heavy demands. They are not torn apart by the stress of their lives because their attachments to people via their public and private support networks enable them to overcome their own limitations and transcend them. The process of forming attachment relationships and bonding with others has its roots in early life and develops throughout life. Understanding this process sheds light on the way executives exhibit healthy bonding with others. In the following section, we explore the lifelong process of developing attachments and how its roots in early childhood may affect adult development and behavior.

THE PROCESS OF BONDING WITH OTHERS

Many of the stresses individuals face stem from the feeling of separate-ness from the world. One of the earliest ways humans learn to deal with the stress of separateness is through attachment behavior and bonding with other humans. Bowlby (1982) and Ainsworth and her colleagues (1978) have described this process, which begins in infancy and con-tinues throughout the lifecycle. These developmental theorists assert that an infant's earliest attachment relationships are the primitive foundation for all social relationships in adult life.

The developmental perspective states that the origin of human social relationships can be traced back to the infant's innate predisposition to form a long-term, affective bond with the primary caregiver. The drive to bond with others is seen as a behavioral tendency which has evolved and persisted in humans because it contributes to the survival of the species. When infants exhibit attachment behaviors such as crying and reaching out for physical closeness, they are seeking proximity to their primary caregiver in order to be protected from harm. The caregiver responds to this move for closeness, and this establishes the reciprocal nature of the attachment relationship. According to Weiss (1982), infant attachments are characterized by three factors:

1. A display of need for the attachment figure and desire for physical closeness to the attachment figure in times of stress.
2. Indications of heightened comfort and decreased anxiety when in the presence of the attachment figure.
3. Indications of increased discomfort and anxiety on discovering that the attachment figure is inaccessible.

Another innate behavioral system is the exploratory behavioral system. When infants display curiosity about the world around them and attempt to explore their surroundings, they are displaying exploratory behavior. This behavior helps to fulfil the human need for competence, which is the need to master or control the environment. These two behavioral systems, attachment and exploration, relate to each other in an important way. The infant who has a secure relationship with the caregiver can venture about in order to explore his surroundings. The attachment forms a secure 'base' to which the infant can return following outings which serve to increase the understanding of, and eventually mastery of, the environment. Thus, a secure attachment relationship developed in infancy supports confidence in exploration and autonomy in later years.

Weiss (1982) contends that our adult attachments meet the criteria above which describe infant attachments, but differ from these factors in three important ways. First, the attachment relationships of adults are usually negotiated with *peers who are of unique importance.* These peers may be sources of strength, or may simply encourage the individual to master challenges which present themselves. Second, the attachment behavioral systems of healthy adults do not overwhelm other behavioral systems as they do in infancy. That is, adults can give energy and attention to other matters when attachment bonds are at issue. The separation anxiety problem has usually been resolved in a healthy adult. Third, in adult behavior, attachments are often formed with figures with whom a sexual relationship also exists; that is, significant others such as spouses play a role in attachment.

The development of attachment relationships proceeds throughout the life cycle. Until adolescence, children exhibit much of the same attachment behavior that they do in infancy. When uncomfortable, they continue to seek out their parents. Parental inaccessibility in times of stress is likely to be met with frustration and despair. This may be recognized as homesickness when away from the parents for a period of time. Children of this age demonstrate that their sense of security is dependent on their parents as a secure base.

In adolescence, children begin to establish their independence from their parents. This period of life is marked by mixed feelings, which reflect the desire on the one hand for freedom from parental control and on the other hand for assurance of parental accessibility and nurturance.

As adolescents develop further, they begin to relinquish their parents as attachment figures. During this time they begin to recognize their parents' weaknesses and regard them as fellow human beings with limitations. The replacement attachment figure is often a peer or a small, reliable group of peers. Relinquishing the parents as attachment figures helps us understand the reasons for substantial feelings of loneliness in adolescence. Eventually, in adulthood, attachment figures become fellow adults to whom the individual can turn, particularly in stressful circumstances.

It is interesting to note what happens in adulthood when infants fail to develop such a secure, positive relationship with the caregiver. Such infants are described by Ainsworth *et al.* (1978) as 'anxiously attached.'

This behavior is displayed in several ways. These infants may avoid their caregiver, following repeated attempts to attach, which were rebuffed. In addition, they may learn to exhibit very little exploration behavior, refusing to detach from their caregiver. These attachments, formed so early in life, have profound implications for the attachments and behaviors in later life.

Morris (1982) has reported the results of years of research which indicates the effects of these attachments on adult individuals. The anxiously attached child spends adult life constantly searching for a secure base. He is isolated, manipulative, and self-protective. Often, these adults are preoccupied with competitiveness and have problems successfully relating to others, especially in relationships which would normally be characterized as intimate. The anxiously attached person is therefore always searching for this secure base *outside of the self*. He learns to rely on others for escape from bad feelings, and to avoid potentially risky commitments because of fear that the other person will not be there for him. Adults who develop from anxiously attached infants have problems with intimacy.

Securely attached infants, in contrast, become adults who internalize the secure base and therefore trust in themselves and others. They approach the social world with confidence and enthusiasm. Their relationships are characterized by cooperative effort, compromise, and balance. Achievement is important, but is not emphasized above social and interpersonal satisfaction. They are able to receive from others and to give to others.

The main thesis of the developmental perspective of attachment is that a person's psychological self is an internal set of expectations which moves one to create relationships that confirm one's sense of self-unity. The secure individual thus forms relationships which are healthy, reciprocal, and rewarding. The insecure person, in contrast, tends to develop relationships which are unhealthy, one-sided, and unsatisfying.

Early life attachments are pertinent to our understanding of adult relationships. If one key characteristic of successful executives is their ability to rely comfortably upon other people, it is important to examine how this ability develops and the processes which contribute to its growth and development. Attachment behavior in infants is the precursor of social support behavior in adults. Healthy executives are those who have developed a secure attachment behavior system and a secure internal base from which they can explore and master their environment. We call these individuals self-reliant. They are willing to acknowledge their own shortcomings and reach out for social support from others. They are also willing to serve as givers of social suport to other individuals in their time of need.

Weiss (1982) argues that attachment behavior has contributed to 'inclusive fitness;' that is, those individuals who possess effective attachment behavior systems in earlier generations have survived in disproportionate numbers in successive generations. Further, he states that attachment is persistent over time, grows more reliable as a relationship persists, and is dominant over our several other behavior systems under conditions of stress and threat. If attachment behavior and social support do indeed contribute to the inclusive fitness of the human species, then our contention that successful executives are the masters of effective social support is a fitting one. The successful executive can be regarded, in essence, as the survivor of the species and as one of the few individuals at that level in American industry who can be regarded as individually healthy or fit. It is intriguing that scholars of business management have paid little attention to these concepts. While the importance of social support is readily acknowledged by stress researchers, the management community, both academicians and practitioners alike, are most probably unaware of the importance of this concept and its roots in attachment behavior theory.

Successful executives turn to a number of individuals for social support. These are primarily secure attachments in that the individual will be there for the executive when needed. Given that attachment behavior is important, the next issue to address is *what types* of social support are important for executive success. Presumably, adults seek close physical proximity with attachment figures when threatened by predators only on rare occasions. Instead, the access to the source of social support in adulthood is of a psychological nature, and the predator is stress. We now turn to the various types of support provided to executives through their social support networks.

FUNCTIONS OF SOCIAL SUPPORT

It can be seen from the developmental psychology perspective that attachments formed in infancy serve to protect the child from predators by permitting physical proximity to the caregiver. Social support relationships, which grow from early attachments, also serve as protection from predators, but the predator in adulthood is distress. In adulthood,

Table 1   Five functions of social support for executives

Type of social support	Function
Protection from stress predators	Direct assistance in terms of resources, time, labor, or environmental modification
Informational	Provision of information necessary for managing demands
Evaluative	Feedback on both personal and professional role performances
Modeling	Evidence of behavioral standards provided through modeled behavior
Emotional	Empathy, esteem, caring, love

there are five basic functions served by social support relationships. These are summarized in Table 1.

Protection from Stress Predators

Executives face demands from multiple sources. In a sense, social support relationships are like a shield which serves to protect the executive against potential distress which may arise from these demands, thereby acting as a natural defense against stress predators. The degree of permeability of the shield affects the amount of distress or strain which the executive may experience.

Subordinates often provide support in this regard. A high ranking military officer was once told by one of his subordinates that he saw his role as protecting the officer from distress—he did not want to hear from the officer unless things went wrong, and otherwise hoped his superior would trust him and assume he was doing his job. Effective delegation to trusted subordinates improves the impermeability of the boundary surrounding the executive.

Executives who report to superiors may also find themselves subordinates, with their superior in a leader/defender role. In management development seminars, asking managers what makes an effective boss elicits the reply 'one who makes my job easier—who buffers stuff from on high from affecting the way I do my job.' Thus the executive as leader/defender also serves as a shield for subordinates against unnecessary distress.

Executives who fail to execute the leader/defender role well are nightmares as bosses. One national-level manager in a division of a large furniture manufacturer reported that, despite the fact that she basically loved her work and was quite effective, she planned to leave because of such a boss. Rather than go to bat for her or run interference between her role and that of the corporate executives, he constantly bombarded her with reports of criticism from higher-ups. 'They don't think you're doing your job,' he would say. When questioned for specifics and ways to improve, he would say 'that's your problem to figure out.' Thus this boss added to stress, and was a stress predator himself rather than providing protection from stress.

This protective support often involves providing direct assistance for an individual in need, in the form of resources, labor, time, or environmental modification. It is similar to the instrumental support which House (1981) describes.

Informational Support

Executives require a wealth of information for effective functioning. They must be constantly aware of the environmental conditions within which their organizations operate, and they must also have readily available the information they need about the internal workings of the organization.

Colleagues can play an important role in the provision of informational support. They can bring to problem-solving a number of independent judgments and perspectives. This type of support is often solicited by members of the academic community in disseminating the results of their research. It is common practice to have several trusted colleagues read and critique a manuscript prior to submitting it to a journal for potential publication. The expertise of trusted colleagues is important in developing effective research skills.

Informational support is a crucial issue for executives, particularly given the advent of management information systems. More control information about the organization is available to the executive than ever before. It would be quite easy to become overwhelmed by the volume of information. The executive must be presented with only that information which is essential to him, and it should be presented in the form needed, in order to be efficient and effective. Consider, for example, an executive in the telemarketing industry. The type of daily activity reports required by the executive is very different from that required by an R & D laboratory supervisor. Effective information management skills are thus important tools for the executive.

Evaluative Support

Executives also need appraisal of their functioning in both the personal and professional spheres of life. This evaluation support provides feedback about behavior which the executive requires for adjusting to the demands of the job. Evaluation support may be deficient for many executives. Subordinates and peers may be reluctant to provide feedback about the executive's behavior because of the nature of their relationships with the executive. There is risk for the provider of evaluative feedback in terms of potential anger, denial, and rejection. This is particularly the case with upward feedback. Still, such monitoring and feedback must take place and be reported in order that the executive be aware of the effects of his behavior on others. The above example of the executive in the furniture manufacturing industry is a case in point. We asked if she thought her boss was aware of the negative impact of his behavior on her, and she replied that she believed he was. When pressed as to whether she told him about her feelings, she cited the potential risk of being fired and her reputation throughout the industry being marred as reasons for not providing such feedback to her boss.

Evaluative feedback is also necessary in the executive's personal life. A health care executive we studied stated that his wife is quick to point out to him that he is under too much stress. She often recognizes his personal signals of distress (psychological withdrawal, preoccupation) before he acknowledges them. When the behavior of the executive becomes out of line, either professionally or personally, he needs to be told of this. Likewise, when behavior is appropriate, effective, and successful, the executive needs to be reinforced. In a research project conducted by Longnecker and Gioia (1988), the authors sought to understand the ways executives appraise the performance of their subordinates. They found that a more important concern is the lack of appraisal feedback *to* executives regarding their own performance. The need for evaluative feedback on role performance does not disappear once one reaches the executive suite; rather, it becomes enhanced while the provision of this feedback may diminish.

Modeling Support

A major way in which individuals learn appropriate behavior is through observing others and patterning behavior after them. Executives often cite models or mentors as important guides to behavioral standards. Mentors serve other roles, such as sharing with protégés the demands to be expected on the job and suggesting ways of coping. They also serve as sounding boards for executives to discuss their career frustrations and are sources of vicarious learning through their own career experiences.

Mentors are not the only ones who serve as models for executives. Peers perform similar support functions through informal exchanges and observations. It is important to note that modeling support may be less available to female executives because of the patriarchal culture in American business. Female executives often find themselves with few models to emulate, and many times must turn to a male superior for this guidance. These modeling relationships are functional but present obvious roadblocks not inherent in same-sex mentoring relationships.

Once at the apex of the organization, the CEO may find a diminished need for models, but an increased need to serve as model/mentor for others in the organization. Subordinates may now turn to the executive for sponsorship and career guidance as well as modeling appropriate behavior.

Emotional Support

Esteem, trust, love, caring, and listening comprise emotional support, another function of attachment relationships. Because individuals often are reluctant to reveal their fears and stresses, emotional support is usually solicited from those people in very close relationships: spouses, family members, or long-term friends. These individuals provide unconditional positive regard; that is, we trust them to care for us regardless of our shortcomings. These are very meaningful relationships in terms of support, because the acceptance and approval of significant others is essential for healthy self-esteem.

Talking over the stresses of the job is an important form of emotional support for executives. Some confide in their spouses, some in trusted colleagues at work, others in friends. An empathetic listener may not be able to help resolve a tough issue, yet his concern and time spent processing the issue with the executive constitutes an outlet which helps the individual manage his response to stress.

There are thus five types of social support relevant for executive stress management: protection from stress predators, informational, evaluative, modeling, and emotional support. The next issue to consider is with whom executives can develop these supportive relationships, and how they form psychological contracts with the various individuals who serve as sources within their well-developed social support networks.

SUPPORTIVE RELATIONSHIPS

No single individual can provide all the types of support we have discussed. Executives who utilize social support well have developed

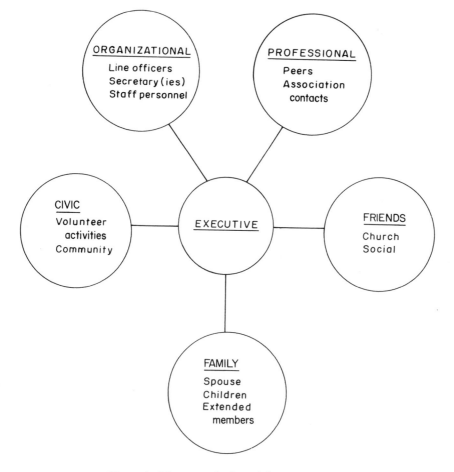

Figure 1   The executive's social support system

relationships over time which are characterized by a high degree of trust and reciprocity. There are a variety of individuals and groups which can provide support to executives. Figure 1 depicts a well-rounded social support network.

The relationships in the social support network are reciprocal; that is, the executive will be both donor and recipient of support in these attachments. Given the reciprocity of the relationships, it is natural that the attachments at times will be *sources of demands*. In any social exchange relationship, there is both giving and receiving.

Civic Involvements

Volunteer activities and community affairs are sources of support for many executives. These involvements are quite reciprocal in that the executives feel a duty to give back to the community some of the benefits their organizations receive from the community.

One individual who feels strongly about the issue is the managing director of a large metropolitan symphony orchestra. He is regarded as a champion of causes and is a volunteer in a large number of civic organizations. In addition, he founded an organization which recognizes and rewards outstanding high school students in the city. This executive is particularly proud of the fund-raising ability he has developed through his involvements. He says the benefit of volunteer and civic work is that it removes him from being the focus of attention (his job is a highly visible one) and focuses his attention outward, toward improving the lives of others. While his work life is creative and satisfying, he contends that the major joy in his life is his community activity.

Organizational Relationships

Line officers, secretaries, and staff personnel are members of the organization with whom the executive establishes supportive relationships. Depending comfortably upon these individuals requires a leap of faith; that is, the executive must trust others to do what he cannot do because of the natural limitations of time, knowledge, ability, or skill.

Personnel selection is a key contributor to building supportive organizational relationships. This does not eliminate the risks, but it does help minimize them. A self-reliant executive surrounds himself with capable, competent people. His self-reliance allows him to select the best and not be threatened by their expertise.

Delegation is another vital factor because of the interdependence of corporate life. The executive with a secure, well-established identity can trust others with important tasks, and turn them loose with authority to work independently and creatively.

Honest communication is also a key to organizational support relationships. Honesty and integrity are important elements in the psychological contract the executive establishes with superiors and subordinates. Uncertainty and ambiguity in the work environment is minimized with honest communication, and trusting, reciprocal relationships are maintained in this manner.

Professional Affiliations

Professional affiliations provide executives with opportunities for dialoguing with peers and sharing experiences about their organizations. These groups often take the form of networks through which the executives can establish a number of associations with others to provide informational, evaluative, and modeling support.

One such organization is the Institute of Business Designers (IBD), a group which consists of architects and interior designers. It is a large organization in which much business is conducted at informal gatherings. One interior designer related her experience with IBD as not particularly supportive in that the sheer size of the organization prevented the formation of close relationships. Some other designers shared her feelings, and they formed their own small group of four designers who meet two or three times per month for informal dinners or outings. She finds this group very rewarding because of the high trust factor developed within the circle. 'I can be candid with them about things in my organization and what goes on there to an extent not possible in my formal business contacts,' she says. These designers alternate as providers of support and recipients of support. 'It seems like each time we get together, one of us has a particular problem and the other three listen and advise, or critique the way it was handled. I've learned a lot from this. It's sort of like doing case studies in school. And each time it seems to rotate to another of us as the one who needs help,' the designer says. This small group of professionals thus provides evaluative, informational, and modeling support to its members.

Friends

Friendships are important sources of support since they provide companionship and nurturance. Executives often use friends as sounding boards for both personal and work-related problems. Their sense of perspective may bring objectivity to situations which the actors in each arena (family versus work) do not possess because of their involvement in the situation.

Some executives form close friendships through their religious commitments. One example of such an individual is a trust officer in a large commercial bank. His primary involvement outside of work and family is in his church, where he has served in various capacities as trustee, deacon, and church school teacher. He cites his religious affiliation as a primary support in that it has built lasting friendships for him and is an outlet which allows him to give support to others as well.

Family

The family and its inherent relationships are perhaps the most intimate bonds in the network. Families are supportive in evaluating and regulating behavior, and can often be expected to be more accepting of the executive's personality as a whole with its flaws and weaknesses. Home becomes a haven for rest and retreat, where the executive can 'let down her hair' without feeling vulnerable or inadequate. In this way, the executive feels protected from the stress predators of work.

Organizations typically do not provide much nurturance or emotional support. Thus the executive turns to the family for meeting this need. The family plays an important role in alleviating loneliness and providing identity, esteem support, and intimacy. An illustration of the contrasting supports of work and family can be seen in the life of a business professor who is described as a 'machine' at work, compulsively productive, highly focused, tightly wound up. His graduate students expressed great surprise on visiting his home, where they found him to be totally different, a warm, relaxed, nurturing family man. The professor's work served as a source of integrated involvement, while home and family life provided him with intimacy.

The extended family also plays an important role in providing support. One of our colleagues has a very meaningful relationship with his maternal grandfather, who has been his mentor and advisor since early childhood.

There are many potential sources of support for executives. Developing a strong network is a process of maintaining these contacts and building new relationships. It is also a process of reciprocity, with the CEO serving as a provider of support to others.

THE CEO AS A SUPPORT RESOURCE

Effective social support relationships are characterized by mutuality. Because the executive is the role model for preventive stress management in the organization, others look to him for support of all kinds. The CEO is a protector/defender for others from outside threats, and provides them with the tools, information, and other resources they need to cope with the demands of work life. Informational support is also provided by the CEO, as others look to the top of the organization for guidance in defining the vision and achieving the organization's mission. The line officers who report directly to the executive look to him/her for appraisal feedback. The CEO is the figurehead for the organization, the model for appropriate behavior and role performance. Inside the organization, in other professional contacts, in the community, and in the personal sphere of family and friends, many people turn to the executive for emotional support and nurturance. Thus, the CEO is a crucial provider of support from a host of other individuals and groups.

An example of one of the many support functions provided by a CEO can be seen in the experiences of a young executive in a large public utility. His job, with extensive public contact, became a source of great frustration, and he began to suffer panic attacks and bouts of excessive drinking. To compound his stress, his wife left him, taking their children with her. His boss constantly pressured him for higher performance, unaware and uninterested in his personal and work problems. The young executive's first supervisor, whom he worked for upon joining the public utility, had just been promoted head of a different division in the company. Upon hearing of the man's problems, he took the young executive on in the new division, gave him emotional, evaluative, and modeling support, and helped the man to cope with his multiple demands and turn his career around.

In this illustration, the executive served as rescuer for the young man, and in a strong role as protector/defender. This is but one of many ways in which CEOs provide support to others. The executive's attachment network thus consists both of individuals who provide support to the executive, and individuals for whom the executive is a major source of support.

FORMING HEALTHY ATTACHMENTS

Instructions: The ten statements below relate to how you form attachments with other people, with your work, and with other interests in your life. There are no right or wrong answers. Circle the number that most accurately describes your response, using the following scale:

> 1—Strongly agree
> 2—Agree
> 3—Uncertain
> 4—Disagree
> 5—Strongly disagree

1.	I make a strong effort to work alone and in a solitary fashion.	1	(2)	3	4	5
2.	My work is the single most important aspect of my life.	1	2	(3)	4	5
3.	I regularly and easily spend time with other people during the work day.	1	2	(3)	4	5
4.	I have a healthy, happy home life.	1	2	(3)	4	5
5.	I have one or two major non-work interests.	1	(2)	3	4	5
6.	I trust at least two other people to have my best interests at heart.	1	(2)	3	4	5
7.	I think I am the only one who can do a job right.	1	(2)	3	4	5
8.	I avoid depending on other people because I feel crowded by close relationships.	1	(2)	3	4	5
9.	I can easily ask for help when I need it.	1	2	(3)	4	5
10.	I am frequently suspicious of other people's motives and intentions.	(1)	2	3	4	5

Figure 2   Attachment questionnaire for executives. (Adapted from J. C. Quick, D. L. Nelson, and J. D. Quick. 'Successful executives: How independent?' *Academy of Management Executive*, **1**(2), 139–46.)

SELF-ASSESSMENT: HOW HEALTHY IS YOUR ATTACHMENT NETWORK?

Part of effectively attaching to others via social support relationships involves introspection. For some of us, bonding is a natural process which takes very little apparent effort. Others must make conscious decisions to attend to relationships and develop reciprocal ties to support both parties. Figure 2 is a tool for executive self-assessment which examines the individual's tendencies regarding the formation and maintenance of healthy attachments. To use the questionnaire, be as honest with yourself as possible and choose the response which best characterizes your behavior.

Score your attachment questionnaire by adding up your answers to questions 3, 4, 5, 6, and 9. Reverse your scores for questions 1, 2, 7, 8, and 10 by subtracting your answer from '6' in each case. Then add these new scores to the total you had for questions 3, 4, 5, 6, and 9 to get a grand total from between '10' and '50'. The lower the score, the more self-reliant this would suggest you are.

Another way to evaluate your use of social support is to perform a network analysis; that is, to appraise your social support network in terms of both *sources* of support and *types* of support available within your current network. Figure 3 is a social support grid for executives. To use the grid, fill in the name of an individual or several individuals from each of the various arenas who provide the type of support indicated. This will involve asking yourself questions such as 'who in my family gives me evaluative feedback about my behavior?' 'Who is it at work that I can count on to protect me from the stress predators of my job?'

The object of the social support grid exercise is to be able to fill in at least one name for every block on the grid. Many of us, however, may not be able to do this. The next step is to examine the empty blocks on the grid. These are voids in a well-developed social support network, and they represent the areas of support which you will want to work on in rounding out your own effective network of attachments.

Sources of social support

Functions of social support	Organizational	Civic	Professional	Family	Friends
Protective					
Informational					
Evaluative					
Modeling					
Emotional					

Figure 3   The executive social support grid

KEY TO THE PARADOX

The paradox of the successful executive is found in his capacity to use the natural drive and ambition associated with the achievement of success without succumbing to any of the risks of distress which all too often occur. Returning to Table 1 in Chapter 3, we can see that a common denominator among the preventive management strategies utilized by the executives we profiled is social support. The effective use of such attachment relationships allows the executives to sustain success, because the personal and professional networks they develop and maintain are essential supplements and complements to their own natural abilities. Self-reliant executives do not face fewer demands or less distress than other executives; rather, they are able to take on additional demands and challenges. Their own self-reliance and support networks makes this possible.

FURTHER READING

Bowlby, J. (1982). *Attachment and Loss, Vol. 1: Attachment*, Revised Edition. Basic Books, New York.
Cohen, S. and Syme, S. L. (1985). *Social Support and Health*, Academic Press, London.
House, J. S. (1981). *Work Stress and Social Support*, Addison-Wesley, Reading, Mass.
Quick, J. C., Nelson, D. L. and Quick, J. D. (1987). Successful executives: How independent? *Academy of Management Executive*, **1**(2), 139–45.

Creating a Personal Stress Management Plan

Popular stereotypes of stress management present a very limited notion of a stress management plan: 'meditation for low-stress living,' 'exercise your stress away,' and so on. But the profiles of successful executives presented in Chapters 4 and 5 highlight the diversity of approaches which can be taken to control the adverse effects of executive stress.

Successful executives understand the nature of their organizations and accept responsibility for individual and organizational well-being. The executive who, through an effective personal stress management strategy, effectively manages stress can serve as an excellent model of success for all employees. Conversely, executives who allow themselves to become overloaded, who are too untrusting to delegate effectively or who exhibit sysiphean 'joyless striving,' themselves become sources of stress in the organization.

For the executives we profiled earlier, effective stress management may appear to have been intuitive, almost preconscious. In fact, the executives describe an evolutionary, trial and error process in the development of their stress management habits. For most people the development of effective stress management habits *is* a continual process of adaptation and modification. The oil executive noted his gradual recognition that working long hours was more a problem than a solution for work demands. The health care executive noted that early in his career he felt guilty if he did not bring home work-related reading every night. In time he found that he was more creative at work and more effective if he maintained a better balance between work life and home life.

Effective management of stress in the workplace takes conscious effort at both organizational and individual levels. A senior manager has a high degree of *potential* control at both levels—the question is whether he or she chooses to exercise this potential control. Whether one is focusing on organizational level efforts to reduce unnecessary and nonproductive stressors or individual level efforts, the development of a stress management plan takes time, systematic effort, and commitment. Five useful steps are (Quick and Quick, 1984):

1. Identify your stressors.
2. Identify your responses.
3. Identify your options.
4. Make your plan.
5. Modify your plan.

A personal stress management plan is a contract which a person makes with himself or herself. It is a plan which contains specific actions a person will take to manage his or her own stress and which is consistent with the person's own values, attitudes, and capabilities. Most people can formulate a basic stress management plan without professional guidance. For people who are unsuccessful on their own or who suffer from unusually high levels of stress and resulting distress, professional guidance may be necessary.

IDENTIFY YOUR STRESSORS

An individual's stressors can be identified through an informal process of self-observation or through more structured assessment techniques. Standardized assessment methods reviewed elsewhere (Quick and Quick, 1984) include Cooper's Management Audit, the Holmes and Rahe Life Events Scale (also known as the Schedule of Recent Life Events), the Stress Diagnostic Survey developed by Ivancevich and Matteson, and McLean's Stressors Checklist.

For most managers and busy executives, however, the first step is usually personal reflection: What are my stressors? What demands at work give me headaches? Are unpleasant? Make me anxious? In general, most work demands will fall into the categories outlined in Chapter 1. These include interpersonal demands, demands from the external environment, role demands, task demands, and occasionally physical demands. Common executive stressors include uncertainty from the external environment (e.g. our real estate and oil executives), overload resulting from accepting too much responsibility or delegating too little, and problem personalities.

Every executive and senior manager experiences stressful demands at work. The first step in preparing a personal stress management plan is to identify these stressors and, in particular, to identify those stressors which are most frequent or most troublesome.

IDENTIFY YOUR RESPONSES

The signs of the stress response and resulting distress were described in Chapter 2. Individuals should learn to monitor their own stress responses and note when, for example, their neck is getting stiff or their cigarette consumption is rising. Simply becoming aware of one's own signals of distress is an important step in formulating a plan. Stress responses can manifest themselves as subtle physiological changes such as a rise in blood pressure, as behavioral changes such as increased smoking or alcohol consumption, as psychological changes such as depression or sexual dysfunction, or as frank medical symptoms such as ulcers or chest pain. It is important for individuals to develop an internal barometer which monitors these responses and tells them when stress responses and distress are increasing.

It is also useful to tune in to one's 'self-talk' patterns. 'Self-talk' is the mental monologue or narrative that most people conduct with themselves—consciously or unconsciously—about the events of the day and their reaction to these events. Self-talk can be positive: 'Gee, you're handling this merger with great finesse.' Or one's self-talk can be quite self-deprecating: 'Boy, you're making a mess of this merger; it's never going to work.' Though some people seem constitutionally bound to negative self-talk, the self-talk of successful people is usually quite positive. When the tone becomes persistently negative, it is usually an indication of increasing stress.

It is not always apparent whether specific symptoms are stress-related. Even an individual's personal physician may have difficulty separating stress from other causes of symptoms. Therefore, individuals should be cautious in attributing new, severe or persistent symptoms to stress without the benefit of a medical opinion.

IDENTIFY YOUR OPTIONS

Most managers have developed their own methods and habits for dealing with stress. Identifying these habits is an important step in outlining the full range of options. Chapter 3 described a wide range of options, highlighting those commonly employed by the executives in our profiles. The left-hand column in the personal stress management plan worksheet shown in Figure A1 contains a summary of these techniques.

An effective stress management plan will depend upon narrowing these options to those that seem to be acceptable, feasible, and appropriate to an individual's particular stressors and stress responses. Techniques vary widely in their focus, complexity, cost accessibility, and effectiveness. It is important, therefore, to take a systematic approach to selecting methods.

Acceptability of a specific method is a prerequisite for including it in a stress management plan. For example, a traditional method such as knitting or mystic technique such as Zen meditation may be wholly unacceptable to a mid-Western bank executive whose life might be greatly improved by a structured relaxation technique such as progressive relaxation. Thus the techniques must be selected and adapted to fit one's lifestle.

Feasibility also limits the available options. Although most methods of preventive stress management require little in the way of specialized facilities, equipment, trained instructors, or counselors, some do. Physical outlets are more feasible, for example, in certain parts of the country or in organizations which provide on-site athletic facilities.

The options should be appropriate to the person's particular stressors and stress responses. The manager who deals well with all aspects of his job except public presentations may benefit from stressor-directed techniques such as more positive self-talk or a behavioral technique known 'systematic desensitization.' In considering organizational stressors, it is useful for the individual to make an assessment of which stressors appear to be changeable, which appear to be avoidable, and which are inevitable. The response is to learn how to change some stressors, to avoid other stressors, and to accept with equanimity those stressors which are inevitable. Managers who successfully deal with the demands of their lives accept stress as a material part of work life and take actions to minimize distress for themselves and their employees.

Some people are bothered more by specific responses than by specific stressors. During an unusually busy period, it may be difficult to control the stressors. If the consequence of overload is, for example, lower backache or neck spasms, then relaxation training, physical exercise, or massage may be the most important elements in the stress management plan.

MAKE YOUR PLAN

Many people, perhaps most people, deal with daily stress without a written stress management plan. But a written plan helps an individual to think more carefully about stress and the manner in which it might be handled. After identifying the range of options available, those options which seem most feasible and most appealing should be formulated into a personal stress management plan. The plan serves as contract with oneself; it can be used as a reminder of the options the individual has identified and it can be used periodically for self-review.

A sample worksheet for preparing a personal stress management plan is shown in Figure A1. Though blanks are provided for the full range of individual stress management techniques, most people will rely on only a subset of these techniques. Though some sections will remain blank, most stress management plans should include some options for improving personal perceptions of stress, for controlling one's personal work environment, for physical outlets, and for emotional outlets.

Space is provided on the worksheet for professional help. The examples of executive suicides cited earlier highlight the fact that the pressures of executive life *can* get out of control. When depression, uncontrolled insomnia, persistent physical symptoms, or other signs of significant psychological or medical illness develop, professional help must be sought. The common misconception that a person must be 'crazy' in order to receive individual counseling or psychotherapy must be countered if individuals are to benefit from professional guidance.

MODIFY YOUR PLAN

Personal stress management is not a science and it is not always possible to anticipate in advance which methods will work best for a particular individual. In addition, stressors change and responses to stress change with time. For these reasons, it is important to view personal stress management plans as trial and error approaches and as being adaptable over time.

STRESS MANAGEMENT PLAN

Name: ———————————————   Date Plan Made: ——————————
                                   Review Date(s): ——————————

Personal Perceptions of Stress
- Recognize the inevitable   (1) ——————————————
- Constructive self-talk   (2) ——————————————
- Change Type A patterns   (3) ——————————————
- Develop hardiness

Personal Work Environment
- Social support   (1) ——————————————
- Time management   (2) ——————————————
- Overload avoidance   (3) ——————————————

Lifestyle Choices
- Maintain a work–home balance   (1) ——————————————
- Leisure time use   (2) ——————————————
- Sabbaticals   (3) ——————————————

Relaxation
- Relaxation response   (1) ——————————————
- Progressive relaxation   (2) ——————————————
- Meditation   (3) ——————————————
- Biofeedback, hypnosis
- Traditional methods

Physical Outlets
- Aerobic exercise   (1) ——————————————
- Recreational sports   (2) ——————————————
- Endurance training   (3) ——————————————
- Yoga, flexibility training

Emotional and Spiritual Outlets
- Prayer   (1) ——————————————
- Talking with others   (2) ——————————————
- Writing it out   (3) ——————————————

Professional Help
- Counseling and psychotherapy   (1) ——————————————
- Medical and surgical care   (2) ——————————————
- Physical therapies   (3) ——————————————

Figure A.1   Personal stress management plan. (Adapted from Quick and Quick (1984) and from J. W. Kertesz, 'Stress Management Plan,' unpublished worksheet, Duke-Watts Family Medicine Center, Durham, NC, 1982)

In assessing the effectiveness of a stress management plan, the bottom line is whether or not the individual feels a sense of relief and achieves what was described earlier as 'eustress'—the healthy, positive, constructive outcome of the stress response associated with an individual sense of well-being and high performance. The essential question is, 'When you follow the plan you've outlined, how do you feel at the end of the day?' If a particular method is not working, drop it and try another technique.

It is also important to guard against turning a releaser into a stressor. Even a simple relaxation exercise can become a source of stress if the person begins worrying about whether he or she is 'relaxing correctly.' 'Leisure' activities such as golf games and vacations can become stressful if tight deadlines are set or if one is overly concerned with winning at golf or getting the most out of a vacation trip.

Finally, personal stress management is an evolutionary process. As one becomes more experienced with stress management, as new or more demanding situations arise, or as one's work environment changes, different stress management methods may be needed.

BALANCING INDIVIDUAL AND ORGANIZATIONAL PREVENTIVE STRESS MANAGEMENT

A personal stress management plan is precisely that: personal—for the individual. But individual stress management should not become a tool for senior management to shift responsibility for a healthy work environment from the organization to the individual. Organizational life should be demanding; if it were not, then there would be little challenge, little accomplishment, and little success. Organizational life should not, however, be unreasonably demanding and individuals should not be expected to work under unnecessarily stressful conditions.

Senior managers as well as line managers and supervisors are in positions to develop both personal stress management plans and stress management plans for the organizational units for which they are responsible. Though our profiles of successful executives focused primarily on their individual styles, it is apparent that they are also concerned with the well-being of their subordinates. Organizational-level stress management aims at reducing or modifying the stressors identified in Chapter 1. These include interpersonal demands, role and task demands, and demands from the external environment. Techniques mentioned by our executives include fostering social support, goal-setting, and participative management. Other organizational-level preventive stress management techniques include task redesign, flexible work schedules, ensuring appropriate career development opportunities, team building, and design of physical settings (Quick and Quick, 1984). Whatever strategies are chosen, they must continually be reassessed and revitalized to ensure that they are suitable to the changing demands of the dynamic organization.

Executives have perhaps the greatest potential for becoming skilled diagnosticians for stress. Everyday interaction provides opportunity to assess the prevalence and consequences of stress within their own organizations. Organizational and individual health will both be enhanced if executives strive to maintain an active approach to preventive stress management, one which balances both individual and organizational needs.

FURTHER READING

Beech, H. R., Burns, L. E. and Sheffield, B. F. (1982). *A Behavioral Approach to the Management of Stress*, John Wiley & Sons, New York.
Davis, M., Eshelman, E. R. and McKay, M. (1980). *The Relaxation and Stress Reduction Workbook*, New Harbinger Publications, San Francisco.
Girdano, D. A. and Everly, G. S. (1979). *Controlling Stress and Tension: A Holistic Approach*, Prentice-Hall, Englewood Cliffs, NJ.
Quick, J. C. and Quick, J. D. (1984). *Organizational Stress and Preventive Management*, McGraw-Hill Book Co., New York.

SELECTED AUDIOVISUAL RESOURCES

American Hospital Association. *Stress!* (Educational package program with a Leader's Package including audiocassette, slides, Leader's Guide, audience participative materials, 16-mm film or videocassette). USCAN International, Ltd, 205 W. Wacker Drive, Suite 300, Chicago IL 60606.
Manuso, J. *Manage Your Stress* (facilitator's guide, film or videocassette, audiocassette, exercise books). CRM Multimedia Module, McGraw-Hill Films, 110 Fifteenth Street, Del Mar, CA 92014.
New Harbinger Publications: Audiocassettes on *Progressive Relaxation and Breathing, Autogenics and Meditation, Self Hypnosis, Thought Stopping*. New Harbinger Publications, 220 Adeline, Suite 305, Oakland, CA 94607.

Bibliography

Ainsworth, M. D. S., Blehar, M. C., Waters, E. and Walls, S. (1987). *Patterns of Attachment: A Psychological Study of the Strange Situation*, Lawrence Erlbaum Associates, Hillsdale, NJ.

Albrecht, K. (1979). *Stress and the Manager*, Prentice-Hall, Englewood Cliffs, NJ.

Anderson, C. R. (1977). Locus of control, coping behaviors, and performance in a stress setting: A longitudinal study, *Journal of Applied Psychology*, **62**, 466–451.

Argyris, C. (1960). *Understanding Organizational Behavior*, Dorsey Press, Homewood, Illinois.

Ash, M. K. (1981). *Mary Kay*, Harper & Row, New York.

Asterita, M. F. (1985). *The Physiology of Stress*, Human Sciences Press, New York.

Bandura, A. (1977). *Social Learning Theory*, Prentice-Hall, Englewood Cliffs, NJ.

Banks, H. (1988). Calmness itself, *Forbes*, March 21, 39–40.

Baun, W. B., Bernacki, E. J. and Herd, J. A. (1987). Corporate health and fitness programs and the prevention of work stress. In J. C. Quick, R. S. Bhagat, J. E. Dalton and J. D. Quick (eds). *Work Stress: Health Care Systems in the Workplace*, pp. 217–34, Praeger, New York.

Barefoot, J. C., Dahlstrom, W. G. and Williams, R. B. (1983). Hostility, CHD incidence, and total mortality: A 25-year follow-up study of 255 physicians, *Psychosomatic Medicine*, **45**(1), 59–63.

Beech, H. R., Burns, L. E. and Sheffield, B. F. (1982). A *Behavioral Approach to the Management of Stress*. John Wiley & Sons, New York.

Bennis, W. and Nanus, B. (1985). *Leaders: The Strategies for Taking Charge*, Harper & Row, New York.

Benson, H., Beary, J. F. and Carol, M. P. (1974). The relaxation response, *Psychiatry*, **37**, 37–46.

Binik, Y. M. (1985). Psychosocial predictor of sudden death: A review and critique, *Social Science Medicine*, **20**(7), 667–80.

Bowlby, J. (1982). *Attachment and Loss, Vol. I: Attachment*, Second Edition, Basic Books, New York.

Bowlby, J. (1973). *Attachment and Loss, Vol. II: Separation Anxiety and Anger*, Basic Books, New York.

Brief, A. P., Schuler, R. S. and Van Sell, M. (1981). *Managing Job Stress*, Little, Brown & Company, Boston.

Bruning, N. S. and Frew, D. R. (1987). Effects of exercise, relaxation, and management skills training on physiological stress indicators: A field experiment, *Journal of Applied Psychology*, **72**, 515–21.

Buck, V. E. (1972). *Working Under Pressure*, Crane Russek, New York.

Burack, E. H., Staszak, F. J. and Pati, G. C. (1972). An organizational analysis of manpower issues in employing the disadvantaged, *Academy of Management Journal*, **15**(3), 255–71.

Burke, R. J., Weir, T. and DuWors, Jr, R. E. (1979). Type A behavior of administrators and wives' reports of marital satisfaction and well-being, *Journal of Applied Psychology*, **64**, 57–65.

Cannon, W. B. (1929). *Bodily Changes in Pain, Hunger, Fear and Rage*, D. Appleton-Century, New York.

Cannon, W. B. (1932). *The Wisdom of the Body*, W. W. Norton, New York.

Case, R. D., Heller, S. S., Case, N. B., Moss, A. J. and Multicenter Post-Infarction Research Group (1985). Type A behavior and survival after acute myocardial infarction, *New England Journal of Medicine*, **312**(12), 737–41.

Chaparral Steel Company (1987). *Apprentice Training Program*, Chaparral Steel Company, Midlothian, TX.

Cohen, S. and Syme, S. L. (1985). *Social Support and Health*, Academic Press, London.

Conway, T. L., Vickers, Jr, R. R., Ward, H. W. and Rahe, R. H. (1981). Occupational stress and variation in cigarette, coffee, and alcohol consumption, *Journal of Health and Social Behavior*, **22**(2), 155–165.

Cooper, C. L. (Ed.) (1984). *Psychosocial Stress and Cancer*, John Wiley & Sons, New York.

Cooper, C. L., Cooper, R. D. and Eaker, L. H. (1988). *Living with Stress*, Penguin Books, London.

Cooper, C. and Hingley, P. (1985). *The Change Makers*, Harper & Row, London.

Cooper, K. (1982). *The Aerobics Program for Total Well-Being*, M. Evans & Co., New York.

Cosper, R. (1979). Drinking as conformity: A critique of sociological literature on occupational differences in drinking, *Journal of Studies of Alcohol*, **40**(9), 868–91.

Davis, M., Eshelman, E. R. and McKay, M. (1980). *The Relaxation and Stress Reduction Workbook*, New Harbinger Publications, San Francisco.

Deming, W. E. (1986). *Out of the Crisis*, Massachusetts Institute of Technology, Cambridge, Mass.

DeVries, H. A. (1981). Tranquilizer effects of exercise: A critical review, *The Physician and Sports Medicine*, **9**, 47–55.

Dorian, D. and Taylor, C. B. (1984). Stress factors in the development of coronary artery disease, *Journal of Occupational Medicine*, **26**(10), 747–56.

Drucker, P. F. (1974). *Management: Tasks, Responsibilities, Practices*, Harper & Row, New York.

Eliot, R. S. (1982). Stress reduction techniques that can help you and your patients, *Consultant*, Feb., 91–112.

Epstein, J. (1981). *Ambition: The Secret Passion*, E. P. Dutton, New York.

Fayol, H. (1929). *General and Industrial Management*, International Management Institute, Geneva.

Flannery, R. B., Jr. (1984). The work ethic as moderator variable of life stress: Preliminary inquiry, *Psychological Reports*, **55**, 361–2.

Folkman, S., Lazarus, R. S., Gruen, R. J. and Delongis, A. (1986). Appraisal, coping, health status, and psychological symptoms, *Journal of Personality and Social Psychology*, **50**, 571–9.

Follett, K. (1983). *On Wings of Eagles*, New American Library, New York.

Ford, D. L., Jr (ed.) (1976). *Readings in Minority-Group Relations*, University Associates, La Jolle, CA.

Forward, G. E. (Interviewed by A. M. Kantrow) (1986). *Harvard Business Review*, **64**(3), 96–102.

Foss, L. and Rothenberg, K. (1987). *The Second Medical Revolution: From Biomedical to Infomedical*, New Science Library, Boston.

Frasure-Smith, N. and Prince, R. (1985). The ischemic heart disease life stress monitoring program: Impact on mortality, *Psychosomatic Medicine*, **4**(5), 431–45.

Freud, S. (1933). *New Introductory Lectures in Psychoanalysis*, W. W. Norton, New York.

Freud, S. (1949). *An Outline of Psychoanalysis*, W. W. Norton, New York. (First published in 1940 in the German language as *Abriss der Psycho-Analyse*.)

Friedman, M. D. and Rosenman, R. H. (1974). *Type A Behavior and Your Heart*, Knopf, New York.

Friedman, M., Roseman, R. H. and Carroll, V. (1958). Changes in serum cholesterol and blood clotting time in men subjected to cyclic variation in occupational stress, *Circulation*, **17**, 852–61.

Funch, D. P. and Marshall, J. (1983). The role of stress, social support and age in survival from breast cancer, *Journal of Psychosomatic Research*, **27**(1), 77–83.

Gal, R. and Lazarus, R. S. (1975). The role of activity in anticipating and confronting stressful situations, *Journal of Human Stress*, **72**, 538–47.

Girdano, D. A. and Everly, G. S. (1979). *Controlling Stress and Tension: A Holistic Approach*, Prentice-Hall, Englewood Cliffs, NJ.

Gentry, W. D. *et al.* (1982). Habitual anger coping styles: I. Effect on mean blood pressure and risk for essential hypertension, *Psychosomatic Medicine*, **4**(2), 195–202.

Handy, C. (1978). The family: Help or hindrance. In C. L. Cooper and R. Payne (eds) *Stress at Work*, pp. 107–23, John Wiley & Sons, New York.

Henry, J. P. (1976). Understanding the early pathophysiology of essential hypertension, *Geriatrics*, **31**, 59–72.

Hillier, S. (1981). Stresses, strains, and smoking, *Nursing Mirror*, **152**, 26–30.

Hinkle, L. E. and Wolf, S. (1952). The effects of stressful life situations on the concentration of blood glucose in diabetic and nondiabetic humans, *Diabetes*, **1**, 383.

Hirschfield, A. H. and Behan, R. C. (1963). The accident process: I. Etiological considerations of industrial injuries, *Journal of the American Medical Association*, **186**, 193–9.

Hirschfield, A. H. and Behan, R. C. (1963). The accident process: III. Disability: Acceptable and unacceptable, *Journal of the American Medical Association*, **192**(2), 125–9.

Hofstede, G. (1980a). *Culture's Consequences: International Differences in Work-Related Values*, Sage Publications, Beverly Hills, CA.
Hofstede, G. (1980b). Motivation, leadership, and organization: Do American theories apply abroad? *Organizational Dynamics*, Summer, 42–63.
Holmes, T. H., Hawkins, N. G., Bowerman, C. E., Clark, Jr, E. R. and Joffee, J. R. (1957). Psychosocial and psychophysiological studies of tuberculosis, *Psychosomatic Medicine*, **19**, 134–43.
House, J. S. (1981). *Work Stress and Social Support*, Addison-Wesley, Reading, MA.
House, J. S. and Wells, J. A. (1978). Occupational stress, social support, and health. In A. McLean, G. Black and M. Colligan (eds) *Reducing Occupational Stress: Proceedings of a conference*, pp. 78–140, DHEW (NIOSH) Publication.
Howard, J. H., Cunningham, D. A. and Rechnitzer, P. A. (1976). Health patterns associated with Type A behavior: A managerial population, *Journal of Human Stress*, **2**, 24–31.
Howard, J. H., Rechnitzer, P. A. and Cunningham, D. A. (1975). Coping with job tension: Effective and ineffective means, *Public Personal Management*, **4**, 317–26.
Hurrell, J. J. Jr., Murphy, L. R., Sauter, S. L. and Cooper, C. L. (1988). *Occupational Stress: Issues and Developments in Research*, Taylor & Francis, New York.
Iacocca, L. (1984). *Iacocca: An Autobiography*, Bantam Books, New York.
Ivancevich, J. M. and Ganster, D. C. (eds) (1987). *Job Stress: From Theory to Suggestion*, Haworth Press, New York.
Janis, I. L. and Mann, L. (1977). *Decision Making*, Free Press, New York.
Jefferson, D. J. (1987). When the heat is on, *Wall Street Journal*, March 20, 209(55), Sec. 4, 26D–27D.
Jenkins, C. D. (1982). Psychosocial risk factors for coronary heart disease, *Acta Medica Scandinavica Suppl.*, **660**, 123–36.
Jones, J. W. (1984). Managing stress to prevent accidents, *National Underwriter*, **88**, 18–19.
Julius, S. (1984). Implications for hypertension. In National Institutes for Health, *Stress Reactivity and Cardiovascular Disease: Proceedings of the Working Conference*, pp. 63–71, Department of Health and Human Services, Washington, DC.
Kahn, R. L. (1987). Work stress in the 1980s: Research and practice. In J. C. Quick, R. S. Bhagat, J. E. Dalton, Jr and J. D. Quick (eds) *Work Stress: Health Care Systems in the Workplace*, pp. 311–20, Praeger Scientific, New York.
Karcher, C. J. and Linden, L. L. (1982). Is work conducive to self-destruction? *Suicide and Life Threatening Behavior*, **12**(5), 151–7. (In *Suicide Abstracts*, **32**, 1983, 386.)
Kasl, S. V. and Cobb, S. (1970). Blood pressure changes in men undergoing job loss: A preliminary report. *Psychosomatic Medicine*, **32**, 19–38.
Kasl, S. V. and Wells, J. A. (1985). Social support and health in the middle years: work and family. In S. Cohen and S. L. Syre (eds) *Social Support and Health*, pp. 175–98, Academic Press, Orlando, Florida.

Kerr, M. E. (1988). Chronic anxiety and defining a self, *The Atlantic Monthly,* September, 35–58.

Kets de Vries, M. F. R. and Miller, D. (1984). *The Neurotic Organization,* Jossey Bass, New York.

Kiev, A. (1974). *A Strategy for Handling Executive Stress,* Nelson-Hall, Chicago.

Kisch, E. S. (1985). Stressful events and the onset of diabetes mellitus, *Israeli Journal of Medical Sciences,* **21**, 356–8.

Kobasa, S. C. (1979). Stressful life events, personality and health: An inquiry into hardiness. *Journal of Personality and Social Psychology,* **37**, 1–11.

Kobasa, S. C. (1982). The hardy personality: Toward a social psychology of stress and health. In J. Suls and G. Sanders (eds.), *The Social Psychology of Health and Illness,* Erlbaum, Hillsdale, NJ.

Kobasa, S. C. (1988). Conceptualization and measurement of personality in job stress research. In J. J. Hurrell, Jr., L. R. Murray, S. L. Sauter, and C. L. Cooper (eds.), *Occupational Stress: Issues and Developments in Research,* pp. 100–109, Taylor & Francis, New York.

Kobasa, S. C., Maddi, S. R., and Courington, S. (1981). Personality and constitution as mediators in the stress–illness relationship, *Journal of Health and Social Behaviour,* **22**, 368–378.

Kobasa, S. C., Maddi, S. R., Puccetti, M. C. and Zola, M. A. (1985). Effectiveness of hardiness, exercise, and social support as resources against illness, *Journal of Psychosomatic Research,* **29**(5), 525–33.

Kotter, J. P. (1985). *Power and Influence: Beyond Formal Authority,* Free Press, New York.

Kotter, J. P. (1988). *The Leadership Factor,* Free Press, New York.

Lawler, K.A., Rixse, A. and Allen, M. T. (1983). Type A behavior and psychological responses in adult women. *Psychophysiology,* **20**(3), 343.

Lazarus, R. S., DeLongis, A., Folkman, S. and Gruen, R. (1985). Stress and adaptational outcomes: The problem of confounded measures, *American Psychologist,* **40**(2), 770–9.

Levinson, H. (1962). *Men, Management and Mental Health,* Harvard University Press, Cambridge, Mass.

Levinson, H. (1963). What killed Bob Lyons? *Harvard Business Review,* **36**, 127–43.

Levinson, H. (1975). *Executive Stress,* New American Library, New York.

Levinson, H. (1978). A psychoanalytic view of occupational stress, *Occupational Mental Health,* **3**(2), 2–13.

Levinson, H. (1981). *Executive.* Harvard University Press, Cambridge, Mass.

Levinson, H. and Rosenthal, S. (1984). *CEO: Corporate Leadership in Action,* Basic Books, New York.

Lindenthal, J. J., Myers, J. K. and Pepper, M. P. (1972). Smoking, psychological status, and stress. *Social Science Medicine,* **6**, 583–91.

Locke, E. A. (1968). Toward a theory of task motivation and incentives, *Organizational Behavior and Human Performance,* **3**, 157–89.

Locke, E. A., Shaw, K. N., Saari, L. M. and Latham, G. P. (1981). Goal setting and task performance: 1969–1980, *Psychological Bulletin*, **90**, 125–52.

Locke, S. E., Kraus, L., Leserman, J., Hurst, M. W., Heisel, J. S. and Williams, R. M. (1984). Life change stress, psychiatric symptoms, and natural killer cell activity, *Psychosomatic Medicine*, **46**(5), 441–53.

Longnecker, C. D. and Gioia, D. A. (1988). Neglected at the top: Executives talk about performance appraisal, *Sloan Management Review*, **41**, 41–7.

Lown, P., DeSilva, R. A. and Lenson, R. (1978). Roles of psychologic stress and autonomic nervous system changes in provocation of ventricular premature complexes, *American Journal of Cardiology*, **41**, 979–85.

Lynch, J. (1977). *The Broken Heart: The Medical Consequences of Loneliness*, Basic Books, New York.

Maddi, S. R. and Kobasa, S. C. O. (1984). *The Hardy Executive: Health under Stress*, Dow Jones-Irwin, Homewood, IL.

Manuso, J. S. (1979). Executive stress management, *Personnel Administrator*, **24**, 23–6.

Manz, C. C. and Sims, H. P. (1988). Superleadership: Leading others to lead themselves to excellence. In J. L. Pierce and J. W. Newstrom (eds) *The Manager's Bookshelf*, Harper & Row, New York.

Maslach, C. and Jackson, S. E. (1981). The measurement of experiential burnout, *Journal of Occupational Behavior*, **2**, 99–113.

Masuda, M., Perko, K. P. and Johnston, R. G. (1972). Physiological activity and illness history, *Journal of Psychosomatic Research*, **16**(2), 129–36.

Matteson, M. T. and Ivancevich, J. M. (1987). *Controlling Work Stress: Effective Human Resource and Management Strategies*, Jossey-Bass, San Francisco, California.

McClelland, D. C. (1975). *Power: The Inner Experience*, Irvington, New York.

McClelland, D. C. and Burnham, D. H. (1976). Power is the great motivator. *Harvard Business Review*, **54**(2), 100–110.

McClelland, D.C., Floor, E., Davidson, R. J. and Saron, C. (1980). Stressed power motivation, sympathetic activation, immune function and illness, *Journal of Human Stress*, **6**(2), 11–19.

McCubbin, J. A., Surwit, R. S. and Williams, R. B., (1985). Endogenous opiate peptides, stress reactivity, and risk for hypertension, *Hypertension*, **7**, 808–11.

McGoldrick, A. E. and Cooper, C. L. (1990). Why retire early? In J. C. Quick, R. Hess, J. Hermaline and J. D. Quick (eds) *Career Stress in Changing Times*, Haworth Press, New York.

Milsum, J. H. (1984). *Health, Stress and Illness: A Systems Approach*, Praeger Publications, New York.

Mintzberg, H. (1979). *The Structuring of Organizations*, Prentice-Hall, Englewood Cliffs, NJ.

Morgan, W. P. (1979). Anxiety reduction following acute physical activity, *Psychiatric Annual*, **9**, 141–7.

Morris, D. (1982). Attachment and intimacy. In M. Fisher and G. Stricker (eds) *Intimacy*, pp. 305–23, Plenum Press, New York.

Moss, L. (1981). *Management Stress*, Addison-Wesley, Reading, Mass.

Mueller, E. F. (1965). Psychological and Physiological Correlates of Work Overload Among University Professors, unpublished doctoral dissertation, University of Michigan, Ann Arbor.

Multiple Risk Factor Intervention Trial (1982). Risk factor changes and mortality results, *Journal of the American Medical Association*, **248**, 1465–77.

Neff, J. A. (1985). Evaluating the stress-suffering role of alcohol consumption: Variation of types of event and type of symptom, *Alcohol and Alcoholism*, **20**(4), 391–401.

Nelson, D. L. and Quick, J. C. (1985). Professional women: are distress and disease inevitable? *Academy of Management Review*, **10**(2), 206–18.

Nelson, D. L., Quick, J. C. and Quick, J. D. (1989). Corporate warfare: Preventing combat stress and battle fatigue, *Organizational Dynamics*, **18**(1), 65–79.

Nowack, K. M. (1987). Health habits, Type A behavior, and job burn-out, *Work-Stress*, **1**, 135–42.

Ojesjo, L. (1980). The relationship to alcoholism of occupation, class, and employment, *Journal of Occupational Medicine*, **22**(10), 657–6.

Pare, T. and Woods, W. (1988). The world's top 50 industrial CEOs, *Fortune*, August 3, 23–6.

Pearlin, L. I. (1985). Social structure and processes of social support. In S. Cohen and S. L. Syme (eds) *Social Support and Health*, pp. 43–60, Academic Press, Orlando, Florida.

Pickens, T. B., Jr (1987). *Boone*, Houghton Mifflin Co., Boston.

Plant, M. A. (1979). Occupation, drinking patterns and alcohol-related problems: Conclusions from a follow-up study, *British Journal of Addiction*, **74**(3), 267–73.

Quick, J. C. (1979a). Dyadic goal setting and role stress: A field study, *Academy of Management Journal*, **22**, 241–52.

Quick, J. C. (1979b). Dyadic goal setting with organizations: Role-making and motivational considerations, *Academy of Management Review*, **4**(2), 369–80.

Quick, J. C. and Gray, D. A. (1989/90). Chaparral: Bringing 'world class manufacturing' to steel, *National Productivity Review*, **9**(1) in press.

Quick, J. C., Bhagat, R. S., Dalton, Jr, J. D. and Quick, J. D. (1987). *Work Stress: Health Care Systems in the Workplace*, Praeger Scientific, New York.

Quick, J. C., Nelson, D. L. and Quick, J. D. (1987). Successful executives: How independent? *Academy of Management Executives*, **1**(2), 139–46.

Quick, J. C. and Quick, J. D. (1984). *Organizational Stress and Preventive Management*, McGraw-Hill, New York.

Quick, J. C. and Quick, J. D. (1990). The changing times of life: Career in context, *Prevention in Human Services*, **8**(1), in press.

Quick, J. D., Horn, R. S. and Quick, J. C. (1986). Health consequences of stress, *Journal of Organizational Behavior Management*, **8**(2), 19–36.

Quick, J. D., Kertesz, J. W., Nelson, D. L. and Quick, J. C. (1985). Preventive management of stress. In D. W. Myers (ed.) *Employee Problem Prevention and Counseling*, pp. 125–57, Greenwood Press, Westport, CN.

Quick, J. F. (1990) Time to move on? in J. C. Quick, R. Hess, J. Hermaline and J. D. Quick (eds) *Career Stress in Changing Times*, Hayworth Press, New York.

Ragland, D. R. and Brand, R. J. (1988). Type A behavior and mortality from coronary heart disease, *New England Journal of Medicine*, **318**(2), 65–9.

Rahe, R. A. (1979). Life change events and mental illness: An overview, *Journal of Human Stress*, **5**, 2–9.

Rosch, P. J. (1989). Dr Stewart Wolf and the Saga of Roseto, *The Newsletter of the American Institute of Stress*, **2**(1), 2–3.

Rosenman, R. H., Friedman, M. and Strauss, R. (1969). CHD in the Western Collaborative Group Study, *Journal of the American Medical Association*, **195**, 85–92.

Roth, D. L. and Holmes, D. S. (1985). Influence of physical fitness in determining the impact of stressful life events on physical and psychological health, *Psychosomatic Medicine*, **47**(2), 164–73.

Rountree, G. D. (1979). Renew your career—Take a sabbatical, *Hospital and Health Services Administration*, Fall, 67–80.

Russek, H. (1965). Stress, tobacco, and coronary heart disease in North American professional groups, *Journal of the American Medical Association*, **192**, 189–94.

Schein, E. H. (1989). Reassessing the 'divine rights' of managers, *Sloan Management Review*, **30**, 63–8.

Schilling, R. F., Gilchrist, L. D. and Schinke, S. P. (1985). Smoking in the workplace: Review of the critical issues, *Public Health Reports*, **100**(5), 473–9.

Schriber, J. B. and Gutek, B. A. (1987). Some time dimensions of work: measurement of an underlying aspect of organizational culture, *Journal of Applied Psychology*, **72**, 642–50.

Schwartz, H. (1987). On the psychodynamics of totalitarianism, *Journal of Management*, **13**(1), 41–54.

Selye, H. (1973). Evolution of the stress concept, *American Scientist*, **61**(6), 692–9.

Selye, H. (1974). *Stress Without Distress*, Lippincott, Philadelphia.

Selye, H. (1976). *The Stress of Life*, 2nd Edition, McGraw-Hill, New York.

Shapiro, A. P. (1961). An experimental study of comparative response to blood pressure to different noxious stimuli, *Journal of Chronic Disorders*, **13**, 293.

Shaver, P. and Buhrmester, D. (1985). Loneliness, sex-role orientation and group life: A social needs perspective. In P. Paulus (ed.) *Basic Group Processes*, pp. 259–88, Springer Verlag, New York.

Sheil, B. (1987). Thinking about artificial intelligence, *Harvard Business Review*, **65**, 91–7.

Siegel, B. (1984). *Love, Medicine and Miracles*, Harper & Row, New York.

Silver, B. J., Goldston, S. E. and Silver, L. B. (1985). The 1990 objectives for the nation for control of stress and violent behavior: Progress report, *Public Health Reports*, **100**, 374.

Smith, L. (1975). Can you cope with stress? *Dun's Review*, **106**, 89–91.

Sorensen, G., Pirie, P., Folsom, A., Luepker, R., Jacobs, D. and Gillum, R. (1985). Sex differences in the relationship between work and health: The Minnesota heart survey. *Journal of Health and Social Behavior*, **26**, 379–94.

Steadan, H. J. and Ribner, S. A. (1982). Life stress and violence among ex-mental patients. *Social Science Medicine*, **16**(18), 1631–47.

Student, K. R. (1977). Changing values and management stress, *Personnel*, **54**, 48–55.

Suinn, R. M. (1982). Interventions with Type A behaviors. *Journal of Consulting and Clinical Psychology*, **6**, 933–49.

Suinn, R. M. and Bloom, L. J. (1978). Anxiety management training for pattern A behavior, *Journal of Behavioral Medicine*, **1**, 25–35.

Sutton, R. I. and Kahn, R. L. (1987). Prediction, understanding, and control as antidotes to organizational stress. In J. Galbraith (ed) *Handbook of Organizational Behavior*, Prentice-Hall, Englewood Cliffs, NJ.

Tache, J., Selye, H. and Day, S. B. (eds) (1979). *Cancer, Stress and Death*, Plenum Medical Book Company, New York.

Taggart, P., Carruthers, M. and Somerville, W. (1973). Electrocardiogram, plasma catecholamines and lipids, and their modification by oxprenolol when speaking before an audience, *Lancet*, **ii**, 341–6.

Tichy, N. and Devanna, M. A. (1986). *The Transformational Leader: Molding Tomorrow's Corporate Winners*, Wiley, New York.

Trell, E., Kristenson, H. and Petersson, B. (1985). A risk factor approach to the alcohol-related diseases, *Alcohol and Alcoholism*, **20**(3), 333–45.

Trice, H. and Roman, P. (1981). Perspectives on job-related programs for alcohol and drug problems, *Journal of Drug Issues*, **II**, 167–9.

Tung, R. L. (1981). Patterns of motivation in Chinese industrial enterprises, *Academy of Management Review*, **6**(3), 487–494.

Vaillant, G. E. (1977). *Adaptation to Life*, Little, Brown & Co. Boston.

Weiss, R. S. (1982). Attachment in adult life. In C. M. Parkes and J. Stevenson-Hinde (eds) *The Place of Attachment in Human Behavior*, Basic Books, New York.

Wells, T. (1980). *Keeping Your Cool Under Fire: Communicating Non-Defensively*, McGraw-Hill, New York.

Williamson, P. B. (1979). *Patton's Principles: The Handbook for the Manager Who Means it*, Simon & Schuster, New York.

Winter, R. E. (1983). *Coping with Executive Stress*, McGraw-Hill, New York.

Wolff, H. G. (1953). *Stress and Disease*, Charles C. Thomas, Springfield, Ill.

Worthy, F. S. (1988). How CEOs manage their time, *Fortune*, Jan. 18, 88–97.

Wysocki, B., Jr (1984). The chief executive's style can have a big impact—For better or worse, *Wall Street Journal*, Sept. 11, 12–14.

Zaleznik, A. (1977). Leaders and managers: Are they different? *Harvard Business Review*, **55**(3), 67–78.

Index

Above-I 14
Accidents 29
Adaptation mechanisms 69
Additional duties 13
Adversity 2
Aggressive behaviour 9
Akers, John 56
Alarm reaction 24–6
Alcohol consumption 27, 28
Ambition 182
    see also Drive and ambition
Anger 130, 152
Anxiety 144, 152
Anxious attachments 152–3
Appetite 29
Artificial intelligence 138
Ash, Mary Kay 49, 51
AT & T (American Telephone &
    Telegraph) 18
Athletics, see Exercise
Attachment figures 152–3, 167
Attachment questionnaire 180,
    181
Attachment relationships, see
    Relationships

Banking industry 95–6, 98–9, 103
Behavior modification 62
Behavioral changes 27
Behavioral consequences of
    stress 27–9
Biomedical model 157–8
Black, Eli 164
Blood lipids 33

Bonding process 167–70
Bradley, General 9
Braniff Airways 8
Brophy, Theodore 56
Burnout 29–30

Cancer 35
Cannon, Walter 24, 26, 133, 134
Cardiovascular disease 33
Challenges 39, 133
    inevitability of 135–6
    response to 135–6
Change, initiation of 144–5
Change makers 136
Chaparral Steel 5, 84
    Apprenticeship Program 89, 138
    see also Forward, Gordon
Chief executive officer (CEO)
    as role model 66
    as source of stress 66
    as support resource 179–80
    stress management by 65–6
Cigarette smoking 28, 33
Civic activities 144, 176
Clinging characteristic 152–3
Cocaine 28
Cognitive appraisal 62
Commitment 39
Communication 12, 177
Community activities 13, 144, 176
Competition 12, 98, 135, 136
Constructive self-talk 62
Control 39, 41, 42
    potential 185

Control (*contd.*)
  see also Power and control
Conversion reaction   31
Cooperative relationship   12
Corporate hierarchy   150–3
Cortisol   26
Crandall, Robert   59
Creativity   21
Crier, Catherine J.   106, 116–23,
    135, 137, 140–3, 145
  biographical profile   116–18
  career challenges and
      stresses   119–21
  career success   123
  civic activities   120–1
  early life experiences and career
      preparation   118–19
  162nd Judicial District
      Court   118
  preventive stress
      management   121–3
  priorities in life   123
  Trot   120, 142
Customer complaints   11
Customer frustration   11
Customer satisfaction   11
Customer service executives   11
Cynicism   34

Dallas Apparel/Menswear
    Mart   125–6
Dawson, Kim   106, 123–32, 136,
    139, 142, 143, 145
  biographical profile   124–5
  career and life stress   127–8
  early life influences   126–7
  preventive stress
      management   128–30
  support for other people   131
  see also Kim Dawson Agency
Decision making process   7, 16–17,
    66, 165
Deere, John   18
Defensiveness   9, 153–4
Delegation   56, 77–8, 171, 177
Demand sources   11
Depression   30–1, 158–9

Diabetes   33
Distress   24, 152
  identifying signs and symptoms
      of   43
  manifestations   27
Diversity   18
Divisiveness   12
Domination   9
Drive and ambition   2–19, 182
Driving forces   16
Drug abuse   28

Eastman Kodak   13
Ebby Halliday REALTORS   108
Education   64, 87, 108, 139
Ego-ideal   3, 4, 10, 14, 15
Eisenhower, General   9
Emergency reaction   24
Emotional deprivation   158
Emotional support   174–5
Endocrine system   26
Energizing forces   5
Ethnicity   42
Eustress   24, 40–2, 191
Evaluative support   173
Excitement   4
Executive stress, *see* Stress
Exercise   58–60, 92, 101, 121, 130,
    139–41
Exhaustion   27
Extension of an ideal   4
External demands   14

Faith   60, 130
Family relationships   30, 178–9
Fantasy and magical thinking   15
Fashion industry   131
Faust, Otto A.   141
Fear   152
  value of   17
Feldman, Alvin   164
Female executives, *see* Women
Fight-or-flight response   24, 133
Flexibility training   36
Forward, Gordon   70, 83–93, 138,
    139, 140, 141, 144, 145
  biographical profile   83–4

curiosity about others   89–90
distinguishing features   92
education and its role in
    individual growth   87–9
preventive stress
    management   90–2
sources of stress and
    challenge   84–7
volunteer work   87
Fraser, Douglas   11
Friendly, Fred   66
Friendships   177
Frist, Tom, Jr   3
Frustration   130
Fuller, Major General J.F.C.   134

Geneen, Harold   149
General adaptation syndrome
    (GAS)   24
Gifted Students Institute   87, 144
Goal directed activity   6
Goal setting   52–3, 122
Grant, Joseph M. (Jody)   70,
    93–103, 138, 140–3, 145
biographical profile   93–5
community demands   95–6
developmental demands and
    opportunities   96–8
financial traumas and
    uncertainty   98–9
preventive stress
    management   99–103
professional demands   95–6

Halliday, Ebby   106–16, 140–3, 145
biographical profile   107–8
community service   108
personal and professional service
    theme   115–16
preventive stress
    management   111–14
stress and challenge   108–11
Hardiness rating   38–9
Headaches   38
Health effects of stress   21, 27–36
Health risk and loneliness   157–60
Heart attacks   33, 34

Heart disease   31, 34, 41, 62
Holiday Inn model   3
Home-work conflicts   14
Honesty   177
Hormones   26, 31
Hospital Corporation of
    America   3
Hostility   34
Hours of work   65
Humor   63
Hypertension   33
Hypervigilance   66

Iacocca, Lee   4, 11, 17, 51, 55,
    164, 166
IBM Corporation   135
Ideographic research   69
Inclusive fitness   170
Independence, myth of   149–50,
    166
Individualism, cultural
    differences   150
Influence attempts and
    responses   8
Influenza   35
Infomedical model   157–8
Information acquisition and
    evaluation   13
Informational demands   13
Informational support   172–3
Insecurity   152
Insomnia   30
Institute of Business Designers
    (IBD)   177
Integrity   177
Intellectual curiosity   137–9
Interference   165
It   14

John Wayne stereotype   164
Joyless striving   34

Kim Dawson Agency   125

Labor–management
    relationship   11
Laughter   63

Leader/defender role   171
Leaders, loneliness versus
    aloneness   154–5
Leadership   3–6
Leisure time activities   50–1, 70,
    191
Loneliness   147–61
    and group life   155–7
    and health risk   157–60
    forces leading to   148–54
    versus aloneness   154–7

McCoy, John G.   56
McKnight, William L.   56
Male executives, profiles   69–103
Management style   7
Managers, loneliness versus
    aloneness   154–5
Manufacturing industry   88
Marital relations   30, 92, 101, 114,
    143
Medical consequences of stress   27,
    31–6
Meditation   60
Mentoring relationships   13, 15,
    174
Model behaviour patterns   14
Modeling support   174
Multiple Risk Factor Intervention
    Trial   34
Musculoskeletal conditions   35–6

Nervous breakdown   29
Nervousness   38
Nomethetic research   69
Nondefensiveness   154
Nutrition   62–3

Occupational stereotypes   41
Omnipotence, fantasies of   9
O'Reilly, Anthony   63
Organizational ideal   4, 5
Organizational outcomes   6
Otis Engineering Corporation   72,
    82–3
    see also Thrash, Purvis J., Sr
Overdependence   152–3

Pace, Stanley   52
Parental model   14
Participative philosophy   4
Patience   11
Patton, General George   9, 17
Peer relationships   12
Personal demands   13–14
Personal exposure   18
Personality and behaviour
    dimensions   2–19, 41, 144
Personnel selection   55–6, 176
Pets   122
Physical activity, *see* Exercise
Physical illness   160
Pickens, Boone   59, 164
Planning   52–3, 78–9
    stress management   185–92
Pneumonia   35
Political activity   114
Popejoy, William   64
Power and control   6–9
Powerlessness   9
Prayer   60
Preventive stress management
    45–67
    as joint individual–organizational
        effort   46
    balancing individual and
        organizational   191–2
    Crier, Catherine J.   121–3
    Dawson, Kim   128–30
    Forward, Gordon   90–2
    Grant, Joseph M.   99–103
    Halliday, Ebby   111–14
    individual-level strategies   60
    ineffective techniques   64–5
    primary or stressor-directed
        level   62
    recommendations from the
        literature   60–4
    secondary level techniques   62
    strategies utilized by
        executives   49
    techniques for   47–60
    Thrash, Purvis J., Sr   75–82
    three-tiered approach   46
    what it is   46

Problem-solving decision
  making 16
Professional affiliations 177
Psychogenic disability 30–1
Psychological consequences of
  stress 27, 29–31
Psychological stress 33
Psychological trauma 31
Psychosomatic illness 36
Putnam, Howard 8
Pyramid Project 87–8

Reading 92, 101–2, 121, 139
Real estate industry 108–16
Reality orientation 5
Reality testing 5
Relationships
  failure to develop 164
  formation and maintenance
    of 163–83
  organizational 176–7
  professional affiliations 177
  reciprocity of 176
  self-assessment 181
  supportive 175–9
Relaxation 60, 191
Resources, control of 6, 9
Respiratory infections 35
Revson, Charles 66
Risk taking 16–19
Risks
  of corporate warfare 136
  of success 21–44
Role models 15

Selection of personnel 55–6, 176
Self, sense of 3
Self-assessment, relationships 181
Self-discipline 101, 102
Self-esteem 41
Self-interest 12
Self-observation 186
Self-reliance 165–6, 169, 176–7,
  182
Separation anxiety 147, 152–3
Sexual dysfunction 30–1
Sexual harassment 41

Sisyphean pattern 34
Sleep disturbance 30, 38
Social misadjustment 159–60
Social support 40, 53–8, 63, 70,
  114, 121–2, 129, 142–4
  evaluating use of 181
  functions of 170–5
  Thrash, Purvis J., Sr 79–80
  see also Relationships, supportive
Southwest Airlines 8
Spiritual aspects 102, 122, 130
  see also Faith; Meditation; Prayer
Stomach ulcers 36, 37
Stress
  behavioral consequences of
    27–9
  dynamics of 22–4
  health benefits of 36
  health consequences of 1, 21,
    27–36
  in decision processes 17
  in executive life 9–16
  major sources of 10
  measurement 42
  medical consequences of 27,
    31–6
  negative consequences of 21–2,
    37
  positive attributes of 10, 21
  psychological consequences
    of 27, 29–31
  staying healthy under 37–9
  symptoms 37
  undesirable consequences of 27
  use of term 22
Stress management 2
  chief executive officer
    (CEO) 65–6
  education in 64
  effectiveness assessment 191
  evolutionary process 191
  identifying options for 187–9
  planning 185–92
  preventive, see Preventive stress
    management
  trial and error approaches 189
  worksheet 189

Stress management (*contd.*)
  written plan   189
Stress responses   23, 24–7, 69, 133
  identifying   187
  modifiers of   40–2
Stressful events   23
Stressors   31, 39
  and their consequences   22
  identifying   43, 186–7
  measurement   42
Strokes   31
Subordinates   56, 171
  demands of   12
  relationship with   12–13
  working to develop   16
Success
  and personal well-being   1
  risks of   21–44
Successful executive
  myths of   164–6
  paradox of   182
Sudden cardiac death   33
Suicide   164
Support sources   11
Sympathetic nervous system   26
Systematic desensitization   188
Systemic change   144–5

Talking it out   63
Tension headaches   11
Texas American Bancshares (TAB)
  Inc   95
  see also Grant, Joseph M. (Jody)
Texas banking system   18
Thrash, Purvis J., Sr   70–83, 135,
  139–45
  biographical profile   70–1
  challenges of adversity   74
  preventive stress
    management   75–82
  social support   79–80
  sources of organizational
    stress   72

Time management   51–2
Trade unions   11
Training activities   138
Trauma   2
Travel   51, 60, 139, 142
TROT   120, 142
Tuberculosis   35
Tung, Rosalie   149
Tunnel vision   18
Type A personality   33, 34, 41, 62
Type B personality   34

Uncertainty in decision
  processes   17

Vacations   191
Violence   29
Vision Group   88, 141
Volunteer activities   176

Wageman, Tom   13
War, principles of   134
War game framework   134–5
Welch, Jack   54
Williams College Executive
  Program   18
Women
  executive profiles   105–32
  risk factors   41
  role stress   41
  stress effects in   38
Work
  as civilized form of warfare   136
  as creation   136
Work-nonwork balance   141–2
Work overload   29
Work perspective   49–50
Workaholic behavior pattern   49
Wyatt, Oscar   7

Young Presidents'
  Organization   94, 96–7, 141